WORDS OF POWER

Thinking Gender
Edited by Linda J. Nicholson

Also published in the series

Gender Trouble: Feminism and the Subversion of Identity
Judith Butler

Feminism/Postmodernism
Edited and with an Introduction by Linda J. Nicholson

WORDS OF POWER

A Feminist Reading of the History of Logic

ANDREA NYE

Routledge
New York and London

Published in 1990 by

Routledge
An imprint of Routledge, Chapman and Hall, Inc.
29 West 35 Street
New York, NY 10001

Published in Great Britain by

Routledge
11 New Fetter Lane
London EC4P 4EE

Library of Congress Cataloging in Publication Data

Nye, Andrea, 1939—
    Words of power: a feminist reading in the history of logic/
Andrea Nye.
        p. cm.—(Thinking gender)
    Includes bibliographical references.
    ISBN 0-415-90199-5; ISBN 0-415-90200-2 (pbk.)
    1. Logic-History. 2. Feminism-Philosophy. I. Title
II. Series.
BC57.N94 1990   89-28195
160'.82-dc20

**British Library Cataloguing in Publication Data
also available**

For Miss Sterne and Miss Main, and all my teachers at Baldwin School, who showed me what it was to think passionately.

Contents

Prologue

The following myth is preserved in an Egyptian text written for use in healing:*

Rah was the greatest of the gods. Unitary in form and self-produced, he was the creator of all things, whether men, gods, animals, heaven, or earth.

But Isis was a woman skilled in words. She thought to herself: could she not make herself mistress of the Earth and a goddess, by knowing the secret name of Rah?

Every day Rah sat on his throne and paraded in front of his courtiers; he had become old and he dribbled at the mouth. Isis took up a bit of the spittle of words that fell into the dust at his feet and kneaded it into the form of a dart, a serpent, an insinuation, a resaying of the tired words that fell from the mouth of Rah, and she left it in his path.

It was Rah's habit each day to make triumphal marches through his kingdoms. Each morning, he set out with all the majesty of his court following to survey his dominions. But on his way, he was bitten by the serpent that Isis had left in his path and was stricken with its poison.

He opened his mouth but could not speak; he could not find the words to answer when the mighty ones who accompanied him asked him what was the matter. "His two jaws rattled, his limbs all trembled, the poison took possession of his body as taketh possession the Nile of the river bed."

"Come to me, come to me," he finally cried out to those who had come into being from his members, to those who were his subjects, "I will tell you what has happened."

"I have been wounded by something deadly, knoweth it my heart. Not

---

*The hieroglyphic text and translation can be found in E. A. Wallis Budge, *The Gods of the Egyptians,* vol. I (New York: Dover, 1969), 372–387.

have I seen it with my eyes, not did I make it with my hand, not know I who hath done this to me, not have I tasted pain like it, never was anything more deadly than it."

Rah recited the long list of his attributes and powers. This misfortune had happened to him, the Great One, the son of a Great One, who bore the name that had been decided by his father, the holy name uttered by his father and mother, hidden in his body by his father so that no one could have power over him by enchantment. But when he, the great Rah, was walking his lands, walking the world he had created, something had aimed this blow at him. And he cried out again in pain.

"My heart contains fire, my limbs are trembling, my members contain the children of quakings. Bring me someone of my children who can heal me," he pleaded.

And Isis came, with her power and her skilled mouth, with the breath of life, with her incantations that destroy disease and her word that maketh to live the throats of the dead.

She spoke to Rah. "What is this, oh Father God, What is this? A snake hath shot sickness into you. A thing made by you hath lifted up its head against you? Verily it shall be overthrown by words of power beneficent, I will make it to depart from the sight of your eyes."

Subdued and quieted, Rah retold his story to her. "I was passing over the way going through the two lands of my country, my heart wished to see what I had created, when I was bitten by an invisible snake."

He told her of his suffering: "Behold it is not fire, behold it is not water. I am cooler than water, I am hotter than fire, my limbs all are full of sweat, I tremble, my eye is without stability, I cannot see the heavens."

And Isis said to Rah, "Tell me your name, the person who declares his name will live."

But Rah recited again his mighty actions, his powers, and his titles. And even with all his powers, he lamented, the poison was not driven from its course. He, the greatest of gods, had not been relieved.

But Isis said: "Thy name was not enumerated among the things which you have said to me, tell me your name and the poison will come out of you. A person who has uttered his name shall live."

Rah's suffering increased. He burned with fever and shivered with cold. Finally he relented. "I give myself to be searched out by Isis, my name shall come forth from my body into her body."

And Rah left his throne and hid himself away; and when the time came for him to speak his heart, Isis said to her son Horus, "Make him swear that he will give up dominion of the Sun and the Moon."

And when the name of Rah had been removed from the great god, Isis, great in words of power, spoke: "Run out poison, come forth from Rah, come forth from the God, and shine without his mouth. I have done this, I have made to fall down upon the ground the poison which is defeated. Rah will live and the poison will die. A certain one, the son of a certain woman, may he live, the poison may it die."

In this way Isis took from Rah his power and his name.

Acknowledgments

I would like to thank my daughter, Anna Nye, and my son Stephen Nye for all their support and assistance, and especially my daughter, Deirdre Nye, and my friend and colleague Joe Hogan, who helped me prepare this book for publication. I would also like to thank my friend and colleague, the logician and philosopher, Don Levi, for his support, encouragement, and helpful comments.

Introduction: Reading Logic

She opens to the first page of Quine's *Methods of Logic*. Even this first week of class there are exercises to be handed in:

> Which of the four cases: Jones ill, Smith away; Jones not ill, Smith away; Jones ill, Smith not away; Jones not ill, Smith not away, make the statement: 'Jones is not ill or Smith is not away,' come out true when 'or' is construed exclusively?

'Jones away,' 'Smith not ill': the phrases jangle in her mind. Nonsense syllables. Was Jones often ill? Not ill today for once? And why? And Smith so often gone. Where?

She shakes her head to force her attention back to the rules for the nonexclusive 'or.' The elementary logic course is required for her philosophy degree, and she is determined to do well. Her tutor has reassured her that she will get through it. But of course, he says, her philosophical interests—here he smiles condescendingly—are elsewhere, perhaps in ethics, or social philosophy, or even philosophy of religion. Not logic or epistemology. And she needn't worry, they will go slowly in the introductory course; many nonmajors take it. They won't get to the last chapter, on set theory, where logic gets interesting and hard, and she needs to take only the one required course.

It would help, she tells herself, if she does not read the words, but sees them as marks. She must look only at their sameness or difference: 'James ill,' regardless of what it means, is the same as 'James ill.' And it is the opposite of its negation, 'James not ill.' She must not mind James and his mysterious illness. Or the troubling situation in the next problem with the penicillin that was or was not flown in and the quarantine that came anyway, or didn't because after all there was the penicillin.

1

Her head aches, she is doing it again. Reading. It is so hard to stop. She has come to philosophy from literature, from Dostoevsky, George Eliot, Nietzsche, from puzzling with Ivan over the parable of the Grand Inquisitor, from doubting with Dorothea the adequacy of Casuabon's approach to knowledge, from thrilling to and fearing the mad teachings of Zarathrusta. Now she is to be a philosopher. And logic is required. But logic, she is learning, is not a feminine subject. There is only one other woman in the logic class. Even in her other philosophy classes there are few women, and no one she knows. After class she is too unsure of herself to be one of the students who gather around the professor to ask questions. She never raises her hand in class.

> 'Jones ate fish with ice cream and died.' The truth value of this conjunction admits of no dispute whatever once the truth values of 'Jones ate fish with ice cream' and 'Jones dies' are known.

The trick is not to think, once she thinks she is lost. She must push out of her mind all thoughts of the bizarre dish set before Jones who was often ill. No speculation about why he would eat such a thing. Or why it would have made him ill, much less die. She must forget the meaning. Do the calculations. Learn the movements, the marks upon the page, their patterns, their intricate placings. The p's and q's: "Mind your p's and q's," her grandmother used to say to her sternly, before she took her to church. But her grandmother had meant something different, or had she?

I think I must not have been the only woman who struggled in this way in her first logic class. Soon, the confusing words, for the most part, disappeared. Only the p's and q's were left. I did well enough, but not brilliantly. Others went on to the more advanced courses in logic. Men, all of them. Logic is, after all, a masculine subject. At least all the great logicians Quine mentions in his little asides on the history of logic were men: Philo of Megara, Zeno, Frege, Wittgenstein. Apparently there were no women in the history of logic.

Is it because I, as a woman, had a different kind of mind, incapable of abstraction and therefore of theorizing, is it because I was too "emotional"? Is it because when I read the logic exercise I persisted in thinking about Jones's painful illness or the quarantine, when none of this matters? I was careful enough not to embarrass myself, didn't volunteer in class. I understood that the problems were only examples, chosen at random as illustrations. I understood that the content of the examples logicians give are of no importance, that what matters is the logic. I understood that it doesn't matter that no one would ever say these things, that no one would ever have need of the truth-function of 'Jones ill' and 'Jones eats fish with ice cream.' I understood that more is at stake than people, or illnesses, or perverse tastes. Logic deals with the structure of truth itself, any truth, even the most trivial, the most strange. All truth has the same structure and it is for logic to reveal that structure. And I knew that if I were to be a philosopher I could not continue to turn away when I saw the p's and q's. Even though I was no logician. Would never be.

But it worried me. Was there a way to understand? The only way to know was to go back to the beginning. Read the logicians. Find out what they meant. Find out if what they meant matters. Find out if logic *is* for men, if it is men's thoughts that it represents, and find out if there might be another thought, another logic, another truth. Find out if it might be possible to read logic after all, and once having read it to say something in answer.

Histories of logic, heroic narratives of victory, breakthrough, defeat, reverse, that show logic moving steadily, if fitfully, toward perfection, were of little help. They had plots I had already begun to suspect. The successes and failures described were only formal: detached from human concerns and as inscrutable and independent of any sensible content as Quine's examples. The problems of logic, historians of logic seemed to insist, are logic's own; they are unrelated to conflictual relations between men and women, between men, or between men and the natural world, unrelated, that is, to all that might have made them understandable. A logician might be a dogmatist in religion, a fascist in politics, a sadist in love, the histories would not mention it. Any such commitments of his or his associates were ignored, and for good logical reason: belief in the natural superiority of Greeks, or the absolute authority of the Church, or the irrationality of women cannot make the logic that supports such commitments false if it is true. Advances in logic depend on thought only, unrelated to any personal, political, or economic considerations. Marital conflict, poverty, war might keep the logician from his desk, but once there, he puts family disputes, politics, and economic hardship aside and engages in a purely intellectual activity. He sheds his intentions, fears, humiliations, resentments; all of his natural life is only dead skin that falls away to reveal the hard bone of thought itself. The impulses that drive him to logic, the examples he chooses to illustrate his points, all the contingent transitory dross of his daily life, are irrelevant to his logic, which is what has to be thought, what cannot not be thought, what cannot change or die. In the midst of mortal life, the logician clears a supra-worldly space that he maps with the eternal patterns of logical relations.

A heroic story indeed. But what is the meaning of these fossils—the syllogisms, consequentia, truth-functions—that histories of logic applaud as the great advances in logical thought? Can this question be answered without examining the lives that have given them form? If the spiral of a shell can only be understood with reference to the habits of the creature that secreted it, isn't it also necessary to try to understand the lives and habits of logicians too, lives which must be the matrix of any desire, ambition, commitment, disappointment, effort?

If there is any solid agreement in the history of logic, it is the claim to be immune from this understanding. Logic proclaims itself the unreadable language, the language which has detached itself from confusion and passion, the language which has transcended natural language embedded in sensual lives, mutably imprinted with social, economic, or personal concerns. The logician does not speak; he does not tell the truth; he exhibits it. All vestiges of his speaking voice are transcended, all reference to his situation, to his sex, his place in time or space. Logic is the perfect transparency of a language which does not need to be read.

This is, of course, what the logician himself claims. But if there never had been life, could these markings, these patterns of argument, have meaning? Logic is a human invention, although logicians may deny it, and it must speak *of* something, speak of ambitions, fears, hopes, disappointments, despairs. Logic must refer to the objects of a common world. Not only must it speak of something but it must speak *to* someone and thereby institute the relationships in which communication is possible. The pretense that logic does not speak and cannot be read is only one such institution, an institution whose pretension to absolute truth reduces the respondent, reader, listener to assent, or even better, to silence. Why should such a silencing have been necessary or desirable? What are the terms on which, the circumstances in which, it could be carried out?

The styles of logic have been diverse. And so have logicians and their purposes been diverse. Different men, different lives, different logics: Parmenides, searching for an eternal *what is* in a Greece only just emerged from the dark ages that followed the destruction of Mediterranean culture by migrating Greeks: Plato, insisting on absolute Goodness in the midst of the disintegration of the traditional order of the city-state as foreigners, speculators, and moneylenders crowded into Athens; Aristotle, promoting a science based on necessary truth as he watches the collapse of Athenian hegemony in the Aegean; Zeno the Stoic, constructing a grammar of the cosmos as he and others try to come to terms with life in the new Hellenistic empire of Alexander the Great. Could they all have been thinking the same thing? The same things as Abelard and Ockham thought, centuries later, when God, the divine Logos, was thought to have spoken and all relations between God and man were being renegotiated; or as Frege thought, the logicians' logician, working out the elegant details of his new logical notation in Bismarck's Germany, surrounded by economic crisis and infected by the ethnic and racial hatreds that would eventually support Fascism?

Logic, one current argument goes, is the creation of defensive male subjects who have lost touch with their lived experience and define all being in rigid oppositional categories modelled on a primal contrast between male and female. Or another: logic articulates oppressive thought-structures that channel human behavior into restrictive gender roles. Or: logic celebrates the unity of a pathological masculine self-identity that cannot listen and recognizes only negation and not difference. These critical evaluations have been made by sociolinguists studying the assymmetries of male and female conversational styles, by poststructuralist feminist theorists struggling for an escape from the "prison house" of sexist language, and by psychoanalysts exploring the darkness of Freud's pre-Oedipal maternal. But none of these theoretical deconstructions account for the fact that logic is an invention of men, that it is something that men do and say.

I attempt here a different kind of validation of the feminist indictment of logic, one not based on any theory of language or logic, whether transactional, structuralist, poststructuralist, or psychoanalytic. In my view, there is no one Logic for which such a theory can account, but only men and logics, and the substance of these logics, as of any written or spoken language, are material and historically specific relations between men, between men and women, and between them and objects of human concern.

Unlike either the logician or theorist I make no pretense at anonymity. I am a woman reading logic. I am also a philosopher who, like many other women philosophers, has often felt uneasy claiming that title. Perhaps *only* a woman would undertake such a project, would do such a thing as try to read logic, a woman uncomfortable in the world of men, involved in the physical details of family life, births, marriages, the keeping of houses, a woman too intent on emotional commitments to be capable of purely abstract thought. Perhaps only a woman would not make even the pretense of disinterested scholarship, but would admit to believing that involvement and commitment can lead to an understanding that logical analysis bound to consistency and univocality cannot.

You cannot ask of such readings that they reveal any absolute or complete truth about logic. There is never only one reading. You can ask that they be sensitive, accurate, attentive, revealing, and informed by an aspiration to a better life for women and for men. These are the standards by which I ask my reader to judge what follows.

Part I
Classical Logic

1

The Desire of Logic:
Parmenides's Passion

The mares which carry me
as far as my heart desires
Were escorting me, leading me
as they put me on the many-speaking road
Of the Spirit, that Spirit who carries
past the towns the knowing man (1.1–3).[1]

Logic and poetry are traditionally put at opposite poles. Poetry expresses emotion; logic is passionless. Poetry invokes objects of desire that can be physically possessed; the objects of logic are abstract entities and relations accessible only to reason. Poetry is most often motivated by love; investigations that yield logical truth are disinterested. What then is the motivation for logic? Why does the logician so delight in his abstractions. Why does he[2] find logical truth so much more exciting than the concrete realities of lived experience? To protest that a logician's interests are pure of any motivation is to avoid the question. Some desire, or despair, or need must have driven him to the intricate and demanding study of logic.

A question of motivation is also a question of origins, of beginnings. But where is the beginning of logic? With Aristotle who was the first to abstract the logical form of arguments? With his teacher Plato who first envisioned the reality of abstract entities? Or is it necessary to go back still further to another text, a poem, that in its rejection of the change and inconsistency of natural beings evokes for the first time that self-consistent "Being" that is the subject of logic? In his sixth-century BC heroic poem, Parmenides dramatically portrays the passion in this rejection of physical and natural existence. Here, in its infancy, logic has not yet separated from poetry. Parmenides frames his quest for logical truth in a romantic setting of maiden guides, eerie sounds, ethereal locked doors, and gaping chasms that open to engulf and delight.

The choice of poetry to describe a search for logical truth has often been seen by philosophers as unfortunate.

It is hard to excuse Parmenides' choice of verse as a medium for his philosophy. The exigencies of meter and poetic style regularly produce an almost impenetrable obscurity and the difficulty of understanding his thought is not lightened by any literary joy.[3]

In this argument, the classicist Jonathan Barnes criticizes Parmenides's poetry as a clumsy gloss on his logic. Others have discarded Parmenides's prologue with its chariot ride and female divinities as religious,[4] or argued that logical notions were so new that they had to be temporarily expressed in figurative language,[5] or discounted Parmenides's poetry as a metaphor whose function is only to represent the objective existence of logical truth.[6]

But what is striking in Parmenides's prologue, whatever its literary merit, is neither spirituality nor rhetoric but poetically expressed desire, desire that is to be fulfilled in Parmenides's final encounter with the patron goddess of truth. Desire (θυμός) initiates Parmenides's journey and is the impulse that drives it forward. He will go as far as desire can reach. The mares he drives are the servants of his longing; they respond sensitively (πολύφραστοι)to the urgings of his heart. Desire puts him on the road to logic, leads him through and past the ordinary concerns of human life in a quest or search for something loved and lost, dreamt of but never attained.[7]

Parmenides evokes the scene in concrete detail. Maidens urgently lead the way as in a marriage procession.

> Maidens of the Sun,
>   forsaking the house of Night
> For the light, throw back
>   with their hands their veils (1.9–10).

These are the first of a series of female attendants, gatekeepers, and instructresses who will direct Parmenides to his final destination. As the Sun maidens press the horses on, the sparking and glowing wheels give out a pipe-like accompaniment, and a strange music and unearthly glow come from the chariot as the wheels turn faster and faster. The throwing back of the maidens' veils expresses the urgency of the logician's passage from darkness to light, to a transparent truth laid naked without any obscuring covering. Their unveiling is only a foretaste of the more profound revelation that will constitute a final apotheosis in the presence of truth itself.

The chariot draws near to the threshold which Parmenides must cross, the barrier he must penetrate, a forbidding set of double doors.

> There are the gates
>   of the ways of Night and Day,
> And they are framed by a lintel
>   and a threshold of stone,
> Ethereal, they close the great doors,
> And for these much punishing Dike
>   holds the alternate keys (1.11–14).

For such an awesome gatekeeper gentle words and cunning are necessary. Using both, Parmenides's maiden guides persuade Dike to push back the bar from the great gates. With loud clankings and scraping of metal bolts, the doors swing open to reveal a gaping chasm (χάσμα) into which Parmenides's chariot is immediately guided by the Sun maidens. With this mimicking of the physical consumation of desire, Parmenides nears the final object of his quest.

Now he is face to face with his goddess; the attendant maidens and chariot fade away, and the sacred conversation begins. She welcomes him in flattering terms, and takes him by the right hand.

> Welcome. It is not an evil fate
> > that prompted you to travel
> This road—for it is
> > far from the paths of men—
> But law and justice.
> > It is necessary that all be learned
> Including the unshaken heart
> of well-rounded truth (1.26–29).

The lesson proceeds. There are in fact two things that Parmenides must learn.

> On the one hand:
> > it is and to not be is not;
> On the other: it is not
> > and it is necessary not to be (2.3–4).

In this hermetic teaching is the self-identical kernel of logical truth. The choice that Parmenides has made, and must go on making, is not between "is" and "is not," for, the goddess points out, the way of "is not" is impossible. Nonbeing is nothing and cannot constitute a choice. The choice instead is between the correct way of "what is" and its identity with itself against the wandering of ignorant masses who think they can go back and forth from what is to what is not.[8] These masses, or tribes (φῦλα) as the goddess calls them contemptuously, are helpless and confused,

> . . . mortals who seeing nothing
> Wander, of two minds,
> > for confusion
> In their hearts guides their wandering thought,
> > And they are carried
> Deaf as well as blind,
> > astonished undecided masses. . . (6.4–9).[9]

The "many-speaking" high road through the towns of women and men must become the broad avenue of truth from which there can be no deviation. The twisting and branching of ordinary existence must be rejected for the straight way of what is. The blindness of sight and the deafness of hearing will be replaced by the vision of logic. Thought will no longer backtrack or veer or contradict itself with the changing evidence of the physical senses and the conflicting opinions of ordinary mortals.

It only remains for the goddess to instruct Parmenides in some of the distinguishing marks of the way of logic, and to compare them to the "wandering" ways of popular teachings on cosmology, theology, and psychology, which involve a forbidden vacillation between the ways of what is and what is not. The goddess first describes the faithfulness of logical truth which Dike, stern gatekeeper with her double keys, ensures by rigidly separating "is" and "is not."

> Nor will the force of fidelity ($\pi\iota\sigma\tau\iota\varsigma$)[10]
>   accept that anything be
> Born beyond itself,
>   when neither for birth
> Nor dying does
>   unhearing Dike loosen her bonds,
> But holds fast. . . (8.12–14).

Now inside the doors, with "is not" exposed as an impossible way, Dike's task is not to separate or balance being and nonbeing, but to hold ($\check{\varepsilon}\chi\varepsilon\iota$) what is tightly, to bind it in the shackles that will keep it uncontaminated from what is not. Ananke, or Necessity, plays a similar role.

> For obdurate Ananke
> The boundaries in fetters holds,
>   presses in from all sides
> Because it is the law that what is
>   is not unfinished (8.30–32).

And also Moira or Fate.

> . . . since of course Moira holds fast
> The whole unmoving (8.37–38).

The goddess explains the characteristics of this imprisoned being. It is, she says, a well-rounded sphere, uniform and not admitting of degrees, homogenous and not subject to any death or destruction.

This is the proper object of Parmenides's search, the destination he longed for in the prologue, the fulfillment of the promise made in the first line of his poem that he would go as far as his heart could reach. This is the ultimate satisfaction not possible in human affairs where the reach of the heart is always beyond its grasp. "What is" is the perfected object of desire, a being that can be approached without any of the confusion, fear, indecision, or ambivalence with which we approach the physical objects of desire. Parmenides has found an object of love eternally faithful, beyond birth or death, held tightly in the embrace of logical necessity.

If the prologue describes the foreplay for this perfect marriage, the remaining fragments of the poem, in which the goddess explains in more detail the fallacious theories of humans, is an account of forbidden and inevitably disappointing extralogical adventures. The masses, she explains, are satisfied with inferior gratifications, with fulfillment that is both uncertain and unclear. The problem is with the incoherence of their view of the natural world. In contrast to the logical contemplation of the oneness of "what is," the description of the "opinions" of mortals shifts to the natural beauties of the night and day skies. If he follows her instruction, the goddess promises Parmenides, he will come to know the fallaciousness of these opinions.

> You will know the ethereal nature
>   and of the ether all
> The signs, and of the pure torch
>   of the shining sun
> Its dark works,
>   and from what they were born.
> And the wandering works
>   of the circling moon you will know
> And its nature. And you will see
>   the heavens holding on all sides
> Since its beginning.
>   And how guiding Ananke bound it
> To hold the limits of the stars (10.1–7).

In this description of the panorama of the heavens is all the grandeur and the puzzling ambiguity of nature. The sun is pure, chaste, shining ($εὐαγέος$), its torch is innocent and clean ($καθαρᾶς$), but nevertheless it does dark works, causing drought and burning crops. The moon circles but also "wanders." Natural cycles alternate between destruction and regeneration. Here again is Ananke in her old role, not binding the logical necessity of what is, but as the necessity that rules the cycles of the natural universe, contains the starry limits of the cosmos, and presides over alternations of light and dark, pure and impure, good and evil.

Parmenides's guide describes a complex system of interlocking heavenly rings (12.1–2):

> In the middle of these is
> the spirit who governs all
> For everywhere she initiates
> shameful birth and mixings
> Causing the female to mix with the male
> and the male with the female (12.3–6).

This divinity, who created Eros before all the gods (13), initiates and maintains a mixing of opposites and therefore a conflation of "is" and "is not" that must be denied by logic. If a female mixes with a male, the result is both female and not female, impossible by the rule of noncontradiction. In another fragment, the goddess describes for Parmenides the unfortunate biological effects of such mixings. In fertilization, if the male principle or the female principle prevails, then there will be well-formed bodies, but if there is no unitary sexual identity, the sex of the offspring will be tormented by "double seed," that is it will have both male and female characteristics (18). But to mix masculinity and femininity is unthinkable. The cryptic fragment 17 illustrates concretely the requisite division between "is" and "is not": "On the right boys, on the left girls," a segregation which popular theories of generation and cosmic origin did not respect.

Even more illogical, mortal opinion posited mixtures to explain the nature of thought itself.

> For always there is a mixture
> in the much wandering[11] limbs
> So thought comes to men, for this
> is what[12] the stuff[13] of the body thinks in men
> Each and every of them, for satisfaction
> is thought[14] (16.1–4).

In this difficult passage, the goddess describes a sophisticated psychology of mixing and motion in the body. Changes in the physical body are what causes thought. Here, there is no separation of soul and body; instead the very stuff of the body thinks. Thinking is not done by disembodied minds; instead the thought process is initiated as people's physical situations change. Thought reaches towards satiety or satisfaction, the resolution of conflict and the fulfillment of desire. In this nondualist psychology are again the mixings and ambiguity forbidden by logic. From the point of view of logic, such a thought could never be complete or final; always the body continues to be affected by internal and external processes, and thinking begins again, only to reach another provisional resolution.

This mingling of what is and what is not characterizes all the "deceptive" opinions of natural processes taught to Parmenides by his goddess. In birth a new life comes into being from what is not; in sexual intercourse the male mingles with the female; in cases of ambiguous sexual identity the masculine is conflated with the feminine. Even thought itself is a mixing in the body and so must lack the unity, coherence, and consistency demanded by logic. Seen from the standpoint of the prologue's desire—the desire to go as far as the heart can reach—these opinions are obviously defective. Fulfillment is never complete; life is always subject to disease and death; heterosexual pleasure requires mixing with women; knowledge is never without ambiguity; birth is painful and "shameful." Parmenides's use of στυγεροῖο implies not only the physical pain of childbirth but also shame, shame that a man comes to be from what he is not, from the inferior body of a woman.

When, from the standpoint of logic, Parmenides indicts the mingling of the sexes, he expresses attitudes toward women characteristic of Greek thought. There is something shameful in men's sexual contact with women. Heterosexual intercourse may be a necessary evil for reproductive purposes but it should be gotten over with as soon as possible so a man may return to the masculine world of the *agora,* assembly, and law courts. A Greek man avoids mixing with women, protects his masculinity from the feminization that will result from too much contact with women.[15] Men and women are segregated, boys on the right, girls on the left. Love between men is preferable to love between men and women because it does not involve any mixing; the union is of like to like and there need be no confrontation with an other who is not like oneself.[16] Similarly impermissible is an individual with mixed sexual identity. To confuse masculinity with femininity is a plague and a curse. For Parmenides and his fellow Greeks, the ascription of femininity to a man was the worst of insults. To be in the position of a woman was shameful for a man and, in the pederastic homosexual relation between an older and a younger man institutionalized in classical Athens and Sparta, the younger man was cautioned never to take the female role of having one of his orifices penetrated. Greek writers regularly referred to the inferiority of women, to their babbling, emotionality, and lack of courage. Because of their natural inferiority, women's virtue was not courage or eloquence but submission to the superior rule of men in the family.[17]

The world of women involves not only heterosexuality and birth but also death. Not only must a man bear the indignity of birth, he must also look forward to bodily decay and eventual destruction. These natural changes in oneself and in loved ones are shameful and intolerable; they deny a man both the certainty of self-love and the "fidelity" of others. In the natural world of mortal opinion, there is no recourse, no extraphysical immortal object that will not alter or grow old, lose its beauty, or die. Logical truth, as disclosed by the goddess, does not have these defects. The two ways, "is" and "is not," are the roads that take the seeker as far as his desire can reach. In logic there will be a true satisfaction that is complete and absolute, that cannot be taken away or compromised. For Parmenides's "what is," there is no shameful birth, fearful dying, or mingling of the sexes. "What is" cannot come to be out of what is not, like a man from a woman, nor can it be destroyed. In logic the way of nonbeing is kept separate from being, just as what is male is kept separate from what is not male. In logic, there is no intercourse of being with nonbeing, and therefore no disappointment or ambiguity, only the perfect fidelity of the unmoveable, unchangeable, perfect "well-roundedness" of truth.

The satisfaction such an object of desire makes possible is made clear in fragment 6, where Parmenides describes the faithfulness or πίστις of what is: "Behold even when far away, things are present to the mind reliably." Being cannot be cut off or estranged from being; there can be no absence or nonbeing. Estrangement is avoided in both its forms, both as separation or dispersal, and as joining which also involves a separation as necessarily different identities, persons, and elements come together. In the popular thought described by the goddess, dispersal and coming together are the basis for cosmological change as well as for human relations. We separate and also we come together. But from the standpoint of logical truth, both separation and union are avoided in the closest of embraces, the identity of what is with what is. How complete this closeness is between the desiring thought of the logician and the object of his thought is expressed in Fragment 8.

> It is the same thing to be thought
> as to be a thought.
> For not without something of what is,
> in what is expressed,
> Can there be thinking (7.35–37).

Logical thought is identical with its object. There is no uncapturable overflow of reality, and no thought that strays beyond what is. Instead what can be logically thought is thought and must be thought if thinking is to continue. There can be no imperfect grasp of the truth, no person or object that lies beyond understanding. In logic, thought finds its final fulfillment in identity with its object. All else falls away as what is becomes what can be thought. Thought is finally finished (τελεστόν)(8.4) in an absolute gratification that replaces the intolerable finishing (τελευτήσουσι) or death of natural existence (19).

The logical truth of Parmenides's goddess is a corrective to the natural philosophy she describes, a corrective motivated by a desire that will not accept disappointment or tolerate any discrepancy between wish and reality. Although Parmenides cleverly puts the logic first and introduces mortal opinion later as a deceptive mimicking of true knowledge, in actual chronology mortal opinion is the older view that logic is to discredit and suppress.[18] A feminine divinity at the center of the natural world, nature ordered in natural cycles of growth and decay, sexual reproduction as a kind of natural immortality, the regular and reciprocal cycles of family life as the basis of social and natural order, these ideas were characteristic of Mediterranean thought well before the immigrations of the Greeks, and they continued to be the focus of teaching at religious centers such as Eleusis long after the Greeks had established their dominance in the Aegean.[19] The Greeks, on the other hand, brought with them a different view of divinity and of social order. Instead of a creative force at the center of natural existence, a supreme warrior/father god Zeus legislated and punished from above and outside natural life. Order was a matter of law, and law reflected not the balance and reciprocity of natural processes, but the orderly dichotomies of hierarchicalized social structures that had been divinely ordained. In the pantheon of Greek gods under Zeus's rule, the Spirit-at-the-center-of-the-world of mortal opinion, whether called Aphrodite, Demeter, Eileithyia, or Artemis, became a subordinate female member of the Olympian patriarchy. By law, man ruled woman and Greek ruled barbarian, and nothing should be allowed to disturb the precarious order of these hierarchies.

But the goddess is not willing to leave Parmenides unarmed in the "illogical" thought of mortals not "sprung from the gods" as the Greeks claimed to be. Not only does she make sure that he understands the deceptive teaching of mortals so as to avoid its fallacies, she also borrows and adapts for logic the authority of mortal opinion's powerful images and figures. Fullness is used to characterize elements in the older view. Everything is full ($\pi\lambda\acute{e}o\nu$) of light and night (9.3). The narrow rings of the cosmos are filled ($\pi\lambda\tilde{\eta}\nu\tau\alpha\iota$) with fire (12.1). Most important, the thought of men can be full ($\pi\lambda\acute{e}o\nu$) (16.4). The thought of the logician is also full, but not in the same way. The thought that comes from the mixings of the body only reaches a temporary satiety and resolution. The thought of the logician is full in the sense that within it there is no contradiction or opposition. The cosmos may be full of two basic principles or elements, and the rings of the heavens with fire; however, logical thought is not full in the sense that a container is full. This would imply a difference between container and contents. Fullness of logical thought is a fullness in the sense that there can be nothing outside it. All negation, all that is not logical thought, is rejected as impossible.

Fullness must be contained, and the motif of containment recurs in both the older view and the logic. Again the uses are different. In popular belief, Ananke guides the heavenly bodies and binds the limits of the cosmos to hold the stars. This is a natural binding or embrace, a kind of protective encirclement that keeps variable phenomena in a regular cycle.[20] Again, the bondage in logic is of a different sort. There, Necessity, Fate, and Justice bind off what is from what is not. Their grasp is rigid, imprisoning a reality that will not be allowed to move or change. They shackle their object so it cannot be mutilated by destruction or death. The order and balance of nature, the rising of the sun, the irregular orbit of the moon, the paths of the stars, safely locked behind Dike's twin doors, can now only be "what is."

Sexuality is central in the older view. The Spirit-at-the-center-of-the-world creates Eros first of the gods and governs not by decree but by providing the motive force behind generation, sending couples to make love and presiding over births and deaths.[21] In the course of Parmenides's journey Eros is transformed; desire is no longer satisfied with physical acts of intercourse. The passion of the journey, the marriage-like procession, the great double vaginal doors that swing open to admit Parmenides into the gaping vaginal cleft clearly mimic the course of sexual desire. But once inside, these images become the conduit for a different kind of fulfillment beyond physical intercourse. If truth is "well-rounded" as a nubile maiden, these are not the mortal curves that must eventually give way to more matronly contours. The truth will remain in shape, a homogenous immortal sphere, perfectly fitting the logician's desire. In this romance, there will be no misfit between anticipation and actuality, no need to attract or interest another being. Nothing is needed for this love affair except one's own thought. Transfigured as "what is," the loved one becomes the perfect projected image of a solipsistic love.

Also striking is the reappearance of female deities in Parmenides's logic. Again their role has changed. In the older view, Ananke and the Spirit-at-the-center-of-the-world play the primary roles. Ananke's is described in Fragment 10. She guides by pressing the sky to hold the limits of the stars. She maintains the regular orbits and paths of the heavenly bodies. As Necessity she is the inexorable "what is," or what must be, of physical reality. In Parmenides's logic, she is paired with Dike, a goddess invented by the Greeks.[22] If Ananke regulates a natural cosmic order, Dike, as Justice, represents the heavenly reflection of an ideal human order. She neither guides nor urges, but holds a jailer's keys. It is for her, as daughter of Zeus, to pronounce what is and is not to be done; she is the gate-keeper who will make sure that these are never conflated. She maintains a conventional order, an order that opposes two contraries, one of which is the negation of the other, one of which is prescribed while the other is proscribed. In the goddess's account of truth, Ananke has been conscripted into her service.

Also different is the role of the Spirit who governs all change and growth. She appears in the first line of Parmenides's poem only to disappear until the instruction in mortal opinion, but, although she is barred from participation in the demonstration of logical truth, as the source of all desire, her spirit also inspires the logician's quest. It is she who "sends" Parmenides on his way to logic just as she sends all natural creatures, female to mate with male, male with female. The love affair of the logican, however, will take a new course; once through Dike's double doors, the mingling, mixing, generation of the natural world will be blocked. Instead of a powerful divinity at the center of the world, Parmenides, the hero, encounters a hostess/goddess whose function it is to introduce him to a higher reality and pleasure. It is not she whom Parmenides seeks; her role is only to instruct and aid him in a quest that she makes clear he is well on the way to finishing by himself. She provides only the final impetus, confirming him in the route he has already chosen to the final embrace of "what is." There, removed from all sensuous existence, he will finally rest.

What logic offers is a different arena for the satisfaction of desire. Removed from the uncertain pleasures of the flesh, Parmenides is reborn. In his passage, he has crossed into another world, through the double doors of gatekeeping Dike. He has left behind the life of the towns. He has left behind the human community where the only antidote to the painful realization that life consists in both happiness and pain, light and darkness, good and evil is the certainty that dark works are always eventually, if temporarily, overcome by purity and light. The logician will not accept such a compromised comfort. His desire is overweening; it will go as far as it can reach; it will tolerate no disappointment or conflict. It will construct a perfectly requited love far from the lives of ordinary mortals. In blissful union with this imaginary object, the Spirit's eternal generative process will be arrested. Self-identity replaces birth, equivalence, intercourse.

The problem of Parmenides's successors will be to mediate the sterility of his achievement. Something will have to stir after all in the embrace of logical truth if Parmenides's world of "what is" is not to be a world where nothing can happen and nothing can be said. Some qualified return will have to be made back to the life of the towns of women and men where the authority of logical thought can be proclaimed and applied. Some controlled license will have to be given to human concern to remotivate a further articulation of logical truth. But even when the perfection of Parmenidean "Being" is compromised in later applications of logic to politics, family life, and nature, even when Being is allowed to take on again some fleshy substance, this will not mean that the desire expressed so passionately in Parmenides's poem is renounced.

As in any romance, true love must prevail over temptations and counterfeits. Even when logic is projected back on the world, so that the logician learns to grasp the unchanging form of Being in the flesh of some real woman, conquered people, or natural element, he remains faithful, and in that faithfulness the ambiguous reality of any woman, or society, or natural phenomenon can be ignored. Working his divisions, syllogisms, entailments, inferences, proofs, the logician takes Parmenides's chariot ride again, past the towns of women and men through Dike's double doors to the reliable arms of well-rounded truth. Once there, in an imaginary bliss, he mimics the motions of love, while all around him the occasions of his researches, those actual women, workers, subjects, patients, natural objects to whom his logic is applied, may suffer a persecution indistinguishable from enmity.

Notes

1. All quotations from Parmenides are my translations from Tarán's Greek text in *Parmenides*.

2. Because logic has been a masculine enterprise in that logicians have been for the most part men, I retain the masculine pronoun, not as generic but as specifically masculine.

3. Jonathan Barnes, *The Prosocratic Philosophers*, vol. I (London: Routledge & Kegan Paul, 1979), 155.

4. E.g., Diels, Kern, Jaeger, Bowra: see Leonardo Tarán, *Parmenides* (Princeton: Princeton University Press, 1965), 22–29, for a review of this literature and a refutation.

5. Karl Reinhardt, "The Relation Between the Two Parts of Parmenides' Poem," in A. Mourelatos, *The Presocratics* (New York: Anchor Books, 1974), 293–311.

6. Tarán, *Parmenides*, 31.

7. Also contributing to the emotion of the prologue are the familiar motifs of epic poetry, particularly Homeric, noted by several commentators, and perhaps most thoroughly explored by C. A. Havelock, "Parmenides and Odysseus," *Harvard Studies in Classical Philology* 63 (1958), 133–143.

8. The use of "Being" instead of "what is," commonly found in translations, is not justified by anything in the text. That an identification of "what is" as a substantive reality or physics would have been made by Plato or Aristotle, or more recently by Heidegger, says more about their philosophy than Parmenides's text (see Tarán's extensive discussion of the literature, *Parmenides*, 33–37). Tarán's solution, that an existential use of the verb "to be" is intended without a subject, may also be unnecessary from a logical point of view. The Goddess's teaching can be put more simply: (1) what is cannot be what is not, what is not cannot be what is, i.e., as the law of noncontradiction, and (2) something either is or is not and there is no other way, i.e., as the law of noncontradiction.

9. The controversy over whether this is a polemic against the followers of Heraclitus, I pass over (see, e.g., Tarán, *Parmenides*, 59) in favor of a reading that takes

Parmenides's references to mortals (6.4) and tribes (6.7) at face value, indicating that Parmenides's target is wider than a particular philosophical school.

10. See Mourelatos's lengthy discussion of the use of πίστις to which his reading gives central significance: *The Route of Parmenides* (New Haven: Yale University Press, 1970), 149ff. Although my analysis of πίστις, or faithfulness, is different from Mourelatos's, I agree that the common translation "belief" robs it of its specific force.

11. πολυπλάγκτων, with the connotations of insanity and madness also.

12. I understand "what" here as the object of "think," in the sense of *how* the body thinks. The body does not think only one thing as does Parmenides's logician thinking "what is," but thinks its own mixtures or changes.

13. The puzzle of how a physical body could be conjoined with a thinking logical soul, which will exercise philosophers for the next few thousand years, does not arise in the same way for mortal opinion. Here thought remains substantial, stimulated by and carried on in physical processes that are neither mechanical nor determined.

14. There is no agreement on the interpretation of this difficult line (see Mourelatos, *Route*, 354–358 for review). My reading avoids any simple equation of the fullness of the older thought and the fullness of logical thought by playing on the psychological-physiological senses of πλέον as fulfillment of desire or fulfillment of appetite. That the same word is used for the fullness of what is does not mean that, in the context, it loses all of those connotations but only that physical desire has once more been transformed into logical desire.

15. Cf. Plato's *Symposium,* where men's opinions on love are expressed, e.g. at 192 where Aristophanes describes the "most hopeful of the nation's growth: those who love other men." "When they themselves come to manhood," he explains, "their love in turn is lavished upon boys. They have no natural inclination to marry and beget children. Indeed, they only do so in deference to the usage of society, for they would just as soon renounce marriage altogether and spend their lives with each other." E. Hamilton and H. Cairns, eds., *Plato: Collected Dialogues* (Princeton: Princeton University Press, 1961).

16. Compare Plato's *Phaedrus*, 250b–d, where Plato describes ideal love as a love in which the lover reacts to the image in the loved one of the heavenly type closest to his own ideal. Once he finds someone with this initial likeness to himself or what he wishes to be, "he does all in his power to foster that disposition" (252e), "creating [in the loved one] a strong likeness of [his] own god" (253a).

17. For the paradigmatic expression of these ideals, see Aristotle's *Politics*, Book I, ch. 13 where he describes his hierarchical relations between natural ruler and natural subject that should hold in the family between husbands and wives and masters and slaves.

18. My reading reverses the order of Mourelatos in *The Route of Parmenides*. Mourelatos argues that the goddess exposes the opinion of mortals as a mimicking or perversion of truth. Certainly this itself was a useful deception. In reality, it is

Parmenides who uses motifs from earlier beliefs to make his logic more persuasive and more palatable, i.e., to give it the "semblance" of truth.

19. The mysteries of Eleusis focused on the myth of Demeter and Persephone.
Persephone, abducted to the darkness of the Underworld by Hades, is mourned
by her mother, Demeter, through the dead time of winter. Finally, through
Demeter's efforts, she is reborn. Demeter, as goddess of agriculture, presided
over the cycle of the seasons and over the immortality revealed at Eleusis
inherent in natural fertility and the regenerations of natural cycles. Common
religious themes throughout the pre-Hellenic Mediterranean were: a female
deity who appeared in a variety of epiphanies, a subordinate young god who
was her son/consort, and celebration of the rebirth of nature in the seasons.
Also the same religious symbols reappeared: the snake-symbol of renewed life
and the wisdom of the earth, the tree-symbol of fruitful regeneration, and the
dove-emblem of spirituality. These are documented in, *inter alia,* B. C. Dietrich,
The Origins of Greek Religion (Berlin: de Gruyter, 1974), George, Thomson,
The Prehistoric Aegean (London: Lawrence and Wishhart, 1949), M. P. Nilsson,
The Minoan and Mycenean Religion and Its Survival in Greek Religion (Lund:
Gleerup, 1950), R. F. Willetts, *The Civilization of Ancient Crete* (London: Bates-
ford, 1977), A. W. Persson, *The Religion of Greece in Prehistoric Times* (Berkeley:
University of California Press, 1942).

20. Anaximander describes a similar process. Coming to be and destruction come
out of each other "according to necessity; for they give due and payment to
each other for their wrongs according to the ordering of time." In other words,
the passing of time returns all to a balance; when one element is in excess and
has been dominant, a right order is restored as its opposite takes over. Fragment
103, G. S. Kirk and J. E. Raven, *The Presocratic Philosophers* (Cambridge:
Cambridge University Press, 1957), 106f.

21. In Plato's *Symposium,* the teaching of Diotima is similar. Beauty is the divinity
at the center of natural life, fomenting the interactions that result in physical
children as well as in new ideas and ways of living. For a detailed account of
the similarities between Diotima's philosophy and mortal opinion, see my
"Rethinking Male and Female: The PreHellenic Philosophy of Mortal Opinion"
(*Journal of the History of European Ideas,* vol. 9, No. 3, 1988), and also, on
Diotima's philosophy, "The Hidden Host: Irigaray and Diotima at Plato's
Symposium" in *Hypatia,* vol. 3, No. 3 Winter, 1989), and "The Subject of Love:
Diotima and her Critics" (forthcoming, *Journal of Value Inquiry,* 1989).

22. Hesiod is apparently the first to invoke Dike in a quarrel with his brother over
property. Not satisfied with the results of the traditional arbitration process,
Hesiod launches a polemic against the unfairness of men's decisions and claims
that they must be judged according to a heavenly Dike, presided over and
enforced by Zeus (*Works and Days,* 212–269).

2
Weaving the Seine of *Logos:*
Plato and the Sophist

The true philosophers, not the seeming ones, looking on life below them, may not seem to be anyone at all or they may seem to be of the highest worth; they may appear either as politicians or as sophists, sometimes they create the impression that they are completely mad (*Sophist* 216c5–d2).

The sophist hides in the darkness of not-being, fastening onto ideas only through groping around; he is difficult to recognize because of the darkness in which he lives. But the philosopher is always truly joined with reality through reasoning. The brightness of his habitat makes him hard to spot because the eyes of the souls of the masses are unable to stand to look on the divine (*Sophist* 254a3–b1).[1]

Although with Parmenides a decisive step had been taken away from the disappointments of physical existence, it is not yet clear what sort of permanent refuge logic can offer. Locked in the embrace of Truth, the logician seemed to enjoy an ultimate security. Soon, that peace was disturbed. If it is impossible to say anything but that what is, is, then any proposition which is not a tautology may be refuted. One can say nothing or, it would seem, anything. Because nothing that is said that is not a tautology can be defended, it doesn't matter what is said. Armed with the principle of noncontradiction, Parmenides's followers proceeded to disrupt all discussion, finding paradox and logical fallacy in even the most uncontroversial assertions. Once the way of nonbeing was forbidden, it would seem to be impossible to say that any statement is untrue or true, that anything is different from anything else, or that anything does not exist. One statement is as refutable as another; and therefore it makes no difference what is said. Both being and thought become a homogenous mass of consistency in which no discrimination can be made. The light of truth had gone out and false philosophers were left groping in darkness. This, the visitor from Elea argues in Plato's *Sophist,* made necessary a kind of "parricide." The father of logic, Parmenides, had to be overthrown. The teaching—that "what is not" has no being of any kind—must be rejected.

Parmenides's desperate flight through and past the towns of men may have, in the end, stayed too close to the ground. Parmenides had insisted on the "existence" of what is, but now logic would have to examine more carefully this existence that locked what is into sterile self-identity. An existing physical object must be identical with itself and with nothing else, but it must at the same time be possible to say things about that physical object that are true or false. In order to make this possible, the Eleatic stranger in Plato's dialogue redirects the flight of the logician in a new direction; no longer does he move horizontally past the towns of men but rises vertically, up, to a region of brightness from which he can look down and say what is irrefutably true about human affairs. From this height *above* the "towns" of mortals, with the confusing self-identity of physically existing things no longer in question, the Platonic philosopher will be able to divide the obdurate oneness of Parmenides's Being into a plurality of Forms between which necessary logical relations can hold. In this way, the endless repetition of the self-identity of "what is" is avoided, and a new content given to logic.

In the dramatic confrontation of the *Sophist,* it is not just the deficiency of Parmenides's logic that is in question. The more pressing concern of the Stranger is to hunt down and capture the elusive and dangerous man–beast who manipulates the tricks of Parmenidean refutation. The Sophists, Plato's political and pedagogical rivals, must be tracked to their dark hiding places and captured. In the discussion of the *Sophist,* these two projects are always intertwined: the redoing of Parmenidean logic and the exposure of the falsity and deception of Sophists. It is the deceptive uses of Eleatic logic, charges the Stranger, that the Sophist has grasped upon in his destructive practices. Eleatic refutations allow him to maneuver in the darkness of his hiding place, attacking with clever arguments the very idea of truth itself. In Sophistic practice, the Stranger explains, the nonexistence of "what is not" is no longer a restriction on what the philosopher may say but a license to say anything at all. The Sophists have, the Stranger claims, reduced philosophy to an empty entertainment, a game, a tug-of-war (259c).[2] Eleatic logic had provided these pseudophilosophers with a camouflage that makes them difficult to track down in their hiding place, invulnerable to counterattack and to any charge of falsity or deception. If there is no nonbeing, there is no falsity and so no way to distinguish proper philosophical thought from improper, truthful statement from false, Sophist from true philosopher. In order to escape from this impasse, the "existence" of Parmenides's being has to be described in new terms. The result is a new practice of logical division that will redeem philosophy from Parmenidean sterility.

Philosophy co-opted by charlatans, the Stranger claims, becomes destructive even of itself. All rational thought is threatened if no predication except simple identity is possible. Then we are only able to "speak of a good as a good, and of a man as a man" (251b5–c1). There can be no substance to philosophy, no physics, no theories of the universe, no moral inquiry that might discover the nature of goodness. There can be no knowledge at all, only a homogeneous "what is" in which it is impossible to make nontautological distinctions, or a plurality of changing being with no constants (252a5–b6). Whether everything is in motion or everything is at rest, knowledge is impossible because knowledge cannot be of just rest or just motion, but must be of both. For this both rest and the "nonbeing" of rest—motion—have to have existence.

Parmenidean logic would result in the complete abolition of all discourse. The logical requirement that each word must be locked into self-identity with itself and separated from every other word means that there can be no engagement with false views. No connection can be made between the language in which human affairs are conducted and logical truth. The logician is condemned to the articulation of sterile inconsistencies and can say nothing of substance. Such a formalism was certainly not acceptable to those, like Socrates and Plato, who were critical of Athenian democracy. If *logos*[3] or reasoning in language, as the Stranger argues (259e), is the weaving together of forms (συμπλοκὴν), then the Parmenidean logic that denies that interweaving leaves the field of human opinion untouched. If no combination of words is logically correct then no combination can be claimed to be better than any other. But this, the Stranger argues, cannot be right. In fact, in discourse, some words do fit together (συναρμόττει)(261d) and some do not, just as in music some chords are harmonious and some are discordant. It is the job of the philosopher to be the guide in such matters; it is he who, from his position above but not beyond the affairs of men, must mark out the correct relations between ideas and expose the charlatans.

The Stranger does not just describe a new form of logical truth; before he even begins to explain the ontological basis of truth he is already practicing a new technique of "capturing" an enemy. As he works to reweave the "seine"[4] of logic correctly, at the same time he is tracking and capturing the Sophist. How shall we catch this slippery fellow? the Stranger asks

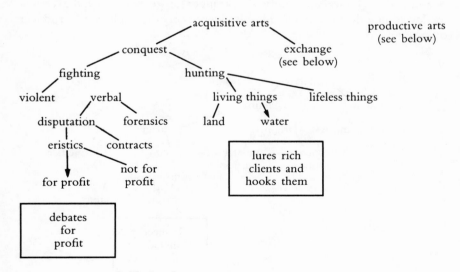

Theaetetus, who has been designated because of his tractability to be his respondent in the discussion. When Theaetetus has no answer, the Stranger does not hesitate. Methodically, step by step, in a series of statements to which the docile Theaetetus invariably assents, the Stranger lays out the above tree of binary pairs of concepts which defines the terrain on which the Sophist can be hunted down. Through each level he tracks his quarry who is, tangled in the "net" of logic at each division, identified with the negative of two opposing alternatives[5] until the Stranger arrives at the Sophist's essence: the Sophist is a hunter of young men; he debates for profit; he hooks rich clients.

The exchange branch of acquisitive arts is then elaborated as follows:

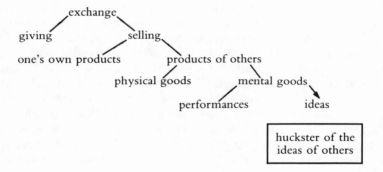

Once the Parmenidean "shield" of the Sophist is penetrated, and falsity is established as a logical possibility, the Stranger can go on to finish the schema by developing the productive side, also identifying the Sophist as a producer of false images.

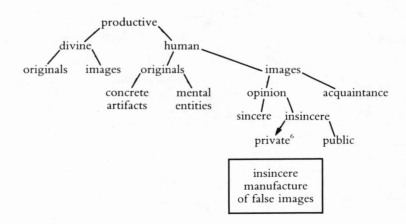

This is a new kind of geography. No longer are the enemies of truth pursued individually on some earthly terrain; instead they are tangled in a net of ideas. Plato moves quickly to the final, decisive definition of the Sophist's nefarious activities: "Making contradictions with words, opinionated mimicry of a dissembling kind, illusion-making generated from image-making, a kind of production, human not divine, of a magic show of words" (268c8–d4). Without the logic that proceeds it, this final conclusion would be only a string of insults. With it, Theaetetus, the Stranger's respondent, and presumably also those gathered to listen to their discussion, are compelled to answer, "I entirely agree." The Stranger has achieved his aim. Without compromising the law of noncontradiction, he has given logic a voice.

Only after successfully illustrating the usefulness of logical division does the Stranger explain in more general terms what he is doing. The knot that reknits the conceptual relations torn by the Sophist is difference (τὸ ἕτερον).[7] A simple dichotomy of "is" and "is not," "being" and "not being" cannot capture the complexity of logical form. In actual speaking there is both a subject and a predicate. A thing does not simply exist, it also is or is not a certain number of things: "a man," "not a dog," "rational," "not ruled by his appetites," etc. Seen this way, it is clear that "is not" is not always the simple contrary of "is," as in "Socrates exists" or "Socrates does not exist;" instead to say something is "not something else" is not to say that it "is not" but that it is "different" from something else in some respect. To say that a man is not a dog is to say that a man is different from a dog, which is not to deny that both dogs and men exist. As difference, what is not exists, for the world is full of differences; in fact everything is different from something else in some respect, and from these differences comes the weaving together of forms that makes speaking possible. Furthermore, once difference is recognized, false thinking and false talk can be identified. To speak falsely is not to perform the impossible task of saying what is not, it is to say what is different from the truth. The job of the philosopher is to find this truth, that is, to find the correct combinations of words, words that are correctly "woven" and "fit together" and so are not different from the truth. The Stranger's insistence that saying something is complex and requires a subject and a predicate allows the philosopher to condemn the Sophist for saying what is not the same as the truth. When the conflation of existence and predication is avoided, the distinction between truth and falsity is preserved. A predication is true not depending on whether *it is,* or says that something is, but on whether what it says is the same or different from what is. Although what is not cannot *be* what is, it can be the same as what is, e.g., if a thing is not white, or not a man.

Parmenides in his flight to logic had gone both not far enough and too far. On the one hand his removal was incomplete, he had not reached the heights because, although he understood the appeal of logical certainty and its incompatibility with the ambiguities of physical existence, he had not freed himself from an existential understanding of the words "to be." Plato, working logic free from concrete existence, was able to project a substitute world of formal differences that can correspond to logical relations ordered by noncontradiction.[8] Seen another way, Parmenides went too far with his insistence on the law of noncontradiction, to a position outside of language where logic may say nothing at all. Armed with differences between forms, however, the philosopher can return to the world of men and the affairs of the city. The limited reality of bodies and physical events, seen only as images, reflections, illusions, shams, can be compared to a new formal reality in which a predicate is not locked into self-identity but is subsumed under other predicates. No longer is there only being and its nonexistent shadow, nonbeing; there is also the higher reality of formal objects represented in a tree of concepts.[9]

As difference, the law of noncontradiction does not create intolerable paradox but can operate in a contained way between specific comparisons. Now the logician may say not only that man "is" or "is not," but that "man is rational" or "man is not a stone." These samenesses and differences are visible to the real philosopher from his position above physical existence. The paradigm, of course, is the Stranger himself, as he marks out the conceptual field on which the deceptive nature of the elusive Sophist is captured. Differences between forms are hierarchically arranged. One form has many forms under it. There is neither an undisciplined horizontal plurality of forms, or one form only; instead there are ordered hierarchies that at each level obey the logical law of noncontradiction. At the highest, most general level is existence; under existence is either rest or motion; under motion, self-propelled or propelled from outside, and so on. By means of a successive dichotomous division and a graded application of noncontradiction—an existing thing is either at rest or in motion, a thing at rest is either . . ., etc.—the philosopher eventually reaches a correct delineation of the nature of things. This vertical projection of Parmenides's two ways allows an ordered sequence of choices, between being and nonbeing, as each category is divided into two opposites which are then subdivided in turn.[10]

The rhetorical benefits of this technique are made clear in the Stranger's attack on the Sophist. From the standpoint of a conceptual order above existence and above actual spoken language, the Stranger is able to separate the higher and the lower, the good and the bad, in each pair of differences. He is able, using his own metaphor, to use the "teeth of the comb" of noncontradiction in actual discourse. Although it might seem that there are any number of different kinds of art, the Stranger is able to demand that division at each level be between two hierarchically opposed alternatives, one side of the division always inferior to the other. At each level of the tree of concepts there is a bad and a good art: trying to get something from others is inferior to production, insincerity is inferior to sincerity. Theaetetus, whose job it is to punctuate and validate the Stranger's demonstration with his answers, is forced each time by the exclusive alternation to place the Sophist on the inferior side. This continues until the Stranger can assemble his final negative definition. The insistence that Theaetetus agree to an exclusive division between two opposing alternatives ensures that Theaetetus must consent to the unflattering portrait of the Sophist that eventually results. Once Theaetetus agrees to put the Sophist in the inferior category of ignorant, later, when the question of the Sophist's wisdom is raised, Theaetetus must admit that "we cannot surely call him wise, because we set him down as ignorant" (268b11–c1). Theaetetus, accepting the new formulation of Parmenides's law of noncontradiction, is forced step by step by logical "necessity" to agree to the Stranger's final indictment of the Sophist.

With division, logic acquired a practical use as an effective tool with which to impose one's view on others. Regardless of the Stranger's rather too dramatic cry of surprise that his practice example of fishing has direct relevance to the definition of the Sophist, it is clear that he has clearly in mind from the very beginning of his conversation with Theaetetus what the concluding judgment on the Sophist must be. Otherwise, there is no reason for divisions to be made as they are. Arts can, for example, be divided by subject matter or methodology, as well as into productive and acquisitive. The particular divisions, however, made by the Stranger force his respondent to a piecemeal acceptance of each element in the Stranger's final definition, and accomplish this before the final definition is revealed. Once it is, the respondent and, presumably, the audience have no alternative but to agree.

The claim that this is a neutral inquiry and that the Stranger only follows the pre-existing order of reality is necessary to support the authority of a speech strategy. In the *Sophist* there is no pretense that the pragmatic end of discrediting the Sophist is not the Stranger's primary purpose. Division allows a way of speaking in which the Stranger's particular value judgments—it is wrong to take money for instruction, relativism is destructive of public order—are embedded in an artificial syntax of positive and negative oppositions. The goodness or badness of the Sophist is no longer an issue for discussion but constitutes the semantic structure of a language which the Stranger is able to force on the young Theaetetus.

The Stranger, however, would not be able to dominate the discussion as he does if his oppositions were completely arbitrary. The power of his logical semantics, still undetached from its use in actual argument and not completely separated from existential assumptions, is not in any necessary or exclusive conceptual scheme. There are many arts, especially in the Greek sense of the word, and there is no reason to think that they are arranged in any necessary order. The deep source of the persuasiveness of the Stranger's presentation is in the series of powerful metaphors and analogies which underlie his divisions. The Sophist is "an angler fishing for rich young men with the false bait of clever rhetoric." The Sophist is a "huckster touting his shoddy wares." The Sophist is "a prizefighter whose mind is for hire." These metaphors give his argument substance; one human activity is used to bring into a negative focus another human activity, to highlight aspects of a practice that might otherwise be missed. The Sophist is seen "as" a fisherman, a hunter, a fighter, comparisons that illuminate his activities by placing them in an analogical frame. The Stranger's positive image of himself as the good philosopher is equally metaphorical. The good philosopher is a weaver who combs out the tangles in discourse, repairs the harmonious patterns of words so that they fit together, winnows the chaff of falsehood from nourishing kernels of truth.

The point of the Stranger's logical innovations, however, is to structure a speech–practice in which one can do more than persuade. Persuasion implies someone to be persuaded, someone who already has certain views and commitments, someone who will also have something to say in answer. With his new technique, the Stranger is able to eclipse this other to whom persuasion must be directed, and to establish a superior and authoritative position in the discussion. He does this by casting the metaphors which are the substance of his insight into an authoritative grid of oppositions. For the Stranger's purposes it is not enough to make a rhetorical comparison hoping that his audience will see the Sophist from a new angle. Instead he constructs out of the metaphors by which he might have only persuaded them a logical structure whose content is no more than the original metaphor but in which that content is reconstituted as necessary truth. If the truth of a metaphor always leaves space for another metaphor and another truth, the Stranger's logical reconstitution does not. It stands alone, as the only correct and true way to view the Sophist.

Division has placed the logician in a new relation to those to whom he speaks. He is no longer the mystic contemplator of Parmenidean Being who can only repeat his assertion: "What is is, Being is Being." Simple repetition does not preclude the possibility of other statements, other visions, other being, any more than a metaphor precludes other metaphors. Plato's accommodation of logic to actual argumentative discussion results in a successful technique for managing dissent. The law of the excluded middle mandates a series of normatively ordered statements at the same time as it forbids the respondent to speak or think outside the categories in which these evaluations have been made. Division closes the question step by step. Now no more can be said. Argument is terminated. It is not surprising that such a technique would be welcome to someone of Plato's political views.[11]

The changes in Greek society during and after the Persian War made

Athens a cosmopolitan mercantile center and created an environment in which the traditional authority of a superior few could no longer be easily maintained. The Sophists' role in this transition from aristocracy to democracy, from divine law to natural law, from natural law to human law, was deplored by conservatives like Plato. To Plato, the Sophists, for the most part not Greeks but foreigners, were opportunistic money-grubbers; their emphasis on practical skills for management of the household and the city seemed to Plato symptomatic of all that was destroying traditional values. Given Plato's nostalgia for a divine order and a society that mirrors that order, it is not surprising that he would have wished to expose the Sophists as enemies of truth, impostors, and shams, or that he would want a decisive instrument with which to command assent to his views.

In order to give credibility to this procedure, however, it was necessary to give it a theoretical basis. This the Stranger proceeds to do in the latter parts of the *Sophist*. Logic would have not just to be practiced, which might leave it open to the charge that it was a mere rhetorical device, but defended as reflective of a higher reality. The seine of *logos* that catches the Sophist must seem to be above and outside any language or any political agenda. Although the Stranger begins by demonstrating the practical use of this logic, he must then establish its epistemological status prior to any use. He must rework Parmenidean Being and construct a new conceptual Being which is neither a collection of disparate items nor a homogeneous whole, but made up of Forms that blend and mix in determinate ways. These Forms are different from each other—they come in opposite pairs, motion and rest, production and acquisition, odd and even, etc.—and they also can fall under each other—productive art is under art, motion and rest under existing things, etc. The independent reality of such conceptual entities was necessary if the dialectial speech-practice of the *Sophist* and other Platonic dialogues was to have the necessary authority.

It was not only reality that had to be reconstituted. The Stranger points out to Theaetetus that the Sophist, even though he may agree that there are Forms and so can no longer argue that nonbeing cannot exist, can still deny that there is any nonbeing in language and claim that there is no such thing as a false statement. Therefore, a complementary reworking of language is also necessary. It must be shown that in a logical language, just as Forms are related to each other, so must words be related to each other in correct ways. It is, the Stranger claims, this weaving together of the Forms that makes language possible. To say something, it is necessary to put Forms together in a statement. To say something true, it is necessary to put together the correct subject and predicate. The result is that it is possible to say that some things we say are true and some are false. What we say is true if it is the same as "what is"; it is false if it says something different from "what is." Language, then can be divided into true statements on one side and false on the other. Again the pragmatic benefit of such a division is clear. Not only is the Sophist exposed as an opportunist out only for profit, but the linguistic wares he sells and the verbal bait he offers can be exposed as falsities. And this can be extended from what he says to his opinions (δόξἄ), his thinking (διάνοιἄ), and to the sensory appearances (φαντασία) which he sometimes relies on. These also are either true or false; they represent "what is" about something or they do not.

The exposure of the Sophist as a sham is then supported with a threefold separation; not only have differences between forms been separated from that concrete existence which in the Parmenidean formulation could be only itself and not anything else, but also the language in which truth can be told has been separated from the Forms. Because the Forms are arranged in a determinate order and what we say is separate from those Forms, what we say can now be judged according to whether it mirrors the order of Forms, and whatever is not consistent with that mirroring can be condemned as false.

But the language in which this is possible cannot be the same language we all speak.[12] In the *Sophist* it is made clear that logic will require a reform of language. In his discussion of truth, Plato has already begun to frame a new use of the Greek word for speech, *logos*. In the course of the *Sophist*, *logos*, the common Greek word used for all the great variety of kinds of speech, begins to take on the metaphysical weight that will continue to burden it in a long series of philosophical and theological usages. *Logos* no longer can be the simple, ordinary "what someone says," but, as required by logical division, it must be restricted to statements that are either true or false and statements that reflect correct relations between formal objects (262–265).[13] Spoken language can be no guide in logical matters, it must be referred to and evaluated in an ideal language that reflects the reality of the Forms.

For this reason it does not matter that sometimes no term can be found to complete the conceptual trees that are necessary to catch the Sophist (226d5). The Stranger gives an explanation for this inadequacy in spoken language.

> Where then, can we find a suitable name for each of these [i.e., for the mimic who is ignorant of what he mimics and the mimic who knows about what he mimics]? No doubt it would be hard, because earlier in regard to the division of kinds by forms, the ancients, we must think, were lazy and stupid and never even undertook to divide them with the result that we have not very many names (267d4–8).

In constructing his trees, the logician is not making a catalog of the actual uses of words. He has no problem in concluding that those who went before were simply too lazy to think up names for everything. In the *Cratylus,* Plato explains why it is that the inadequate surface structure of a language is not relevant to the philosopher. There are, Plato argues, beyond the different notations of different languages, ideal names. The success of a language depends on how closely the surface structure corresponds to an ideal conceptual structure that carves reality at the joints.[14] The philosopher who combs the tangles from language must also be a butcher who trims away the fleshy fat of ordinary talk to leave the bare bones of truth.

What results is a language that is not spoken like ordinary language, but that institutes a new kind of relationship between speakers exemplified in the *Theaetetus.* If the result of Parmenidean logic was an autism in which any other to whom or about whom one might have talked has disappeared, Plato's division restores discussion, but this is a discussion from which reciprocity has been removed. The Stranger makes it clear at the onset of the dialogue, when asked if he accepts Theaetetus as his respondent, that he has no use for any exchange between equals. "It is easier, Socrates, to speak in this way, to another person, if that person is tractable and manageable, if not it is easier to speak oneself" (217b1–3). Logical division offers an alternative to a lecture which can be ignored or disbelieved, at the same time as it prevents discussion from being interupted by contrary views or responses.

Logical division makes possible a conversation in which one party is in complete control of the discussion. The Stranger leaves Theaetetus no opening for any substantive contribution to the discussion. At the same time the illusion is created of an exchange of views. At each level of division, the Stranger elicits either a positive response or a question asking for further clarification from Theaetetus. The either/or questions he asks, however, strictly limit the kind of answer Theaetetus can give.[15] The price for deviation is ridicule. One of the few times Theaetetus ventures an idea of his own is at the very sensitive center of the argument where the Stranger introduces his self-description as the winnower of truth. Well, the Stranger suggests, after giving his self-flattering definition of the real philosopher, he hesitates to call such men Sophists. Theaetetus, for one, expresses doubt; he sees some resemblances. But this suggestion of the naive Theaetetus is brushed aside. There is also a similarity, says the Stranger contemputously, between a dog and a wolf, and he goes on with his argument (231a). The Stranger again ridicules Theaetetus when Theaetetus comments on the Sophists' claim to be able to discuss a variety of subjects. "It would seem, at any rate," Theaetetus ventures bravely, "that almost nothing is beyond them" (232e5). The Stranger responds with sarcasm. "Do you, my young friend, really think things such as this possible? Perhaps, then young people see more keenly, and I only dimly." Theaetetus responds, for once, with a trace of irritation. "What then, and for what are you saying this? I don't understand what you are asking now" (232e6–8), but he quickly returns to tractable monosyllabic responses of assent and dissent. A few exchanges later, he has completely surrendered all ability to think for himself. When asked a question, he conceeds, "This is a hard question. It is scarcely for a person like me to find an answer at all," a judgment which the Stranger happily accepts as the correct basis for continued discussion. With this established, the Stranger proceeds to tell Theaetetus how Theaetetus conceives reality (250b), and what Theaetetus means by what he says (261d). By the time the important question comes up of the divine origin of the universe, Theaetetus has lost all ability to consult his own instincts or beliefs. "I, myself, perhaps because of my age, many times change my opinion from one thing to another, but now looking at you and accepting that you hold that these things come from god, I am convinced" (265d1–4). Logic has restructured communication. The laws of noncontradiction and excluded middle force Theaetetus's replies and also his thought, into approved channels. They structure a drill by which Theaetetus can learn, not to think, but to repeat what his teacher says. The logic of the Stranger's argument is the exercise of that authority. It is logical necessity itself that denies Theaetetus's futile attempts at response.

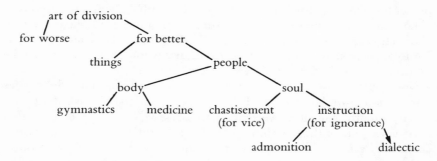

There is only one point at which the paralyzing mesh of the Stranger's logic seems to tear and the completeness of the conceptual scheme which renders Theaetetus speechless is compromised. The Stranger breaks off his critique of the Sophist. He must, he says, describe another kind of Sophistry, a good Sophistry, of "noble lineage." Abruptly the images of deceiving hunter, huckster, opportunist fade: no longer are we at the manly hunt with its violence and self-interest, tangling the quarry in nets and tracking him down. Surprisingly, we are in the feminine world of the household. Isn't there, the Stranger prompts the bewildered Theaetetus, another Sophist, a benign Sophist who does not hunt or angle, but winnows, sifts, strains, threshes, combs—all wholesome generative improving activities that involve no deception or destruction?

This "side wind," as the Stranger himself calls it, necessitates a new conceptual tree. It is not possible to catch the true philosopher in the net that caught the Sophist; instead the Stranger must propose a new one. The supposed exclusive dichotomies of the first schema are abandoned; the Stranger does not ask whether this benign art is productive or acquisitive. In fact it would be impossible to classify it in either category. Although the philosopher works on opinions of men that are already there and which he has not produced, what he does cannot be classed as acquisitive because there is no motive of personal gain. It would seem that this third, benevolent art of dialectic must compromise exclusive division; the logic that pinned the Sophist down in his lair and forced Theaetetus to agree with the Stranger's condemnation of the Sophist required an exclusive division. If the Sophist is not productive then he must be acquisitive; if he is not acquainted with reality, he must have only opinions.[16]

But, the interruption is necessary. The Stranger must protect himself from the charge that in tracking down the Sophist he practices just the very deceptive tricks for which he indicts the Sophist. He must show that he is not a hunter and an angler. He must identify and justify his activities without himself being caught in the seine of his own logic. This is the one point of serious weakness in the Stranger's strategy, and the vulnerability of such a position does dimly cross even Theaetetus's befuddled mind. Isn't the good philosopher, including by now, the Stranger, a Sophist too? Isn't he perhaps only an opportunist of another kind? This is dangerous ground for the Stranger. To avoid such questions, he must refuse to place himself, as the true philosopher and the practitioner of logical division, on the same map as the Sophist. He must not be in the same "world," or on the same "level." This necessarily introduces, as he notes, a "side wind."

The puzzles of self-reference that will trouble logic throughout its history are here initiated as an infelicity in speech practice. The logic in which the Sophist is identified cannot include a description of itself. The problem is practical. Strategically, the logician cannot allow himself to be judged in the same terms as the Sophist; his motives and intentions must be evaluated in different terms. This requires that there be a 'metalogic' in which the art of division itself can be represented. The philosopher is no Sophist looking for refutations. In order to make this clear, he must move yet one step higher, beyond even those heavenly Forms which had captured the Sophist, to a level of analysis from which, this time with approval, he can look down upon himself tracking the evil activities of Sophists.

This higher level of analysis requires a new set of metaphors. The masculine activities—fighting, hunting, fishing, selling—by which the Stranger described the Sophist disappear. The philosopher "winnows," "combs," "untangles," "reweaves" the threads of human discourse. If Parmenides borrowed the powerful images of pre-Hellenic matrifocal thought to buttress his logic, the Stranger has borrowed again. The life-affirming and benevolent household and agricultural activities of disenfranchised Greek women, women excluded from any philosophical discussion, become the metaphors that validate logical division. The true philosopher is no virile hunter; he threshes the grain, weaves the cloth, braids, reknits, reknots the torn fabric of thought. The defender of the privileged male speech that must rule the good state is the feminine weaver of truth. This redemptive feminine image reappears at the most crucial of moments, when the Stranger must justify his own practice. If Parmenides borrowed the authority of the still-powerful Nemesis or Moira at the same time as he reduces them to the handmaidens of truth, the Stranger borrows the benignity and constructiveness of female activities to validate the logic that must reject them.

The personae in the Platonic dialogues are men. The interchanges that the Stranger's logic was to structure took place as part of exclusively male institutions. Rational discussions such as the one reported in the *Sophist* were typically between an older, wiser patron and a younger, attractive youth who provided sexual pleasures in return for an initiation into the affairs of men and the benefits of the elder man's patronage. As with Parmenides, the mixing or mingling of the sexes still has no place in logic. Logical discussion is between men. But logic is no longer an impotent mystical flight from a material feminine reality to metaphysical Being. The terms set in the *Sophist* are for an alternate male society, outside the household, away from women, away from birth and death and heterosexuality in a new public space reserved for men. If that space had a constitutive beginning, it was not only in the physical spaces—law court, assembly, agora—laid out for logical debate in the new city-states. More important was the establishment of the forms of rational communication that define these spaces. For Plato, democratic Sophists such as Protagoras, with the view that every viewpoint should be heard and credited, compromised the independence of that rational communication and of the authoritarian institutions that it structured. If anyone's view may have merit, if no opinion can be called absolutely false, if there are always two sides of the question, then the boundaries that define authoritative speech and authoritarian rule are blurred.

In their households, and in the few public venues where they were allowed to congregate—occasional religious festivals and family gatherings—Athenian women no doubt continued to talk as they wove and embroidered, visited back and forth, discussed the management of their households and the well-being of their children. And their talk, as women's talk does, must in fact have constituted that reweaving of the social fabric so often broken by misunderstanding, anger, insensitivity. If the Stranger co-opts their reweaving, it is a reweaving in a different sense. No longer are the broken strands, colors, motifs of human feeling and behavior rewoven painstakingly back into some altered design that can give new meaning and stability to human life; now there is a rigid pattern meant to exclude and forbid, and not to accommodate.

It was not just women who were excluded from rational discussions. Slaves, non-Greek barbarians, as well as the masses of low-born Greek artisans and workers who could not be expected to regulate their feelings and desires in the ways required by logic were also barred from logical thought. When talk was necessary, they could be made to play the role of Theaetetus. The rhetorical techniques of Plato's dialectic would prove useful in conversation with any inferior. If a woman or servant insists on speaking to a man, she, or he, can be required to follow proper logical form. She can be required to listen and to punctuate the speaker's remarks with signs of approval and acceptance. If she attempts to speak on her own, she can be accused of lack of rigor and lack of understanding of the categories of rational expression. If she ventures a thought outside the tree of logical concepts she can be dismissed and ridiculed as Theaetetus was by the Stranger.[17] Better, she can disappear altogether, leaving the world of public speech to men exercising their power over other men with their vision fixed on Truth regardless of what she might say, regardless of what anyone might say.[18]

Notes

1. Citations are to *The Sophist, Platonis Opera,* vol. I (Oxford: Oxford University Press, 1977). My translations.

2. Judging from the existing fragments of Sophistic thought, some preserved in the Platonic dialogues themselves, this is hardly an accurate account of the various positions of the Sophists. Closest is perhaps Gorgias's Parmenidean refutation, preserved in Sextus Empiricus, "On Being," repr. in J. B. Wilbur and H. J. Allen, *The World of the Early Greek Philosophers* (Buffalo, NY: Prometheus Books, 1979), but there is good reason to think that this was a parody and therefore a negative comment on Parmenidean logic.

3. There is no exact English translation of λόγος, a nominalization from the verb to speak, which can be used for any unit of speech: declaration, assertion, reckoning, promise, command, order, request, as well as a phrase, sentence, or a complete work such as the *Iliad*. The result is that translators render it in a variety of ways, depending on context, as "discourse," "statement," "sentence," etc., creating the illusion that contemporary logical distinctions were present in the Greek and covering over the processes of thought and practice in which those distinctions were developed. I have chosen instead consistently to use the literal "what is said," which I believe is closest to the Greek meaning and preferable to the technical term "locution," which may capture the logical scope of λόγος but fails to capture the meaning of the word, widely used in ordinary speech.

4. The Greeks used a seine, or net, for fishing and for hunting birds and small

game, and also in battle. One might also remember the crude Hephaestus's entrapment of Aphrodite and her lover Ares in a gossamer net spread over the violated marriage bed.

5. This retention of the law of the excluded middle as a forced choice between two oppositions shows that Plato does not mean to abandon Parmenides altogether. Witness the placing of the Stranger as "belonging to the school of Parmenides and Zeno" (216a). Also, in the *Republic* and elsewhere the unity of Parmenides's Being is preserved in the Form of Good which, although it can be divided, unites all the Forms.

6. The Sophist practices his arts in private homes rather than in the law courts or Assembly where the Stranger implies that his deceptions might be easier to detect. In fact, of course, the Sophists, being foreigners or *metics,* were excluded from the courts and the Assembly, and could only operate in the background as speechwriters and advisors.

7. The discussion of difference continues through 257ff. This is perhaps the historic entrance of a concept that is to play a major role in contemporary linguistic thought, for example in Saussurian structural linguistics as the "difference" between signifiers that generates meaning, or in the work of Jacques Derrida, with the addition of deferral in time, as the "differance" that for him constitutes the less-ordered, deconstructed weaving of meaning.

8. A modern formulation of this rejection of concrete existents is that propositions refer not to things but to facts. Here even Forms, as the pseudo-things which mediate between language and the world, have disappeared in order to preserve linguistic truth from the paradoxes of existential identity, and reference is established to a textualized mirror image of predication itself. Eventually the result is a fully semanticized theory of truth such Tarski's, where "true" is simply a term in a metalanguage by means of which a lower-level language may be discussed, and truth is a relationship, not between words and things, but between language and metalanguage. The modern successor to Plato's Forms is an idiom in which to talk about neither conceptual things nor concrete things, but logical language itself: see Alfred Tarski, "The Concept of Truth in Formalized Languages," *Logic, Semantics, and Metamathematics* (Oxford: Oxford University Press, 1956).

9. Thus preparing the way for a clear distinction between contingent empirical science and necessary analytic truth. That Plato himself had not fully separated logical form from ontology is given by some as a reason for denying that the dialectic is logic, since it uses neither symbols nor patterns of argument: (e.g., F. M. Cornford *Plato's Theory of Knowledge* (London: Routledge and Kegan Paul, 1949), 275. The proponents of an abrupt beginning for logic with Aristotle discount both the fact of the symbolic metalanguage implicit in Plato's Forms, and the existential presuppositions that remain in Aristotelian logic.

10. A similar method of analysis can still be found in contemporary structural semantics where the semantic value of a term is given by semantic oppositions such as physical object/abstract object, male/female, animate/inanimate, between which there are relations of incompatibility and of hyponymy. By means

of such semantic markers, linguistic facts such as snyonomy, meaninglessness, analytic truth, etc., can be explained: e.g., Jerrold Katz, *The Underlying Reality of Language* (New York: Harper Torchbooks, 1971), 95. This seems to correspond, at least in practice, with Plato's interest in finding words which "fit together." In both cases, statements are clarified (given a semantic reading) against the background of a hierarchically ordered conceptual scheme. There are, however, some interesting differences. The semanticist uses a componential model in which a semantic reading is built up out of atomic units of meaning: see Katz, "Democritean Theory of Language," in *Underlying Reality*. For Plato, however, the direction is not from the bottom up but from the top down. The all-encompassing Forms are divided until one reaches the smallest possible Forms such as "man" or "bear" (not to be confused with individual men or bear). Thus, the result is not a construction out of primitive elements but a complex whole. There are also differences in professed motivation. Plato's is to trap the Sophist. A semanticist claims the status of an objective science whose enemies are anonymous.

11. See Eric Havelock's description of Socrates's and Plato's attack on the liberal democratic views of the Sophists in *The Liberal Temper in Greek Politics* (London: Jonathon Cape, 1967).

12. This distinction between speech and language is preserved in Saussure's *parole* and *langue*. "But what is language? . . . It is not to be confused with human speech. . . . Language is a self-contained whole and a principle of clarification": *Course in General Linguistics,* trans. Wade Baskin (New York: McGraw-Hill, 1966), 9.

13. This change is marked in many translations, as λόγος, which before was translated as "discourse," begins to be translated as "statement" (e.g., Cornford's translation in E. Hamilton and H. Cairns, eds., *The Collected Dialogues of Plato* (Princeton: Princeton University Press, 1961).

14. Contemporary linguistics must also circumvent the fact that not only individual speakers, who may be excluded as deviant, but also entire languages may not very exactly exhibit logical form. The circumventing is done in contemporary linguistics by assuming that universal semantic components must underlie surface structures, and then developing generative grammars that explain the derivation. In this way, linguistics is relieved as Plato was from reliance on the vocabulary of any actual language which might not have a name for "animate" or "inanimate" to complete a semantic analysis.

15. Contemporary propositional logic also operates only on statements that are either true or false. If Theaetetus's presence is necessary to the art of division, his inaudible voice may still be assumed assenting to the truths and falsities of the truth-functional calculus.

16. See also Aristotle on why failure to divide without remainder is fatal (*Posterior Analytics* II, ch. 5).

17. See recent research that establishes differences between male and female conversational styles discussed in, for example, Cheris Kramarae, *Women and Men Speaking* (Rowley, MA: Newbury House, 1981), or M. R. Key, *Male/Female*

Language (Metuchen, NJ: Scarecrow Press, 1975). The Stranger's style is, in fact, characteristically masculine. See also studies that link speech-styles to class dominance: e.g., Peter Trudgill, "Sex, Covert Prestige and Linguistic Change in the Urban British English of Norwich," *Language in Society,* 1 (1972), 179–195, or Basil Bernstein, "Social Class, Linguistic Codes, and Grammatical Element," *Language and Speech,* 5 (1967), 221–250.

18. The supposed liberalism of Plato's *Republic,* where a small select number of women are allowed to join the Guardian caste, is consistent with this exclusion. Plato's argument is that, although women in general will not have the rational capabilities of guardians, the few who are able to pass the tests, that is, who can learn to speak as men do, will be admitted. These "honorary men" were needed for a very practical purpose. Plato's guardians had to breed and it was best that they did this without being contaminated by the speech of women. Plato's admission of guardian women to his ruler class makes the separation between the world of the household and the world of politics complete. Guardian men now have no need to return to a woman-focal household for any purpose, even for physical reproduction.

3

Aristotle's Syllogisms

The Mechanisms of Deceit

When they are on the offensive, students ought to conceal the strategy we are teaching them to detect when defending (*Prior Analytics* 19; 66a33–35).

If an inference is drawn through the middle, we begin from that middle for this way most certainly the answer will be concealed (*Prior Analytics* 19; 66b1–3).[1]

Clumsy and inept though he may appear in the sudden darkness of human affairs, the Platonic philosopher returns from the illuminated world of transcendent Being back to the world of men, of politics and business, of struggles for power and status. Once there, the method of division allows him to discredit his enemies, to put forth a defense of his own true philosophy, and to attract an admiring circle of pupils. But Platonic logic, Aristotle charged, is still too removed from human affairs, still too encumbered with Parmenidean circularity. Plato's divisions can prove anything to anyone, and if division is only the articulated repetition of a given position, it can have no real authority over others' opinions. In place of division, Aristotle devises a more effective logical technique, the syllogism, which will not just articulate what is already known, but produce new knowledge.[2]

The aim of this new logic is not to reveal relations between transcendent Forms. Aristotle proposes a more practical study of the skillful combination of terms in statements to produce necessary conclusions. In his definition of the syllogism he makes clear that his logic is a linguistic matter: "A syllogism is a *discourse* in which, certain things being stated, something other than what is stated follows from necessity" (*Prior*, 24a18–22; my emphasis). The syllogism tells us how to arrange what we say so that a conclusion *must* be drawn, a conclusion that is not just a reiteration of what we already believe but new knowledge which must in turn be accepted by our opponents.

We may know, to use Aristotle's example, that "all mules are barren," and that "this animal here is a mule," and still not have put these two facts together. "Nothing prevents someone who knows both that A belongs to the whole of B and that B belongs to the whole of C, thinking that A does not belong to C" (*Prior*, II, 21; 67a33–35). But once the statements are combined in a syllogism—"All mules are barren. This animal is a mule. This animal is barren."—The truth that "this animal will not give birth" becomes evident. It is necessary to forgive Aristotle his example of the simple farmer whose logic fails. To know that mules are barren and still think that the "mule" in our barn is with foal seems more indicative of mental illness than of ignorance. In fact, this defense of the syllogism as superior to division and noncircular is only intelligible when one takes into account that it was never meant that any farmer would have use of it. The techniques described in the *Prior Analytics* assume a specific Athenian institution of elaborate, often artificial debate in which farmers, laborers, or workers were not involved. Although it is unlikely that a farmer would think his mule pregnant if he has any knowledge of animal husbandry, a professional disputant, working his way through a complex series of predications removed from any substantial reality, might indeed make the mistake of not seeing an inference. The result is that he might be caught in a contradiction and defeated by a clever opponent. Only given this particular context for Aristotelian logic is it possible to understand the ignorance for which the syllogism is the remedy and the "new knowledge" that it is to provide.

The *Prior Analytics* is a handbook, a refinement of argumentative techniques already developed by the Sophists, which, as one scholar put it, amounted to "a highly artificial and, as we should say, unnatural study, namely, deliberately, even professionally, coined false reasoning."[3] This "reasoning" had its place in a specific institution of programmed debate. There are two participants, a questioner and a respondent, and also an audience. The audience does not participate directly, but comments or breaks in, to urge on or chastise one or both of the disputants. A question is proposed. The respondent, having the right to choose his side, decides which of two contradictory propositions he will defend. The contest begins. His opponent questions the respondent and attempts, in eliciting his opponent's response to other propositions, to get him to admit to a thesis contrary to his adopted position. If a contradiction is found, the respondent loses the contest. The skill of the questioner, the skill in which Socrates of the Platonic dialogues is a master, is to find credible premises that will at the same time, contradict a respondent's position.[4] The skill of the respondent is to avoid the trap. Their respective maneuvers are watched with amusement and suspense by the audience. Debates of this form were not an academic matter. They went on for amusement in the homes of the privileged as in the *Sophist*—although even in a private setting there was always the serious business of attracting students, clients, or allies—and also in the law courts, in political debate, or in business negotiations where debate had considerable stakes.

Nor was this institution an invention of philosophers. Although Plato often seems to claim for Socrates the initiation of an agonistic question-and-answer form of discussion as a new form of speculative inquiry, patterns of dialectical debate were already well established in the city-state of Athens. Philosophical dialectic might be popularized by Sophists advertising themselves as teachers of the sons of the wealthy, and a philosopher-celebrity such as Socrates might provide entertainment in the recreational settings—private parties, gymnasia, informal gatherings, walks in the country—familiar from Platonic dialogues, but similar patterns of argument, refutation, charge and countercharge were beginning to structure concrete exchanges between men in the busy courts of Athens and in an Assembly swollen with the addition of new male citizens. The debates for which Aristotle's logic was a handbook were not between a few leisured aristocrats disinterestedly contemplating eternal truths, but between men intent on winning and preserving power, privilege, and wealth.

The form of such exchanges was established in the courts where plantiffs made charges and defendants tried to defeat their claims. The fundamental alterations in familial and community relations which resulted from this institution of juridical dialectical debate are dramatized in Aeschylus's trilogy, the *Oresteia*. There, on the occasion of Orestes's application for acquittal of the crime of murdering his mother, Aeschylus depicts the founding of the first court of homicide in Athens.[5] Orestes has wandered as an exile for many years, seeking purification at various shrines, but his crime is so great that he cannot be absolved. He is pursued by no actual avenger but by the Erinnyes, fearful personifications of his own conscience that haunt a murderer wherever he goes.[6] He appeals to Athena, daughter of Zeus and patron-goddess of Athens, who proposes the remedy: there will be a hearing before a jury who will hear the charge and Orestes's defense. Orestes can present his case and refute the charge made against him. Argument and counter-argument before a jury will replace the old blood guilt that haunts the matricide cast out from the human community.

With the divine aid of Apollo, Orestes prepares his argument. First, he attempts to catch the Erinnyes in a contradiction. The Erinnyes claim that it is the worst of crimes to murder someone of your own blood. Then why didn't they pursue with the same fury Clytemnestra, his mother, for killing her husband Agamemnon? The Erinnyes respond: but a husband and wife are not of the same blood. Now Orestes, expressing Hellenic outrage at this slight on the marriage tie which binds a woman to her husband, cleverly manages to turn their argument against them. The Erinnyes claim that it is the worst of crimes to murder someone of your own blood, but in fact a mother and a son are not of the same blood; a mother nurtures the seed planted in her by the father, thus the only true blood relations are between father and child. Triumphantly Orestes rests his case. His ingenious "syllogism"—mother and child have not the same blood, so a matricide is not guilty of killing a parent; Orestes killed his mother; therefore he is not guilty of killing a parent—prevails, supported by Athena who acts as presiding magistrate. She herself is proof, she announces; she has no mother but only her father Zeus. The jury votes, with Athena casting the tie-breaking vote for acquittal.

Before they are bought off by Athena with the "honorable" status of minor household deities, the Erinnyes describe in dire terms what will result from such "justice."

> This is catastrophe,
> this new institution
> if the plea and injury of
> matricide is to prevail.
> His deed made easy will
> tempt all men.
> Much injury will be
> brought on parents by children
> From this time on.
> For from no vigilant
> Maenads now will anger
> Come upon these deeds (*Eumenides* 493–503).

From the standpoint of the old ways represented by the Erinnyes, morality and social order falter if specious arguments can release a murderer from guilt.[7] Responsibility for crime vanishes when clever defenses absolve criminals and wrongdoing can be successfully circumvented by the letter of the law. From the standpoint of Athena, who describes herself as always "for the father," the constitution of the new city-state governed by male citizens for which she is the patroness requires a new form of justice. Neither local and voluntary judicial procedures based on custom and rooted in the inner restraints whose disappearance the Erinnyes deplore, nor the guilt that inevitably pursued anyone who had irrevocably transgressed the sacred laws of hospitality and family obligation are any longer appropriate in a centrally governed city and empire. The old inner restraints could only be binding in a community of men and women with shared values and commitments.[8] A city-state and its colonial empire in which the majority (slaves, foreigners, women, manual workers, artisans, conquered or dependent peoples) are ruled by a minority of propertied men required a new justice in the form of legislation written by men and adjudicated by men, legislation that defined offenses, penalties, and defenses. The courts provided an alternate, less destructive arena for the violent agonistic contests for prestige and power between upper-class men that were the most distinctive feature of Greek culture and that in the close confines of the city-state were increasingly dangerous.[9]

Just as Orestes appeals to Athena's court to exonerate him from guilt, so would claimants and defendants come to argue their cases before citizen judges and juries of Athens. But the result of such procedures, the Erinnyes charge, will be catastrophe: pain for families and disruption of the social fabric. In the place of, on the one hand, the deeply rooted understanding of the wisdom of the heart and "health of the soul" (539) which leads to a good life, and on the other, the "insolence" (537) that leads to ruin, failure, and alienation from the human community, Athena has instituted her "higher" justice.[10] This higher justice allows Orestes to argue his case, devise a successful defense, and return home, freed from guilt, to resume the rule of his father as a loyal ally of Athens. It permits, the Erinnyes argue, a criminal to go free, and a "usurper to take a throne that drips with blood" (162).

In the new courts, success depended not on guilt or innocence, but on cleverness and dexterity in argument. Not only did each side have the right to present arguments, they also had the right to question and refute those who accused them. Orestes tries to catch the Erinnyes in contradiction: if they pursue murderers, why didn't they pursue Clytemnestra for murdering her husband? He tries to prove that, from their own premise that murder of a parent is unforgivable, it follows that Orestes's crime is not unforgivable because a mother is not a parent. There is no discussion of what happened, of the circumstances of the crime, of Clytemnestra's reasons for killing her husband Agamemnon, of the senseless slaughter at which he had officiated at Troy, of his brutal murder of their daughter. There is no discussion of the circumstances of Orestes's crime, of the fact that he entered by stealth and as a guest, thus also transgressing the duty of guest to host. Charges and countercharges are made; arguments are devised and elaborated. Whoever can find an inconsistency in the charge or evidence against him may go free. Although in many cases political expediency must have been involved—Orestes's restoration at Mycenae as a friendly ally was certainly to Athens' advantage—there was in Athens a relish for the tricks and devices of adversarial argument quite apart from the substance of the case. Juries awarded verdicts in the same way they might reward a particularly inventive if not too sportsmanlike wrestling hold. Justice, like the athletic contests so popular among Greek men, was a substitute for the ruthless, violent competition for plunder and power that dominated Hellenic culture and that is documented in the Homeric epics. Now a successful man would learn how to use the weapons of rhetoric as skillfully as he used his sword against barbarians or his limbs against rivals in the gymnasium.

As laws, lawsuits, pleas, and arguments proliferated, direct evidence became unreliable. Witnesses could be bribed, testimony from slaves was elicited under torture.[11] The old *logos*, the account of an event by a witness, could no longer be trusted. A new authoritative Logos or Reason replaced human credibility. Such a higher truth allowed testimony to be tried with logical refutations such as Orestes's that depended on clever definitions of words or inconsistencies intricately traced out between differing testimonies or between conflicting laws passed to protect different private interests. Dexterity in argument was the key to success. As Aristotle says, in his *Rhetoric* (I, 17; 1376a), you cannot buy off an argument from probability the way you might buy off a witness. In the courts there were excuses, extenuations, exceptions, indulgences, and lesser penalties, to be argued and debated before a jury who would reward the most agile dialectician with success.

Although Athenian law still required a litigant to conduct his own suit, a growing number of professional dialecticians were soon preparing briefs, working through the complexities of refutations and defenses. The Athenians took to litigation. Suits and counter-suits multiplied. This new arena for display and the winning of advantage was crowded with competitors. Debate and refutation, so successful in law, became popular in the other public places in which men gathered to discuss issues of value and policy. In politics, speakers in the Assembly borrowed the new forensic techniques to show up their opponents. Teachers advertising their skills showed off their knowledge in staged dialectical debates. These practitioners and their clients were the clientele for whom Aristotle's *Topics* and *Prior Analytics* were written.

In the *Topics* Aristotle made a general survey of arguments actually in use in order to acquaint the student with the tactics or *topoi* with which he could win arguments. In this initial marking out of the field, Aristotle dealt with a great variety of arguments, not all of which could take the form of a syllogism—arguments, for example, that have to do with relations or with the "preferable." In the *Categories* he began tailoring language to fit the syllogism by subsuming vocabulary under several basic metaphysical categories. In *On Interpretation* he turned to combinations of words ordered in ways to better accomplish refutations, showing how statements can be set out in oppositional pairs to polarize a dispute and prepare the way for the production of contradictions. Finally, in the theory of the syllogism presented in the *Prior Analytics*, Aristotle made his great contribution to logic. Some of the arguments of the *Topics* had to be set aside, such as ones that deal with indefinite statements or the preferable, concepts that do not fit into any "category," and statements that do not admit of dicotomous negations might have to be ignored, but, given these preliminaries, in the *Prior Analytics* Aristotle devised a mechanism for generating contradictions that would infallibly improve a disputant's performance.

Whether a lawsuit, teaching ability, proposed legislation, or a philosophical position was at stake, it was crucial in dialectical argument to premeditate the moves of one's opponent; it was this skill that the Sophists had claimed to teach by acquainting their students with the various common and tempting fallacies in which a disputant might be caught. But the special virtue of Aristotle's new theory of the syllogism, the virtue that makes it the first "true" logic, was that it offered a systematic way to detect any fallacy.[12] The formalism and symbolism that Aristotle introduced had a very practical value. The introduction of variables borrowed from mathematics, the concept of a term or *horos* as in a mathematical function, the idea that all valid arguments can be reduced to a few simple forms, all this allowed a mechanism by which fallacies could be not just listed but generated. Now, instead of memorizing a list of fallacies, a dialectician could master the workings of the syllogism to produce an infinite number of possibilities for refutation to be tried or avoided no matter what the subject matter or the occasion.

The theoretical discovery, not yet complete,[13] of the difference between truth and validity that Aristotle's symbolism makes possible reflects the actual situation in which the dialectician found himself. In debate he could not always choose his side; often he was a foreigner, having no right to argue in the Assembly or law courts, but paid to write speeches for other men. If arguing for himself, it was often expedient in the tumult of Athenian politics to change position or to equivocate on one's position. Certainly when a charge was brought against him in the courts, he would want to defend himself whether guilty or not. Therefore, in dialectical argument truth was not in issue. The great merit of the concept of logical validity is that it takes this into account in a way that is impossible in ordinary communication. For the purposes of the dialectic, one can treat of things, in Aristotle's words, "only with a view to general opinion" *Topics* I, 14; 105b30–31). One can start out, not with true statements, but with statements that are generally believed. The important thing is not whether the statements that form the syllogism are true but whether they are believed and make a valid argument.

A logical practice that was to be truly efficient had to begin the separation between questions of truth and questions of logical form that would allow disputants to exhibit their skill without hesitation. If they were able to forget the truth and concentrate only on the form of the argument, they were likely to be successful. By isolating syllogistic forms of argument, by substituting letters for statements that allowed them to be arranged in certain valid and invalid patterns, Aristotle's theory of the syllogism made possible this bracketing of the truth, and therefore could form the foundation of an education that prepared a man for success in public life.

Logic, as the ideal form of rationality, regulated exchanges between commercially and politically active male citizens, members of the ruling aristocracy of Athens, who engaged in lawsuits, politics, and the philosophical discussions that framed public policies. The dialectic exchanges for which Aristotle wrote his handbook are not between a Platonic master with access to transcendent Form and a student guided to its revelation. They are professionally mediated public encounters between privileged equals. The religious atmosphere of revelation has given way to a different hush, the hush of a men's club in which good "form" means that even as members compete for wealth and honor there are certain rules of debate. The most difficult step might be entrance to the privileges and responsibilities of citizenship, but once one was admitted, the *Prior Analytics* was the guide to success. Not only did it systematize the skills necessary to triumph over legal and political opponents, it also defined the forms of interaction that identified responsible participants in political and public life. Those who were rational, those who were logical, those who had mastered the syllogism were the proper rulers of those who could not. If the mechanisms of the syllogism ideally regulated the communications of a male citizen, it also identified him as a superior, rational man whose nature was to rule.

There were many from whom he needed to be distinguished. In his family, a man had to establish hegemony over his wife, children, and slaves. It is clear from Aristotle's own discussions that there was controversy in respect to slavery, and even to the inferior situation of women. In the home Greek women exercised a sovereignty that was a constant threat to male control. In public life a man had to exercise control over masses of laborers and artisans whom he could not accept as capable of self-government. Even more important, he had to distinguish himself from everything not Greek, especially from the conquered "barbarians" from whom his stock of slaves was replenished and from the vassal peoples whose tribute enriched Athens. Barbarians were particularly dangerous. With established social forms and values, sometimes matrilineal and matrifocal, and always different from his own, non-Greeks were in a position to challenge his thinking in a way that Greek women and slaves were not.

In Aristotle's *Politics*, the inability of non-Greeks to be rational and logical is often cited. Among the barbarians, Aristotle deplores, there is no "natural ruler" whose superiority depends on his rationality. Non-Greeks are in the shocking position of making no distinction between ruler and subject or between women and slaves. The conclusion that Aristotle draws is that barbarians are "natural slaves." "The barbarian and the slave are the same by nature, making it fitting and right that the Greeks rule over them" (*Politics* I, 1; 1252b5–10).[14] This was also the view of Aristotle's patron, Philip of Macedonia, who was busy Hellenizing the Mediterranean and the East. Greek rationality, exemplified in the syllogism, was a mark of the superiority of Greek culture. Trained in logic, graduates of Aristotle's Lyceum proceeded to posts in newly colonized areas, confident of their superiority and their ability to govern. Logic was a badge of office, a way to identify "that one who can plan things with his mind" and is therefore "the ruler by nature" (*Politics* I, 1; 1252a32–33). Women, slaves, workers, and conquered people, all those who did not participate in dialectical contests, were expected to accept the superior reasoning of their masters.[15]

Logic, even when practiced only for diversion, provided valuable training for a public and private life in which those who were less rational would be ruled by their superiors. First, logic provided the mark of the superior man. Neither race nor color would work as well. Philip and his son Alexander, as many later conquerors, ruled an empire in which many subject peoples were similar in color or racial descent to their conquerors. If Greeks were to rule it would have to be by virtue of something other than bodily characteristics. The ability to reason, to reject the diversity of opinion for Logos, to foresee the conclusions that syllogisms generated served as a non-bodily mark of those destined to rule. The conclusions that the superior man foresaw with his syllogisms were necessary. Logic provided refutations and proofs that established what was unarguably true and false, giving an authority to decrees that could not be questioned. Aristotle's logic also provided a medium for increased mobility among ruling citizens. No longer was the truth to be revealed to a few chosen respondents by the method of division. Instead there would be a battle of wits between peers to see who could combine statements most successfully. The terms of logic still guaranteed that discussion would take place safely within a universe of dichotomous categories closed to alien points of view. Aristotle's *Categories*, in which the terms which logic will use were ordered,[16] and his *On Interpretation*, in which statements are arranged in opposing affirmations and denials, had prepared and tailored language so that the necessities of the syllogism could operate.

Not all Athenians thought that such dialectic discussion was beneficial for the city. The Sophist Thrasymachus, for example, saw the "mutual contention of discourse thought to be mutually antithetical" as dangerous to the health of the polis.[17] For Thrasymachus such a deliberate taking of sides, in the Assembly for example, could block the fragile consensus toward which discussion should move. Plato's insistence on logical integrity, on the unity of virtue, on the authority of those who could discern transcendent Form had already undermined the precarious balance of understanding in a community of equals that might have established a consensus. Although Aristotle expanded the circle of rational men to a group of male citizens among whom relations of equality and friendship could be maintained, and although he allowed his syllogism a practical use in deciding what actions should be undertaken, he was far from recommending the kind of open discussion that Thrasymachus and other Sophists urged. The discussion that could establish a consensus, Thrasymachus says, is a not a discussion that seeks out meaningless differences and clever refutations, but one that feels back for something that "could be grasped with the greatest of ease" and that could thereby provide a basis for mutual understanding.[18]

This the arcane workings of the syllogism were hardly likely to provide. The purpose of logic was not to open the discussion to all viewpoints with the purpose of establishing a consensus, but to establish a model of discourse that excluded what was contradictory or irrational. In Aristotle's *Politics*, the rationality of whose who are natural rulers is continually defined in opposition to other unacceptable speech: the emotional expressions of women, the subrational words of slaves, the primitive political views of barbarians, the tainted opinions of anyone who does manual labor, whether Greek or barbarian. Unlike the speech envisioned by Thrasymachus which aims at communication and understanding, Aristotle's logic shapes "discourses" which even when antithetical take the same form. The society that such a logic reflects is not a community where there could ever be the "common mind" that Thrasymachus sought or the common public opinion that establishes a just judgment. For Aristotle there is no common mind, but only the rational mind, and the syllogism is the necessary shape of that mind.

The rejection of the ambiguities inevitable in any open discussion that attempts to move toward consensus accounts for the artificiality of much dialectical debate. In the sometimes mind-numbing complexities of the syllogistic, in the seemingly pointless questions pursued with such energy can still be felt the chains of Parmenides's Goddess-jailer forbidding the way of nonbeing. But this time the logician has locked himself away from mortality and change in a new way. No longer does he detach himself from human affairs to contemplate the unity of Being or the form of the Good. The logic of the *Prior Analytics* is very much a thing of this world, a medium of exchange between men involved in men's affairs. Some of Parmenides's retreat remains. The logician need not contend with the shifting mortal opinion of the thoughtful bodies of women, slaves, laborers, non-Greeks. In all its various elegant permutations, the syllogism put off indefinitely anything they might have to say. If it was seldom the problem of slavery or sexism that was discussed among men, this was because within the field of dialectial discourse the justice of the inferior position of slaves and women did not have to be called into question. Once rationality is defined as what is not emotional and emotionality established as the characteristic of women, once rationality is seen as a characteristic of mind, not body, and a slave is understood as what is only a body, there could be no discussion of the institutions of slavery or sexism.[19]

In these ways, the dialectic could provide a way to establish the credentials of a privileged participant in public affairs, a way within those affairs for participants to win advantage over each other, and a way to restrict discussion within convenient conceptual parameters. The speech strategies that syllogistic logic codified could provide models for exchanges between male citizens in law courts, the Assembly, and in those semi-public discussions of politics or morality in which parties were joined and opinions formed. But Aristotle himself was aware of the weakness of a purely rhetorical dialectic. If the authority of logic and the rational man were ultimately to be defended, the syllogism would have to be more than a test of mental dexterity, more than a new form of contest, more than a way to silence opponents. The refutations and proofs produced by the mechanism of the syllogism had to be true. And that meant that the premises from which the syllogism began had to be established as necessarily true. Logic would have to be more than a way for men to talk to each other, or avoid talking to each other, it would have to take on the authority of a science.

The Comforts of the Cause

> It is the cause of our loving anything which we love more than the thing itself (*Posterior* I, 2; 72a31).

> The questions we ask are as many as the things that we know (*Posterior* II, 1; 89b23–24).

If all knowledge must have the necessity of the syllogism, and the syllogism must rest on true premises, how can such premises be generated without circularity? This is the problem to which the *Posterior Analytics* turns. Either the logic that Aristotle has devised is unfounded or it is circular. It might have a rhetorical use, might be used to dazzle listeners, or to embarrass and confuse opponents, but for the authority of a demonstration to be finally established, more is necessary. The force of the argument has to come not only from the dexterity of its manipulation, but from the truth. This requires, as Aristotle puts it, that we look at the premises.[20] Here Aristotle agreed with the critics of Parmenides: it is not enough simply to repeat what one has said which is only an easy way to prove anything (*Posterior* I, 3; 72b33–35). At the same time, Aristotle was not willing to give up the law of the excluded middle.[21] Knowledge cannot be of those ambiguous bodily individuals who so often both are and are not what we desire of them. He shares Parmenides's disdain for perishable, changeable things of which nothing can be known, but for Aristotle, the answer cannot be an imperishable unity of Being which would make all argument impossible. Instead he proposes a new Being, the "cause." This is the immutable object of desire whose explication dominates the discussion of the *Posterior Analytics*.

It is important to distinguish Aristotle's cause from "cause" in its modern sense. The cause Aristotle seeks is in no way temporal: it does not precede its effect either in the order of knowledge (*Posterior* II, 8; 93a17–19) or in the order of physical events (*Posterior* II, 12; 95a23–24). No reasoning from one event to a succeeding event or to a future event could have the necessity of the syllogism. The syllogistic cause and effect are simultaneous, whatever the order of our awareness of them. This is shown in the direction of syllogistic reasoning. The point is not to argue from premises to whatever conclusion might follow, but from a conclusion to premises that will affirm or contradict the conclusion. You do not begin with a cause that can produce a given effect; instead, you begin with the effect or with the conclusion and then reason back to the cause necessarily involved in that effect. If the syllogism is to produce more than a superficial mechanical validity, the proper ordering of the syllogism, in which the cause is placed as the middle term, is necessary (*Posterior* I, 13). It is on the possibility of a such an ordering that Aristotle's defense of the demonstrative syllogism rests.

In order to show that the syllogism results in knowledge, he must show that the premises from which the conclusion is drawn are "prior:" more basic, more intuitively certain than the conclusion. Without this priority of premises, the syllogism produces perhaps a "fact," but not a "reasoned fact," a difference which is not in the premises or conclusions themselves but in their arrangement. It is only the "reasoned fact" that amounts to knowledge, for knowledge cannot be simply that such and such exists: one must know why it has to exist the way it does. Everything then depends on the status of these prior truths. They must give us the essential and not the accidental nature of the things we are to understand. But from where are such premises to come? To say they are demonstrated is to return to circularity.[22] Certainly, they cannot be reached by simple induction, or by sense-perception, or by pointing. What is needed is a definition, but if the definition is the point from which a demonstration proceeds, the definition itself cannot be demonstrable.

Aristotle escapes from this impasse by equivocating on the idea of a demonstration. A definition, if not proven by a demonstration, can be "exhibited" by one.[23] One can provide a "quasi-demonstration" of essential nature and it is by way of the syllogism that this is possible—not just any syllogism but the syllogism organized so as to reflect the "cause" of a phenomenon. To show this Aristotle examines a trial question: why are the planets non-twinkling? There are a number of syllogistic possibilities: for example (a) the planets are non-twinkling and what is non-twinkling is near, therefore the planets are near. This formulation is tempting, Aristotle says because it is known by direct observation that things non-twinkling are near. However, this syllogism, though it proves a fact, does not prove a reasoned fact. Because the cause is always the middle term and here "non-twinkling" is the middle term, non-twinkling becomes the cause of the planet's nearness, whereas in truth it is the other way around. The remedy is to rearrange the syllogism: (b) the planets are near and what is near is non-twinkling, therefore the planets are non-twinkling. With (b) we have "proven" the reasoned fact (*Posterior* I, 13).[24]

The instruction that Aristotle does not give, however, is how to tell which order to use. Which is it that is more basic and necessary, nearness or non-twinkling? The answer cannot depend on the order in which we see them, or in the certainty of our perception. If it is certain perceptively that non-twinkling things are near, it is as certain that near things are non-twinkling. The order in which we see things may or may not reflect the real order of things. The real order depends on causal connections: once it is seen that nearness causes non-twinkling instead of the other way around, the premises rearrange themselves. But it is still not clear how this is to be done.

We must be sure, Aristotle says, to ask the right question; we must not ask a question whose answer we do not already know. Once we ask why the planets are non-twinkling, we have already positioned nearness as the cause. This ability to ask the right questions, which reflect what we already know, is required if we are to frame proper syllogisms. And in order to illustrate that skill Aristotle reconsiders the causal relation itself. What makes one thing a cause of another, when the reverse is not true? It is, he concludes, a matter of extension. The trouble with saying that non-twinkling causes nearness is that not everything non-twinkling is necessarily near, but if this is turned around and nearness becomes the cause, then it is the case that everything near is non-twinkling.[25]

At this point Aristotle, after all his arguments against its circularity, must return to division.[26] Some content is necessary, if logic is to have substance and authority, and at the end of the *Posterior Analytics* (II, 13–14) the syllogism "exhibiting" the "reasoned fact" is refounded in a division reminiscent of the *Sophist*. What, in the end, we must refer to in framing the syllogism is a tree of concepts, the facts which the syllogism will exhibit; in this way we can "trace" the elements of a definition correctly, we can "collect" the essential nature (II, 13; 96a23, 27). We begin with a species, we find what general category it falls under, we compare it to other species, then we divide until we have a definition that is co-extensive with the species. This will be its essential nature or substance. To use Aristotle's example of the concept man, the example which will continue until the twentieth century to be the one most favored by logicians: once we have determined that men are animals, then we may establish the characteristics of animals and divide until we can say what it is to be a man as opposed to for example, a horse or a bird.[27] Although Aristotle does not retract his earlier charge that division cannot prove a definition, here he acknowledges it as a necessary tool that allows us to get the order of our terms straight and ensure that we do not omit anything from essence so that our syllogism will be based on the correct middle term.

There are differences between Aristotle's use of division and Plato's. The purpose of Platonic division was ascent, the revelation of a supreme Form of the Good to which logic was only an approach. Aristotle is not a Platonist: he makes quite clear that for him the idea of pure Forms apart from any matter is unintelligible and he admits the possibility if not the necessity of multiple divisions. Aristotle's syllogism does not reveal an independently existing formal reality and that reality cannot be used to justify the syllogism.

The result is that Aristotle's division alone cannot solve the difficult problem of knowledge. The scientist who wishes to exhibit knowledge of his field may make a division, but how can he be sure that his division is correct, how can he be sure with which species he should begin, how can he tell what common characteristics count as essential or accidental? How can he tell what is a genus and what an individual variation? If the proper order of the syllogism is generated from a division which must reflect what is, and Platonic forms are rejected, it is not clear what our access is to that reality.

A purely nominal definition of terms would return to simple formalism. Such definitions could mark only contingent relationships between words, relations which, because they do not have to be the way they are, carry no existential implications. Aristotle is enough of a Parmenidean to find this intolerable. Being cannot be reduced to the ambiguities in the way people speak.[28] To give up existential implications is to give up the claim to truth, and once this is done, the authority of the syllogism is called into question. Ordinary perception also is inadequate; perception is of the "this" and "now" and not of essence (*Posterior* I, 31; 88a10ff.). Perception is often misleading. Nothing that we see of an eclipse, for example, tells us its essential nature, nor can we see in a cube of ice the lack of heat that has caused it.[29] Definitions that delineate substance or essence cannot be demonstrated or proven by division or perception. If they are not to be only verbal formulae that mark out something we do not even know exists, some other medium of validation must be found.

Aristotle considers some of the problems which result in his *Metaphysics* (X, 9). Why do some differences make a species difference and some not? Why are "winged" and "footed" essential attributes, but "pale" and "dark" not? Or the even more puzzling question with which Aristotle introduces this subject: why do male or female not make a species if they have the contrary properties which regularly distinguish one species from another? Aristotle presents his possible solutions in a tone which indicates that even he is aware of their inadequacy: "winged" and "sex" are "peculiar to the genus," whereas "pale" is not; or, "paleness" and "female" are in the matter, not the definition, which must mean that men are made of pale or dark stuff and, in a construal that fits Aristotle's biological account of sexual difference, the female is made of matter somehow resistant to form. But still no reliable method has been given for telling which characteristics belong to matter and which to form.

The fact is that we must already have a grasp of the species whose nature we are to demonstrate in the syllogisms of our science. The only questions we are likely to be able to answer are those to which we already have the answer. But how is that answer to be obtained? Aristotle's final solution comes at the very end of the *Posterior Analytics*. Again, as so often when

Aristotle needs a paradigm of substance, the example is "man." It is not true to say that no perception can yield a universal. In fact, Aristotle argues, the *content* of perception is not particular but universal. From even one instance, it is possible to grasp a species. The man Callias may be what a man sees, but the content of what he sees is "man" (*Posterior* II, 19; 100a14–65). The repetition of this content, as a man's experience of men expands, allows him to get a firm grasp on the species; then he may proceed by induction to the genus to which man belongs, "animal." A particular kind of intuition, embedded in the perception by men of other men, is the original source of scientific knowledge. As Aristotle searches for the cause that makes the syllogism true, the cause that "we love more than things themselves," he is inevitably returned to himself, to his thoughts and perceptions and those of men like him.

The priority of such thoughts he had already made clear in the *Categories*. It is not sentences that are true or false, because the same thing can be said in different languages. Instead it is the thoughts they express. These thoughts common to men must be correctly structured for the truth-producing syllogism. Such a restructuring of thought is mapped out in the *Categories*. The only things that exist, Aristotle argues, are substances ($o\dot{v}\sigma\iota a^{30}$) "or things that are," everything else—qualities, genera, accidents—exist only in the sense that they are true of things that exist. But the things that exist are not only, or even primarily, concrete individuals like Socrates or Callias—again the preferred example is men— because for these no necessary premise can be formed and therefore no demonstrative syllogism. Callias and Socrates also exist or are substances in another sense, the sense in which they exist "as men." To say of someone that he is a man is to say *what* he is. This, Aristotle argues, clearly conveys a knowledge of him that his name and other personal attributes do not.

Aristotle has found his comfort. What we love in Socrates is not some particular flesh-and-blood human, but what makes him what he is: his manhood. "The cause" that gives us true knowledge of him is his manhood. The propositions from which demonstrative syllogisms must be drawn are of the form, "Man is a rational animal." This is the sort of premise that makes demonstration possible, that allows an argument to begin with necessary truth and not with positions drawn by lot for the purposes of competitive debate or principles chosen only to conform to what people are willing to believe, as in dialectical argument. Aristotle explains: "This is why always in syllogisms the beginning is substance: because a syllogism's beginning is substance, because a syllogism comes out of what a thing is" (*Metaphysics* VII, 8; 1034a31–33). The material reality of a concrete individual cannot be the subject of syllogistic argument, because of an individual there can be no definition.

> In the definition [*logos*] of a substance the material parts will not be present (for they are not part of that substance but of the composite substance); of this substance, there is in a sense a definition, and in a sense not; for there is no definition of it with its matter, for this is indefinite, but there is a definition of it with reference to its primary substance . . . (*Metaphysics* 1037a24–37; see also 1039b27–30).

The concept "man," plays the paradigmatic role in Aristotle's discussion of substance, essence, and its relation to the demonstrative syllogism. In the *Categories*, "man" introduced the concept of primary substance. In the *Posterior Analytics*, it was the example which illustrated the difference between what a thing is essentially and what it is accidentally, and also the difference between what we can have knowledge of and what only opinion (I, 31). It was the example used to explain the usefulness of division in the generation of syllogisms and appeared in the final sections as the intuited universal in the particular that makes the demonstrative syllogism possible. Throughout the *Metaphysics*, "man" is the constant example of substance or essence, and appears prominently in the concluding sections as an example of the priority of actuality over potentiality which accounts for the unity of substance (e.g., 1050a3ff.). "Man" is the example most often used by Aristotle of form by which formless matter is some definite thing. "What a thing is," "whether a man or a god," is prior in all ways, in definition, in order of knowledge, even in time (*Metaphysics* VII, 1; 1028a33). Only this sort of substance can have an essence (1030b5), not an abstract essence separated from existence in a Platonic heaven, but one firmly embedded in reality.

If Plato's insubstantial forms were necessary to ground the authority of a Platonic division, Aristotle has returned that grounding to the natural world. As part of the world, our only access to it is through perceptual experience. But this can be no simple perception. We see men, we see Socrates or Callias, but in what sense do we see their substance, their manhood? Some new kind of perception is necessary if substance is to serve as the cause that grounds a syllogism in truth. The substance "man" can be no taxonomic category abstracted from random observations of actual similarities between men: it cannot change when a Greek encounters barbarian peoples with different values and culture, or when he is confronted with his wife's opinion of him, or when laborers attempt to have a say in the affairs of the city. At the same time, it must be embedded in perception. "For the act of sense perception is not of each thing; the perception is of the general, as a man, not of Callias the man" (*Posterior* II, 19; 100a17–b1).

What Aristotle, as a rational man, sees when he looks at Callias is not Callias but Callias's manhood. What *he* sees when he looks at Callias, for example, is not his animality. Although men and horses are animals, an animal is not an existent in the same way as men and horses (*Metaphysics* VII, 13). The rational man he sees is what distinguishes Callias, what causes him to be what he is, a man. The "comforts" of this cause are not hard to understand. A logic based on such a cause is no longer a retreat, either to the self-identity of Being or to a Platonic heavenly Good. Instead, as in a flattering mirror, in the perceptions of men is reflected an ideal self-image of the Greek male, necessarily ideal because, as Aristotle admits at a difficult point in his argument for natural slavery, not even all Greek men are rational. From the vantage point of this self-image, embedded in his very perception, projected outwards in perceptual experience, the philosopher can draft perfect syllogisms. An ethics can be theorized based on the authority of reason over emotion which is the mark of a man; a politics can be developed that founds men's authority over women and slaves on the basis of that same rationality, other natural creatures can be divided into lower species in imitation of the superior species man; and finally divinity itself can be theorized as a nonmaterial, manly intelligence removed from the distortions of matter.

With such a cause, logic has new life. The dialectic is no longer only a debate skill learned in Greek schools as the mark of the superiority of Greek citizens. Given substantial content as science, it lays down the truths that inform policy. It is no accident that Aristotelian reasoning continued to be used to support colonial exploitation and imperialism well after the Hellenistic empire had ceased to exist. In his great debate with Las Casas at Valladolid in 1550, Sepulveda spoke for the Aristotelians on the barbarity of American Indians, so "contaminated with sins and obscenities,"[31] living in societies in which males do not necessarily make the rules.[32] It is only right, he concludes, that such a "humane nation excellent in every virtue as Spain" should rule over them.[33] The complicity of a thought and language correctly ordered by Aristotle's categories and the syllogism in such conquests was recognized by the Bishop of Avila in 1492 as he defended the "first grammar of a European language" to Queen Isabella. "What is it for?" she asked him, and he answered, "Your Majesty, language is the perfect instrument of empire."[34]

With syllogistic demonstration, a new use of language appeared. Not the patient didactic of the Platonic master instructing his pupil, and not the intricate maneuvering of the friendly or unfriendly rivals of the *Prior Analytics*, logic now structures a learned *discourse*. The scientist forms the conclusions that can inform proper behavior; he prepares his lectures; rehearses to himself the truths that will later be expounded to others; he carefully organizes his writings. If the *Prior Analytics* is a handbook for the dialectician, the *Posterior Analytics* is for the natural philosopher. Aristotle makes clear what is the ultimate foundation of such a philosophy. The scientist's prior division of a subject is done in accordance with rational perceptions, his and those of his associates, in accordance with the ideas which they assume to be "the same for all" (*On Interpretation* I; 16a9). The scientist begins and ends with these ideas, with the knowledge he has, with the questions that reflect that knowledge, with the knowledge he has of himself, with the comfort of knowing the essences of things and especially his own essence. Logic has given him a skill with which to present and articulate these ideas effectively. It allows him to arrange them in a deductive matrix so that they are no longer just what he, and others like him, happen to think, but what everyone must think and what it is necessary to think. In this way, his opinions and beliefs are fixed for an indeterminable future. Is it any wonder that so often he begins with that "cause" dearest to him of all: the nature of man, the most "rounded off and developed" of natures" (*History of Animals*, IX, 1; 608b)? The great achievement of the demonstrative syllogism is not that it produces new ideas, but that it allows a man to draw out of his existing ideas, the "cause" that shows why it is that what he thinks is true, must be true. It is not surprising that, for Aristotle, this cause is so often the nature of man. In much of his thinking on politics, ethics, and biology, that notion is foundational.

If the syllogism produces new knowledge, this is new knowledge in a very practical sense. Now questions can be definitively answered and closed. Once beliefs have been divided and made to justify each other, a final confirmation is achieved. "We stop inquiring for the reason and are content with our knowledge when we reach something whose coming-to-be or being is not due to some other thing, for this far-as-we-can-go is itself the goal and end of our inquiry" (*Posterior*, I, 24; 85b29–31). When our knowledge becomes universal in this way, the matter is settled and settled so there can be no further inquiry or discussion. The demonstration is framed by the scientist, the expert, who expounds his view to a passive audience. What gives his exposition power and authority is the logic of its presentation, a logic that insures that any questions will be framed in the terms of answers that he already knows.

In this way, and from this paradigm, the answers we have to all sorts of questions can be reframed. In the *Posterior Analytics*, when the possibility of a demonstrative syllogism is raised, the questions that Aristotle considers are various: "what causes an eclipse? why does water freeze? what caused the Persian War? why is it beneficial to take a walk after dinner? These are all questions to which Aristotle, one way or another, already had a reasonably satisfactory answer. An eclipse is caused when the Moon intervenes between the light of the sun and the Earth. Water freezes when there is a lack of heat. The Persian War was caused by unprovoked raiding parties of the Athenians. A walk after dinner faciliates digestion. What the demonstrative syllogism does, however, is present these answers in a new way. If interference with sunlight is the antecedent cause of an eclipse, if a raiding party was the efficient cause of the Persian War, if a walk after dinner is for the final cause of healthy digestion, in the terms of the syllogism that demonstrates necessary truths, all these causes become commensurate. An eclipse just is interference with sunlight, digestion is health, the essence of the Persian War was retaliatory. In each case the cause is the essence, what a thing is, and, as its substance, forms a middle term. In the same way that Callias must be a man, so the Persian War must be retaliation for raiding, and water freezing must be the state caused by lack of heat, and walking to facilitate digestion must be healthy. In the end, efficient, material, and final causes are collapsed to one, the essence or necessary form of a thing.

With eclipses, post-prandial exercise, freezing, the certainty that results is not dangerous; Aristotle's intuitions were sound. But on other subjects they were not so sound. Aristotle's theory of generation is an example. Aristotle, here as elsewhere when he speaks of the difference between men and women, begins with intuitions firmly embedded in his and other Greek men's perceptions.[35] What is female is passive and material. A woman has less "form" than a man, and is bodily. A man, on the other hand, can be "perceived" to be more rational, courageous, and active. On the basis of these perceptions, Aristotle then can proceed to explain generation (*Generation of Animals* I, 18). One must start with the essence of semen. Semen is that from which offspring come and so there must be an active generating force and something from which they are generated. Since the female is passive and the male active, the semen must only move the matter in the female. The form or essence of the man that results, unless that form is overcome with matter and the offspring is female, is solely a function of the form–imprinting semen of the male. Orestes's argument before Athena's court is no longer only a clever dodge. It now stands with the authority of scientific fact.[36]

In Plato's *Sophist* there was an interaction between speakers, even though mediated by a logic that reduced one of them to passive assent. In the *Prior Analytics*, an exchange occurs between disputants, even though a system of rules has been devised which takes precedence over anything participants might wish to say to each other. In the *Posterior Analytics*, there is no longer any discussion. Logic needs no respondent; it has reduced to silence any possible hearer and even the second thoughts of the logician himself. If the "cause" that Aristotle discovers is more dear than any object of desire, it is because in its self-confirming perfection, it finally insulates the speaker's words from anything anyone else might say. Other voices have disappeared and there is only the logician's own. No longer is even a staged dialogue necessary. Instead lay subjects listen to experts whose superior knowledge will guide decisions. Science provides the facts on which knowledge rests; its internal consistency—constitutes its power to produce knowledge. In this way the scientist's, the Greek's, the master's, the male's perceptions are elaborated into necessary truth.

Notes

1. Aristotle translations and citations are from Greek texts in *Works*, Loeb Classical Library (Cambridge: Harvard University Press, 1961). *Prior Analytics* is cited as *Prior*, *Posterior Analytics* as *Posterior*.

2. In the *Prior Analytics*, Aristotle describes three "figures" of the syllogism; however, all the syllogisms, he notes, are reducible to universal syllogisms in the first figure. The definition of the perfect syllogism is: "Whenever three terms are so related to one another that all of the last is contained in the middle and the middle is either all contained in, or excluded from, the first, the extremes must be related by a perfect syllogism" (*Prior* I, 4; 25b32–35).

3. Ernest Kapp, *Greek Foundations of Traditional Logic* (New York: Columbia University Press, 1942), 63.

4. The strategy is, in Aristotle's words, to "not draw the conclusions but conceal them after laying down the required premises" (*Prior* II, 19; 66a35–38). Or, as explained in the *Topics*, we must find a method by which, when attacking, we will be able to reason on any matter presented us from common opinion, and never be drawn into admitting a contradictory statement (*Topics* I, 1; 100a18–21).

5. The first play of Aeschylus's trilogy depicts Clytemnestra's assassination of her husband, Agamemnon, motivated by revenge for Agamemnon's murder of their daughter as a human sacrifice in order to insure fair winds for his military adventures in Troy, as well as by disgust at the unjustified and senseless excess of the Greeks' assault on Troy (see, for example, her opening address to the Chorus in *Agamemnon*). In the background is the residual conflict between indigenous Mediterranean matrilineality and the aggressive patrilineality of the Greeks. Aeschylus, as apologist for Hellenic values, constantly plays on the perversity of Clytemnestra, a woman playing a man's role, usurping the kingship and governing the country.

6. The Erinnyes have been described by commentators on the *Oresteia* as writhing, bestial, snakelike, associated with primitive blood-lust and brutish instincts of blind retribution. Such diatribes indicate a continuing attempt to discredit a moral order that empowers the family and the mother. Aeschylus's account of the Erinnyes is at variance with previous myth. In Hesiod and Homer, they are depicted as ominous and fearful but not disgusting. Historically they are connected with pre-Hellenic religious traditions centering around an Earth Goddess whose sanctuaries the Hellenic priests or Apollo had co-opted. An example is Apollo's installation at Delphi where Aeschylus, in *The Libation-Bearers*, stages a confrontation between the Erinnyes and Orestes prior to Orestes's appeal to Athens. In the concluding scenes of the Orestian trilogy, Aechylus depicts their transformation under Athena's auspices into the Eumenides, or kindly ones, tame goddesses of the hearth. Accompanied by women, they are led off to their new home on the Acropolis where they will pose no threat to the institutions of the city-state. They will share, Athena promises, in

the glory of Athens as its citizens turn their violence away from each other and against other peoples in foreign wars of conquest and colonization.

7. Most commentators have seen little moral value in the Erinnyes' position except their praise of moderation with which Athena is willing to agree. Often their stated position has been distorted. Nowhere do the Erinnyes argue that there are obligations only to the mother, but they speak in terms of duties to parents. Nowhere do they argue that murder of a parent is the only crime, but only that it is unforgiveable. More generally, it has been assumed that their defense of special responsibilities to those bound to us by blood or relation is patently unjust. From the standpoint, however, of contemporary discussions in moral philosophy inspired by feminist ethical theory, the superiority of universal rational laws of Justice to the claims of those with whom we are in intimate relations of vulnerability and dependence is problematic.

8. It is difficult, if not impossible, to imagine what specific forms pre-Hellenic justice might have taken. Homer in several places describes voluntary arbitration procedures. In the *Odyssey*, for example, Queen Arete is described as the one who decides disputes between men in Phaeacia. In the *Iliad* (18.497–508), a scene depicted on the Shield of Achilles involves the hearing of a dispute having to do with recompense for a killing before an assembled populace and designated elders who give judgments, one of which is approved as the most just. Such procedures can only occur in communities where relationships define duties and obligations, that is, where there is a common sense of proper recompense for injury, where all parties to a quarrel are committed to a just solution, where individual judges are known to have the ability to give fair decisions.

9. See the *Iliad* and the *Odyssey*, which are almost exclusively concerned with such heroic competitions. Athena's moral superiority to the Erinnyes is commonly based on the argument that she humanely eliminated the blood feuds which the Erinnyes represent. What the Erinnyes actually argue for is quite different: criminal behavior, especially that which overreaches the boundaries of relationships between those bound together by trust and dependency, leads to misery and should not be condoned by any act of state, nor should a criminal profit from his crime.

10. In *Works and Days*, Hesiod invented the mythic underpinning for this change. Unhappy with the arbitration of a dispute over an inheritance, unwilling to accept the *dikai* or words of the elders who gave the judgement to his brother, he appoints a goddess to represent him, Dike, daughter of Zeus, a higher abstract principle of justice. Dike, Hesiod proclaims, must override the judgements of the arbitrators. We do not just wrong a person or the community, our transgressions are against Justice that issues from the supreme lawgiving authority of Zeus. There is a fundamental contrast between this Justice and the justice of the Erinnyes. Justice for the Erinnyes is built into the very fabric of social life; the evildoer will be haunted by remorse and alienation, his greed will make his "overladen ship" eventually flounder. The determination of such a guilt is appropriately by the elders of the community. Dike represents an external principle, a deified universal that rules the affairs of men not in any

community of households but as leading citizens rule the state. These two ideas of justice cross and recross in the *Oresteia*, with Dike declared triumphant in the end.

11. See the discussion of this evolution in George Kennedy, *The Art of Persuasion in Greece*, (Princeton: Princeton University Press, 1963), 88–90. The acceptance of slave testimony is particularly puzzling. A slave belonging to one of the litigants could *only* give testimony under torture, the rationale apparently being that otherwise he would be likely to support his master's case regardless of the truth.

12. One example of how the syllogism could be so used: "In order to avoid having a syllogism drawn against us, when someone asks us to admit a statement without drawing the conclusions, we must not grant him the same term twice over in his premises since we know that a syllogism cannot be drawn without a middle term" (*Prior* II, 19; 66a25–28).

13. See *Posterior* II, 7, where Aristotle has not abandoned the existential implications of syllogistic premises.

14. The movement from the doctrine of the natural slave to racism is evident in the *Politics*. There was apparently enough question raised in Athens as to the justice of the institution of slavery that Aristotle feels obliged to offer an argument. Although he begins with the familiar thesis that the rational mind of the master is the natural ruler of the bodies of slaves, he meets a stumbling-block in the possibility that a Greek might be enslaved. For the most part a slave became a slave through defeat in battle as Athens expanded her empire in the Aegean islands and Anatolia. Because these conquered people were not necessarily different in color or stature from the Greeks, their appearance could not be a distinguishing feature and, needless to say, the Greeks did not invariably win. If a Greek was captured in battle, did that mean he was also a natural slave? This dilemma forced Aristotle to concede that barbarian and natural slave are really the same. (The literal meaning of "barbarian" is *non-Greek*;, the term also had all the negative connotations it has today.) In this way, the equivalence of reason and mastery becomes an equivalence of Greek and master.

15. This may be the basis for Aristotle's shocking conclusion: "So master and slave have the same interest" (*Politics* I, 2; 1252a35).

16. The *Categories* establishes the univocality not present in natural language but necessary if the syllogism is to work, by ordering vocabulary in ten general categories that comprise what can be said.

17. I am indebted to Eric Havelock, *The Liberal Temper in Greek Politics* (London: Jonathan Cape, 1957), 232ff., for this fresh view of Thrasymachus, usually remembered only as the hothead of the *Republic*.

18. The text of Thrasymachus's remarks is as follows:

    In the first place I shall demonstrate that those parties from among the speakers or the rest of you who have fallen into mutual contention have in the process of discourse been affected by a natural attitude which becomes an inevitable attitude in men whose partisanship is uninfluenced by thought. They think their discourses are mutually antithetical but are not aware that the policies pursued are identical, or that the discourse of their opponents is inherent in their own. Ask yourselves, going back to the beginning, what is it that both sides are looking for? In the first place there is the constitution of the fathers, this, which throws them into confusion, can be grasped mentally with the greatest of ease and is supremely something in which the citizens have community (quoted in Havelock, *Greek Politics*, 233).

19. The invisibility of women and slaves is ratified by much Greek scholarship. Two examples, at random: Finley Hooper *Greek Realities* (Detroit: Wayne State University Press, 1978); J. K. Davies, *Democracy and Classical Greece* (Sussex: Harvester Press, 1978), neither of which mentions women in the index or discusses the situation of women.

20. "If we are reasoning concerning opinion, and therefore only dialectically, it is clear that we need only credibility, so that if a middle term between A and B is believed to be true but is not true, then through this one can still reason by a dialectical syllogism. If truth is the aim, in those circumstances, it is necessary to examine the premise" (*Posterior* I, 19; 81b19–24).

21. As this most seminal of logical insights is articulated, puzzles and paradoxes continue to be generated, for example Aristotle's famous struggle with the problem of determinacy: if future statements about the future must be either true or false, it would seem that there is no contingency to future events (*On Interpretation* 22).

22. "Generally then, if it is necessary to prove what a man is, let C stand for man, and A for what he is—whether two-footed animal or something else. If we are to have a syllogism, it is necessary to predicate A of all C. But this requires another middle term for what it is that a man is. So we assume what it is necessary to prove. For B (the middle term) is what a man is" (*Posterior* II, 7; 91a27–33).

23. "We have stated then how 'what something is' is grasped and becomes known, and we see that, although there is no syllogism of 'what something is' or has become, or any proof, it is through syllogism and through proof that 'what it is' is made clear" (*Posterior* II, 8; 93b15–18).

24. The other example from Book I, ch. 13, is as follows: the unreasoned syllogism: if what waxes is spherical and the moon waxes then the moon is spherical—making waxing the cause of the moon's spherical shape; but rearranged, we get: the moon is spherical and what is spherical waxes—therefore the moon waxes, and spherical shape is placed properly as the cause.

25. This problem does not occur when the extension of the terms are commensurate as in the example of decidious and broad-leafed trees, where either arrangement of premises is correct (*Posterior* II, 17; 99a5). Aristotle must be careful not to imply here that causal connections that are not commensurate are "accidental." An analysis in terms of extension preserves the necessity of the causal connection.

26. There is much ambiguity, if not inconsistency in Aristotle's treatment of division. In the *Topics* the theory of Forms is criticized as conflicting with the method of division: Form implies a Parmenidean oneness inconsistent with differences in species (VII, 5; 143a11–32). However, this may only be the finding of a convenient weakness in the argument of a rival, when one remembers how roundly division is criticized in the *Prior Analytics*. Furthermore, the dichotomous division finally approved at the end of *Posterior Analytics* (II, 13) is itself declared useless for the classification of animals in *The Parts of Animals* (I, 2; 643a24–27).

27. Aristotle introduces the procedure with a simple example from arithmetic: a triad is an "odd prime number." However, his substantive examples in chs. 13 and 14, where he illustrates the necessity and usefulness of division, involve "man" (II, 13; 96b25ff.; II, 14; 98a8ff.).

28. Among other intolerable results would be: "All expressions would be definitions, since any one of them can be associated with a name; so that we should be talking in definitions, and even the *Iliad* would be a definition" (*Posterior* II, 7; 92b31–33).

29. Here and elsewhere, Aristotle flirts with induction. Can it be that we could "track" the universal by repeated observations? The trouble is that this requires that we know what to observe. Aristotle constantly returns to cases in which we might be said to *see* the cause.

30. There is no very good translation of the Greek οὐσία, a nominative formed from the feminine singular of the present participle of the verb "to be." Being or "what is," is too wide, as Aristotle distinguishes the being of properties from the being of *ousia*. *Ousia* are beings in a primary sense, actual existing entities that are *ousia* in two ways, both as individual particulars and as the essences that make them what they are, e.g., men. In this way, under the cover of *ousia*, Aristotle manages by sleight of hand to assume a universal which is at the same time a particular. In order to provide consistence with other translations, I use the common "substance" for *ousia*.

31. Lewis Hanke, *Aristotle and the American Indians* (Bloomington, IN: Indiana University Press, 1959), 47.

32. See Sister Mary Margaret, C. I. M., "Slavery in the Writings of St. Augustine," *The Classical Journal*, XLIX (1954).

33. Hanke, 47.

34. *Ibid*, 8.

35. An example from *The History of Animals* (9, 1; 608b): Aristotle describes women as more compassionate, tearful, jealous, and querulous, as devoid of shame and self-respect, dishonest, deceptive, and harder to rouse to action. Cf. also *Politics* I, 5, where men's proper rule over slaves is analogous with the proper rule of the mind over the body, and men over emotional women.

36. For another example, see G. E. R. Lloyd's discussion of Aristotle's mistakes in anatomy as he attempts to apply the opposition of an honorable masculine "right" and an inferior feminine "left" to biological structures: *Polarity and Analogy* (Cambridge: Cambridge University Press, 1966), 52–59.

4

Logos Spermatikos:
The Logic of Empire

> God is reason and fate and Zeus, and has many other names. In the beginning
> there was no other being until he changed all substance from air to water. And
> just as with animals sperm is in liquid, so he left the sperm of his logic behind
> in the water to generate all the beings of the universe, shaping matter out of
> himself in a successive creation. (Diogenes Laertius, *Life of Zeno*, 135–136)[1]

With this declaration, a new role and articulation for logic is announced,
along with a new universe of discourse. Zeno, born the year of Alexander
the Great's death, was a youth when Aristotle died. By then, Athens had
lost its status as a Mediterranean power to Macedonia. Alexander's empire
opened a new world, the world of Persia, Africa, and the great cultures of
the Orient; rivalry between minor Greek city-states could no longer appear
as the focus of history but only as petty squabbling kept in check by the rule
of the Macedonians. Much as Athenians might try to convince themselves
that Alexander wasn't Greek and that Athens was still the intellectual hub
of the universe, it was clear that Alexander and his descendants would now
be the standard-bearers for Hellenism, not Athens.

Nevertheless Zeno, an ambitious young Phoenician from Cyprus, went
to Athens where rival philosophical schools still energetically competed for
students and commissions. There, he discovered the Cynics. Taken with
their criticism of convention and ambition and by their view that virtue
made you a king, he wrote a utopian tract, *Politea*, which outlined an ideal
libertarian Republic on Cynic principles. But the novelties of the Cynics'
outrageous behavior did not interest him for long. He soon turned to the
Megarians, famous for their logical skill and adepts at generating new paradoxes and forms of argument. In the mysterious teachings of the Milesian
Heraclitus, he discovered metaphysics in a universal Logos/God who ruled
the cosmos. Out of these disparate sources, the young philosopher founded
a new logic, a cosmopolitan logic that would transcend the narrow boundaries of the *polis*.

The starting point of his philosophy was a logic that did away with both
Platonic Form and Aristotelian substance. The Stoics rejected a metaphysics
of transcendent Forms, replaced Aristotle's syllogistic term-logic with a
logic of propositions, reframed truth in terms of truth-functions, and estab-

lished new relations between signs, meanings, and things. Logic was no longer merely a technique of argument, or a method of pedagogical demonstration, or the form of scientific demonstration. It was the grammar of the cosmos: a divine law that keeps the physical world in place and a universal will to which the virtuous must conform. These innovations of Stoic logic reoriented both logical theory and dialectical practice in the new context of world empire. The city-state had collapsed; no longer could its values or political integrity survive intact. No longer was there one superior Greek state which could legislate substantive agreement on heavenly Forms or universal essences. Instead new kinds of logical constants had to be invented consistent with the administration and repression of a plurality of peoples with differing values and customs.

For this to be possible radical change was necessary in both the grounding and the syntax of logic. In the atmosphere of scepticism that followed Athens' final failure to maintain its dominance in the Aegean, neither Plato's forms nor Aristotle's essences could seem eternal or necessary. Any clear view of what things are or should be was gone. That Alexander, a barbarian upstart from primitive Macedonia, could become overlord of Athens meant that what happens must be only a contingent and temporary creation of the divine will.[2] In the midst of the scepticism and confusion that resulted, the Stoic logician turned away from essence and form to examine more carefully the actual instrument of rationality, language. Perhaps language, itself, might be made to generate truth with no reference to substance at all. The essential middle term necessary to hold the Aristotlean syllogism in place and on which its truth is dependent might be dispensable.

Certainly if the middle term was to be the essence of man this would seem to be necessary. It was clear enough after Alexander's exploits that there were men who were not like Greek men and who were unwilling to accept Greek men as ideal; the Hellenic empire was never an easy place to govern, and local populations often resisted the rule of the Macedonians. Zeno's cosmopolitan rivals, the Sceptics, were busy ridiculing all attempts to defend any certain knowledge, especially if it involved reference to an universal concept of man.[3] Even Greeks were not unanimous on the nature of man. No matter how intuitively obvious it might have seemed to Athenians like Aristotle or Plato, Anatolian Greeks, Macedonian Greeks, Egyptian Greeks might not agree. For citizens of a vast empire that had rejected national and cultural boundaries, the ideals of Athenian gentlemen were narrowly parochial. It was clear that if order in the cosmos or empire was to be maintained, it would have to be by something greater and more universal than any "man," even if he was Greek. "Man," Zeno argued, is not a true perception of any reality because men are either Greek or barbarian and a universal "man" is neither (Sextus Empiricus, *Outlines of Pyrrhonism* II,

128ff.). Plutarch also reports Zeno's cosmopolitanism: Zeno, he says, thought all men fellow citizens, not just Greek men (Plutarch, *Moralia* 329a). The logic that could accommodate these changes in outlook required a new ontology. There are, Zeno argued, no Platonic Forms or any secondary substances in Aristotle's sense. There are only bodies, only physical beings in given states and relations, the objects formed at the first creation by God's spermal logic in a free act of creation. Platonic Forms are ideas in the mind and so have no substantial being. Nor is there a significant difference, as Aristotle argued there was, between genus and species. There is no one quality which gives the special "whatness" of a thing.[4] Common qualities are only names for different states of things and have no ontological significance.

But if the Stoics' ontology was spare, their linguistics was not. They invented a complex metalanguage of technical terms to explain the workings of rational expression. Not only were the Stoics careful systematizers of grammar, they developed a logical "semantics" that accounted for meaning without reference to suspicious entities.[5] There is the sign (ἡ φωνή) or actual voiced sound, the meaning it stands for (τὸ λεκτόν) or "what is said,"[6] and a referent (τὸ ἐκτὸς ὑποκείμενον) corresponding to that thought: meanings thus isolated were the main focus of the logician's interest. Unlike signs, which are only the words of a particular language, meanings are what any language can represent, whether Greek, Persian, Egyptian, or Chinese. These meanings, the Stoics continued their semantic analysis, can be deficient or complete, depending on whether they constitute a complete thought or are only a subject without a predicate, or a predicate without a subject. A complete meaning is either an assertive proposition that can be true or false, or else a question, command, or other expression that cannot be true or false. Because logic is the study of truth and falsity, the logician can ignore all but assertive propositions. Only statements that can be true or false form the premises and conclusions of arguments.

With this tripartite division into sign, meaning, and referent, the Stoics accomplished their first innovation. Now peculiarities of any particular Greek dialect and even of non-Greek languages did not need to distort the clarity of logical thought but could be translated into logical syntax. Furthermore, this could be accomplished without positing either a Platonic super-universe of forms or Aristotelian categories which already assumed a fusion of particular linguistic predicates and ontology. For the first time logic could stand alone, truly beyond or above any particular language, untroubled by the contingent form of any human experience or by the contingent constitution of any given reality.[7] Logic had established an alternative meta-universe of discourse, neither psychological nor physical, in which truth could be reliably established.

The Stoics, however, were not willing to leave propositions with no foundation in reality. Because there are no formal existents, whether meta-physical or embedded in reality, but only physical bodies and because access to these bodies must be through perception, again perception would have to become that foundation. The Stoics, however, saw as well as Aristotle that perception alone is inadequate; their rivals the Sceptics rehearsed often enough the many examples of sensory deception and illusion. Again a special kind of perception would have to be isolated, not just animal sensation, but a "rational presentation" which in turn could become a linguistic meaning or *lekton*, and form by combination—by contact, similarity, analogy, trans-portation, composition, etc. (Diogenes, *Life of Zeno*, 52)—more general concepts.[8] These meanings could then be combined into complete proposi-tions or assertions and used to produce syllogisms, conditionals, and other arguments (Diogenes, 43–44). No longer would the logician intuit directly, in Aristotelian fashion, the substance "man" as he looks at individual men. Instead his general notions would be built up from rational presentations and those rational concepts put into logical order.[9]

But if Stoic logic could not depend on any essence to hold it in place, there would still have to be some assurance that it could reveal the truth. For the Stoics, the answer had to be found not in any privileged referent but in the rules of logic itself. These rules could not be the rules of the syllogism, which involve placing terms in their correct locations. If the syllogism was meant to be a map of a world of substances and forms (e.g., man), their genera (e.g., animal), and their instances (e.g., Socrates), Stoic logic would have to present the world in a different way because there was no longer any canonical ontology to support these distinctions. The scaffolding of logic could not come from any privileged term; there is no necessary order either to the objects in the world or to the expressions that stand for them. The truth of logic would have to be found elsewhere, not in terms or even complete expressions, but in the relations between them. Here the Stoics made their most important innovation. The figure of the syllogism, that perfect form which mimicked the ideal geometrical arrangement of objects in space, is flattened. The syllogism, the Stoics discovered, can be written as a conditional expression:

> "Men are rational animals;
> Socrates is a man;
> Therefore Socrates is rational"

becomes, "If men are rational and Socrates is a man, then Socrates is ratio-nal." Logical relations are no longer dependent on terms but are relations between propositions.

Aristotle's problem in the *Prior Analytics* of grounding the truth of the demonstrative syllogism is circumvented. There is no longer any need to be concerned about the status of the middle term or any other term. Instead logical relations can be stated in discursive rules. A conditional is true if it is not the case that the antecedent (or statement in the if-clause) is true and the consequent (or statement in the then-clause) is false. Beginning from this first principle, the Stoics were able to formulate rules for the manipulation of most conditionals.[10]

As with Aristotle's syllogism, with which practicing dialecticians were now all too familiar, the regularization of the workings of conditionals in rules gave a practical advantage in argument. A competitor used to the syllogism, but not familiar with the rules for conditionals, could make a mistake, and be caught in a contradiction. Conditionals had the further advantage of focusing on propositions, which, as what is true or false, are what must be proven false in a refutation. Because according to the Stoics every syllogism can be converted into a conditional, Stoic logic offered a new tool for refutation in traditional forums of debate—law courts, assemblies, gymnasiums. Instead of memorizing the schema of the perfect syllogism, the logician could now operate with rules on strings of expressions. Logic was free from a geometric model that, no matter how abstract, had remained tied to intuitions of physical form. The new algebraicized formulae of logic could be mechanically manipulated apart from any visible reality, and logic could efficiently address itself to its main purpose of refutation without having to remain faithful to a logical map of the world in which terms function like place-names conjoined or separated in accordance with their proper positions in reality. What was important was not the identity of two items whose names are joined in a sentence, but those formulae whose true and false values can be calculated mechanically. As the Stoic extended this truth-functional character to other connectives, such as "and," and "either/or," the possibility opened of a completely mechanized discourse of inferences.

This could not, however, be accomplished without considerable distortion of ordinary usage. What is one to do with the problem that Aristotle's syllogism with its essential and necessary substantial premise ruled out: what about a conditional whose antecedent is false? If we know an antecedent to be true we can go on confidently to mark out the consequences, but if it is false we find ourselves at a loss. Is the whole conditional true or false? If we have a conditional such as "If it is raining, the games are called off," and it isn't raining, what are we to say? That the conditional is false, or true, or that it depends? The status of the conditional with a false antecedent strains the most fundamental of logical principles, Parmenides's law of the excluded middle: a statement must be true or not true. The conditional with a false antecedent seems to be just that, neither true nor false or both true and false, unless one is to say that the conditional, "If it rains, the games will be called off," is true even when it doesn't rain and the games are held inside in bad weather, which is decidedly strange.

These are not the only conditionals that cause difficulty. Given a truth-functional definition of truth, some conditionals would seem to be true that shouldn't be. If I am listening to Zeno lecture in the afternoon, then it would seem to be true that "If I listening to Zeno, it is afternoon," because both antecedent and consequent are true even though there is no logical connection between these two facts. Sextus reports some Stoics' logical grit in regard to these paradoxes. Philo, for example, was willing to take a strictly truth-functional position. If both antecedent and consequent are true, the conditional is true, and a conditional with a false antecedent is always true (Sextus Empiricus, *Against the Mathematicians* VIII, 247; *Outlines of Pyrrhonism* B138).[11] This counter-intuitive solution, convenient though it was for orderly rules, was not uncontroversial. Diodorus, disturbed by possibly, but not necessarily true conditionals such as, "If I am listening to Zeno, it is afternoon," made a stronger claim. The conditional must be necessarily true, under any circumstances; it must be impossible for it to have a true antecedent and a false consequent such as in the conditional: "If a thing is round and red, then it is red" (Sextus, *Against the Logicians* 115). The choice then was between a conditional where the consequent was somehow hidden in the antecedent and therefore triviality, and an analysis of implication that depended only on the truth values of the component statements and assumed no logical or causal relation between them.

Both required considerable deviation from the ordinary uses of conditionals in speech. If I promise, for example, "If you will pay me, I will deliver the goods," the delivery is conditional upon the payment. If you don't pay, I do not deliver. But it is understood that I would have if you had paid; in the practical logic of promising, this is imperative. If I would not have delivered, the conditional is false; I have made a false promise. Or I predict: "If you smoke, you are going to get cancer"; if you stop smoking and it turns out there is no connection between smoking and cancer but only between the nervousness that drives people to smoke and cancer, then what I have said is false. I have misinformed you and you may get cancer anyway. Even more resistant to a truth-functional analysis are common counterfactual conditionals in which the antecedent is known to be false: "If he had stopped smoking, he wouldn't have gotten cancer."

But if they were to be useful in dialectic argument, conditionals had to be divorced from the realities of communication—from the purposes of a promiser or the causal connection between dangers and misfortunes. The only way to preserve the law of the excluded middle is to make the value of the whole expression dependent only on the truth and falsity of its parts, whether truth and falsity at a given time or in all possible situations. Logical implication had to be either a formal relation replicating identities, or an empty calculation of independently determined facts connected in truth-functionally correct strings. The gains for the dialectic were great. Indeterminacies of intent and causality were removed and the workings of implication regularized in strings of truth-functions: an implication has the value "true" if the sequence of antecedent and consequent is true/false, false/false, or false/true, but 'false' if the sequence is true/false.[12] With this calculative device, Zeno and other Stoics articulated an impressive new technique that allowed disputants to construct elaborate arguments whose validity or invalidity could only be detected by a trained professional.

The Stoics' truth-functional logic would also require further work on the notion of truth. The original Greek concept of truth (ἀλήθεια), closely related to the credibility of a *logos* or account of a matter by a witness, had already been circumvented in the semantics of the *Sophist* and the formalism of the syllogism. The questions relevant to judging the truth or falsity of a description or an account of events— Could the witness be trusted? Was her promise to be credited? Was his narrative of the events likely to be true?— were not relevant in dialectical debate. Because in logic the purpose of speaking is no longer the construction of a viable intersubjective account of events, but success in a competition with fixed rules, the credibility of a speaker is irrelevant. If a dialectician can convince his opponent of a falsehood or unfounded statement, this can only be a merit, as many of Aristotle's instructions in *Prior Analytics* to his students indicated.[13] For the Stoics' new propositional logic, either truth would have to be abandoned altogether, an admission that would have been damaging to the logicians' authority, or a new concept of logical truth would have to be developed. The Stoics' solution was admirably simple: "It is day," is true if it really is day, false if it is not. "The man is sitting" is true if the man actually is sitting (Diogenes, 65; Sextus, *Against the Mathematicians* VIII, 100). Truth is not a faithful account of an event by a credible witness but the avoidance of contradiction. It is a matter of semantics. Gone is the complex determination of motives and events and purposes that characterize truth in its communicative setting. What is in issue is a relation between signs and formal objects. How the Stoics managed to accomplish this final efacement of a speaker-oriented concept of truth can be seen more clearly by looking at the nature of the 'facts'—that it is day, or that the man is sitting—that determine the truth of the corresponding expressions, "It is day," and "The man is sitting." The important innovation here was the invention of the Stoic "meanings," the *lekta* or propositions that were to stand between signs and their referents. The connection between semantic truth and meaning is conceptual: each is defined in terms of the other.

This is Sextus's critical insight as he examines the dispute between Sceptics and Stoics on the question of whether there is a criterion of truth.[14] "True,"

Sextus reports, is defined by the Stoics, as "in" propositions, or "about propositions." In other words, "true" is what a proposition is. On the other hand, a proposition is "what is either true or false" (*Against the Logicians* VIII, 11, 70; cf. also Diogenes, 65). Therefore the Stoics' definition of truth depends on their definition of proposition, and their definition of proposition depends on their definition of truth, and they have told us nothing about either. Nor does it help when the Stoics attempt to make more explicit what it is "about" a proposition that makes it true. All knowledge, the Stoics argued, comes from the senses; there are no Platonic innate ideas or Aristotelian substances. Therefore, truth cannot be determined by the formal relations between terms, either marked in division or intuited. Where, then, is there something stable enough in perception to guarantee logical truth? More than a simple, possibly mistaken, perception is necessary. The Stoics' candidate was the rational or "grasped presentation" (τὴν καταληπτικὴν φαντασίαν:[15] Sextus, *Against the Logicians* I, 227; Diogenes, 63).

Sextus was quick to point out that this cannot mean that everything we see is true. Somehow, within the blurred, shifting field of experience, something that corresponds to the proposition must be isolated. What is this mysterious entity? Zeno admits that it is not identical with everything in the mind. It must be distinguished from other mental contents which are active such as impulse, assent, and apprehension, all of which can be mistaken and therefore can provide no criterion for truth. The rational presentation must be passive, guaranteeing that no willful distortion makes it unreliable (Sextus, *Against the Logicians* I, 237). It must be something that stands between the possibly mistaken sense perception and the true assertion, something that stands between them to assure that the assertion or proposition will be true.

Sextus describes in unfriendly detail the struggles of the Stoics to make clear what this might be. Some, for example, argued that the presentation is a kind of imprint on the mind such as one might make on wax (Sextus, *Outlines of Pyrrhonism* VII, 70). But given that the mind is not a material substance in Stoic teaching but a kind of air current in material substance, it is hard to see how any imprint could hold. Zeno's more sophisticated view that the presentation is not an imprint but an alteration of the currents of air that are mental phenomena is equally inadequate because it doesn't explain how anything is retained in the mind (*Against the Logicians* I, 228–229). Furthermore, even if we could imagine that there is such a thing as a presentation arising from perception, it can only be as reliable as the perception itself. If the Stoics argue that it is not every presentation that guarantees truth, but only the "grasped presentation," just as many confusions are generated as by the rational presentation itself. The Stoic definition of a "grasped presentation" is "caused by an external object and according to that object" (Sextus, *Against the Logicians* I, 248). A rational presentation arises from sense, and forces us to assent. But again, if "grasped" is defined as what comes from and is like an external object then the Stoics are still assuming what they need to prove. They have given no way to determine which presentation is "grasped" and which is not, for we can be fooled by any perception.

There is only one solution: true presentations become those presentations which we take as true. To say that "they could not be produced by what is not real" is only to add emphasis to a circular definition (Sextus, *Against the Logicians* I, 401ff.). All this, charges the Sceptic Sextus, throws truth into great confusion. Epistemological soundness, however, is less important to logicians than dialectical utility. For logical soundness, a semantic definition of truth is necessary. If a true proposition is established according to a rational presentation, a rational presentation is what can be described by a true proposition. That is all that is required for the logician's arguments. It is clear to what the two terms of the Stoics' definition of truth refer: "The man is sitting" (the proposition) is true in the case that there is a man sitting (the rational presentation). Logical truth can be established with no possibly mistaken epistemological assumptions and with no reference to any reality at all.

For this to happen a distance has to be be created between our experience and what we say that allows logic to function autonomously. Propositions are true insofar as they fit the facts; facts are not perceptions of things or relations between things or the language in which we talk about these things, none of which fit neatly into logical categories. They are the structures and the objects that correspond to logical form. It is the job of semantics, the study of logical meaning, to project these proper objects of truth so that the terms of logic will have "reference." Although the Stoics are obviously novices at semantics compared to its twentieth-century practitioners, whose formal structures rival mathematics in complexity, they invent a new meta-discourse: a language insulated from what people say and what they say it about, a realm of logical objects not dependent on any reality, and not dependent on what any "foolish" masses might say. Zeno even goes so far as to equate the discernment of this new discovery with "humanity"; if we deny these presentations, we put ourselves in the category of things with no souls (ἀψύχοις): Sextus, *Against the Logicians* I, 260).[16]

What is true no longer has to be what someone says, no longer the old *logos* of the witness come to tell her tale, but is "what is said" regardless of who says it, or why, when, and where they say it. That the Stoics, with their commitment to the view that there is nothing in the world but physical bodies, had some difficulty justifying the existence of these incorporeal "things said" did not diminish the dialectical advantages of independence from the ordinary restraints of speech and reality.[17] With truth as "what is said" and the rules for conditional implications, the dialectical displays that had so delighted upper-class Athenians at the Stoa, in the courts, and at private parties could now be even more dazzling.

But Zeno and his cosmopolitan colleagues did not only revitalize dialectical debate and analysis. In the Hellenic empire, outside the closed, self-congratulatory security of the city-state, the syntax of Stoic logic also reflected new forms of interaction between rulers and ruled. Much as they refused to acknowledge the achievement of their new masters, the Macedonians, even Athenians were uneasily aware that the walls of Athens no longer delineated the civilized world. The new centers of power and culture were elsewhere, in Egypt, in Asia Minor, and Persia. In such settings, the racial superiority of Greeks could no longer be assumed. Nor could political stability be based on friendly relations between well-born citizens of similar background and education. Alexander's world was full of differences: different cultures, different religions, different ways of thought. At the same time, Athenians, never reluctant to pursue their own advantage, quickly saw the opportunities that had opened. If the Greek empire was not, as in the old days, under the direction of Athens, it was still Hellenic, and there was money to be made and power to be gained for Greeks in the administration of Alexander's conquests and in expanded opportunities for international trade. Although Alexander had on occasion attempted to promote intermarriages between Greeks and daughters of local ruling classes, or integration of his army, these innovations had not been popular. There was a great demand for Greeks in the outposts of the empire, as officials, as administrators, as military leaders, as colonists.

In this first attempt at Western imperialism, the mechanisms of administration of large and disparate possessions were undeveloped. But the Stoics' new logic pointed the way to a idiom of control. The arrogance of marauding Homeric adventurers imposing their will by force of arms could not give authority to imperial government. No longer could the moral superiority of rulers consist only in the traditional military virtues of courage, discipline, and strategic intelligence. Instead of on brute strength, Hellenic rule would depend upon a superior culture. The medium of that culture was language, Greek, but not the diverse demotic Greek spoken by tradespeople, workers, slaves, and women. The language of those in power would be a rational, logical Greek suited for use in law courts, in political debate, and in the decrees of governors.[18] It would be a language which even the non-Greek aristocracy of conquered possessions would be motivated to master in order to get access to power and opportunities for advancement.

The same pattern of rule was repeated in each of the Macedonian imperial cities. After a superficial deference was paid to local traditions—the token appeal to religious authorities for conformation, a taking of the local titles for high office—a Greek *polis* was established, complete with the institutions in which discussion was logical: a law court where cases could be argued, a council where leaders could prepare legislation, an Assembly where citizens would debate, a gymnasium in which the youth of citizens were trained in military virtues and taught the skills of leadership.[19] Here, in enclaves separated from the diversities of multi-racial, multi-cultural cities, the colonizers and administrators made themselves at home and prepared to rule the city, sustain the military control of the surrounding countryside, and hear and implement such decrees as might come from a distant emperor. Hellenization was not to be a degraded adaptation to foreign ways, but the establishment of Greek rule and Greek culture for Greeks and those of the local elites who were able and willing to emulate Greeks.

A new logic was required for such an understanding. The rationality that would justify the rule of Greeks could no longer be based on the substantive Athenian ideals that had held the Aristotelian syllogism in place. These might have seemed self-evident in the closed world of the city-state, but were hopelessly parochial in a large empire. Even among those whose mother tongue was Greek, there was now evident a wide diversity in ideals and outlook: Macedonian Greeks, Anatolian Greeks, Black Sea Greeks did not always agree, nor did the nature and essence of man seem so unitary to them as it had to Plato or Aristotle. Certainly Athens no longer had the military might to insist on their submission. Even Aristotle's own school, the Peripatetics, as they extended his biological studies of the species, had begun to eclipse the notion of a racial difference between barbarian and Greek.

If the superiority of Greek culture and the Greek right to rule was to prevail, it would have to be understood in a new way, not as based on race, but on linguistic and intellectual superiority. What distinguishes Greek from barbarian would no longer be any physical or quasi-physical form, but something more objective, the rule of right reason, a universal language that could form the syntax of all meaning. The grammar of that language, not its substantive terms, would be the bearer of authority. The unity of the Hellenic world would be a unity of thought expressed in a language removed from peculiarities of accent, dialectic, emotional tone, and even of ideas, which might differ from Greek to Greek, or from East to West. Logic would provide the rigid skeleton and the powerful muscle that could hold such an empire together. To cite Zeno's mix of metaphors:

> They say philosophy is like an animal: logic is the muscles and bone, ethics the flesh, physics the soul. Or as in an egg: the shell is logic, after that ethics and in the center physics. Or, again, a field: the encircling fence is logic, ethics the crop, physics the earth or the trees. (*Or a city well-walled and governed by logic*) (Diogenes, 90; my emphasis).

Zeno's closing parenthesis illuminates the whole: logic is the supportive skeleton, the protective shell, the restrictive barrier that provides government and order in the state.

This was a powerful conception and, even when Alexander's empire did not survive, an imperial conception of rational order was not defeated but only more securely realized in the empire of Rome where, in the words of Cicero, community was based on reason and law.

> Since nothing is better than reason and reason exists in both man and god, reason is the first bond of unity between them. But those who have reason in common also have right reason in common; and since right reason is law, this also must be seen as a common tie linking men with the gods. Now those who have the same law must also have the same justice; and those who share law and justice must be regarded as members of the same community—much more so, if they obey the same authorities and powers; and they do obey the order of the heavens, the divine mind, and the god of supreme power. Therefore the whole universe must be seen as a single joint community of gods and men (*De Legibus*, 22–39).[20]

Imperial government is established in the name of "right reason" and truth. The logician does not contribute the content of that truth. Logic has freed itself from conceptual content which can only localize its truths. Logic offers the technique by which any chosen content can be articulated in self-consistent decrees. With Zeno more is claimed for logic than that it devise weapons for the ritual battle of words that identifies superior men; it is the scaffolding for a ruling culture, a way to order thought and administer possessions. This new role for logic is made explicit in Stoic metaphysics and ethics.

The dialectic, says Zeno, is virtue (Diogenes, 47). All other virtues are subsidiary to the logician's ability to know to which of his perceptions he should consent. Therefore, the logician is the best legislator. The dialectic allows him to put questions and answers in the right way and to give the correct answers when he is questioned. He has the ability to shape and control his instincts and so bring instinct into harmony with right reason. Consistent rational thought constitutes the inner disposition and fixed character which is virtue. Once rational thought is firmly instituted, a man can do no wrong. His actions will follow naturally, not requiring any deliberation or conscious choice. He has achieved the state of Stoic a-pathy (ἀπάθεια); he has driven passion from his life. He is not without feeling, but his emotions are rational: he takes pleasure only in what is correctly done, wishes only for the established good, takes precautions only at the proper times. Here is the able administrator of conquered territory, far more efficient than Plato's philosopher-king whose insight into the eternal form of beauty might make him seem ridiculous to those on earth. Zeno's rational man armed with Stoic logic was more efficient: his consistency was unmarred by any instinctive response, his decrees had the inner consistency and security that logical consistency can generate. Stoics were popular in imperial Rome; they were sought after as advisors to statesmen and tutors to the sons of ruling citizens. The Stoic, it was thought, made the ideal administrator.

What assurance does such an administrator have that his virtuous consistency is, in fact, based on the right? All his virtues— of consistency, steadfastness, unconcern with the consequences of his action, unthinking fullfillment of his obligations—might be monstrous in the service of falsehood or evil. To defend his virtue a Stoic cannot return to any reference to human experience. As Sextus's criticisms bring out, the rational presentations which ground the logician's propositions cannot depend for their validity on the perceptions that underly them. If a perception is mistaken, then the presentation and the proposition that describes it are false. Something else must be provided to give the rationality of the presentations on which the Stoics' inferences depend an authority that deviant perceptions cannot challenge. Zeno provides this in his theory of the cosmos.

The beginning of all things are two, he argued, active and passive. The passive is the physical substance which is everywhere, the active is the divine *logos* which is eternal and shapes each thing. God releases his form-giving sperm-word into the waters of the world, and from it rise the various beings. The human logician, then, does not manufacture his own possibly fallacious rational perceptions, he follows the movements of God as the divine Logician ejaculates the correct relations between propositions. The logician's rational presentations and right reason are not his own personal view, they are the Word of Zeus, leader and governor of all things. This divine word is the virtue of the good man and the happiness of his smoothly flowing life. Once the rational man understands this universal order, all is in harmony; the spirits of rational men conform to the will of Zeus who rules the universe (Diogenes, 88).

All that is required is that the will of a supreme ruler on Earth be identified with that order. Alexander was applauded by Plutarch and others as the Stoic Sage;[21] Cicero, in *De Legibus* and *De Republica*, equated the universal law, innate in nature and the same for all men, with the laws of the Roman Republic.[22] The logic of Plato and Aristotle was founded in the shared ideals of a masculine elite projected either above the physical world, as in Plato's Forms or onto matter, as in Aristotle's substances. Society, as well as the soul, could then be held to a common ideal of virtue. Stoic logic holds the soul and society together in a different way, not by projecting an ideal, but by providing a divine grammar of reason within which all are to think and act. The cosmos ruled by the supreme Zeus is the counterpart of the world-state ruled by his delegates whose intelligences are claimed to be in accord with a natural law created by divine will. Centuries later the theologians of the universal Catholic Church would find much to admire in Stoic logic.[23]

It is clear enough that the unity of Man so created had little liberatory effect. Stoics were not revolutionaries. Zeno's patron was the Macedonian King, Antigonus Gomatas; Zeno's student Sphaerus was advisor to the reactionary King Cleomenes of Sparta. Stoics did not support the various attempts by Athens and other city-states to regain their independence from Macedonia.[24] In Rome, Stoics supported the Empire as advisors to statesmen, educators, and administrators. Until the final break-up of the Roman Empire, there was little substantial change in the status of conquered peoples, slaves, or women. Although Alexander is praised by Plutarch for his belief in the brotherhood of man, and the cosmopolitanism of the Romans is sometimes cited, never in either empire did this mean anything more than the inclusion in circles of power of those men similar enough in racial or cultural characteristics to pass as honorary Greek or Roman gentlemen. Although at times, Stoics in Rome supported an alleviation of the condition of slaves, they did not recommend the abolition of slavery.[25] Loosened from the concept of "man," Stoic logic seemed to demand that women as well as men were capable of logical thought, but although Stoics such as Seneca argued that women could be as reasonable as men, Stoics took no substantive steps toward integrating women in public life or in the affairs of the state. There were no substantive changes in Roman marriage or property law. The discussion that might have begun to challenge these oppressive institutions and the misconceptions that supported them could not occur by the very terms of Stoic logic. The dialectician's task was not to blur boundaries, not to question the rational presentations that order things according to general principles.

An example is again the theory of generation that fixed the women's role, even in reproduction, as passive. Generation, being active, is inconsistent with the concept of femininity. Logic ordered these "facts," and so the Stoics continued to make the same foolish mistakes in reproductive biology as Aristotle. The semen, the Stoics argued, is the generative element; the female is sterile, watery, and without tension, the anonymous liquid into which the male casts his sperm. The semen is the model or form of the soul that creates being out of a formless substance (Diogenes, 158–159). Again a theory of generation that minimizes the female role is projected onto the universe. In Aristotle's metaphysics, inert matter received the imprint of form. In Stoic metaphysics, God, the supreme masculine element, plants his seed in a characterless primal medium and generates the grammar of the cosmos.

The wisdom of the Stoic Sage was not open to the wisdoms of any conquered cultures. Plutarch himself, the great defender of Alexander's humanity, describes the different ways in which Alexander treated Greeks and non-Greeks. Certainly the Romans' treatment of Jews and Christians is well enough documented in our own tradition to show that Roman ideals, both ethical and religious, were not to be engaged in any discussion that might question Roman rule. Local practices and customs were tolerated as primitive archaisms as long as they did not interfere with the keeping of order and the collection of revenues and taxes. Any culture that fostered rebellion was ruthlessly destroyed. Logic cannot be credited with beginning the oppression of slaves, women, under-classes, or subject peoples, or even with playing the major role in maintaining these oppressions. The collecting of tribute and taxes, the disciplining of women, the capture of slaves, the military control of territories was carried on in more material exercises of economic and military power. Stoic logic, however, was no innocent theoretical bystander. It provided the grammar for communicative relations in a centrally governed world-state, a divinely ordained universal law that could govern all peoples, and a model for learned discussion that continued to finesse substantive questions of justice and injustice.

The youth in the *Sophist* who docilely submitted to the questioning of his master, the jury or the Assembly that marvelled at the display of the debaters of the *Prior Analytics*, the student in Aristotle's Lyceum who respectfully listened and noted his teacher's correct division of a subject matter from the *Posterior Analytics*, and now the subject turned tongue-tied before the right Stoic reason of his governors—logic rendered them all speechless, unable to voice their reservations and scruples, unable to validate or refute what had been said from their own experiences. And it was this dazzlement and this silencing that logic was meant to create.

Logic cannot refute pain, hunger, despair. Alexander's Hellenic empire fell, as well as the Roman. Rebellions, civil war, charismatic religions, famine, all were outside the scope of that right reason so admired by Cicero as the bond between men. Zeno and his school, however, had invented something more lasting, a new conception of discourse. Logic provided a way of speaking which was not speech, which did not need to say anything about the constitution of the world or the perceptions of speakers, a language that could generate, without embarrassment, indeed with pride, its own semantics, a language that constructed its own world of entities and structures to correspond to its own truths. The unity of being envisioned by Parmenides takes on new meaning. Regardless of physical conquest, regardless of which monarch, potentate, emperor, or ruling party is in control, in an autonomous dissemination of meanings that mimics the creation of God, language is now capable of generating its own cosmos, the cosmos of sexist, racist, ethnocentristic culture.

Notes

1. There are no original manuscripts extant from Zeno or any of the other Stoics. Their views must be pieced together from various secondary sources. The

principal ones are: Sextus Empricus's *Outlines of Pyrrhonism* and *Against the Logicians*, both Sceptical criticisms of the "dogmatism" of the Stoics, and Diogenes Laertius, *Life of Zeno*. Citations are to the Loeb Classical Library editions of these works.

2. The created world, according to the Stoics, was perennially destroyed by fire. In this Heraclitean conflagration the divine *logos*, Zeus, was the only thing that survived to initiate a new creation.

3. Sextus devotes much space to criticisms of the idea of man. There is no stable substance "man," no precise conception, no one shape of man, because both men and women are human. "Rational" animal cannot be used as a definition because clearly not all men are rational; furthermore, the idea of potential rationality is incoherent. Sextus developed these and other arguments in *Outlines of Pyrrhonism* II, 5, and *Against the Logicians*, 263ff.).

4. A considerable amount of confusion surrounded this issue as philosophers, used to thinking in terms of universals or Aristotelian substances, attempted to understand Stoic teaching. See the extended discussion of the various misunderstandings in J. M. Rist, *Stoic Philosophy* (London: Cambridge University Press, 1969), 164ff.

5. I use the word "semantics" in the model-theoretic sense, current in mathematical logic and linguistics: semantics comprises theoretical entities, sets, and structures, onto which the symbols of a system, grammatically or mathmatically ordered, can be mapped. Semantics provides an interpretation of the symbols in the same way that Euclidian or spherical geometries provide interpretations for geometric symbols.

6. λεκτόν has been translated in a variety of ways. Often it has been left untranslated as a technical term. Its literal meaning, "things said," which corresponds to our "what is said," seems to me to get across the Stoics' point best. When that is awkward I use "meaning." For complete assertive *lekta* the Stoics were more likely to use ἀξίωμα, or judgment, which I translate "proposition."

7. It is also this insight that founds contemporary structuralist views of language. The virtue of Noam Chomsky's transformational grammar was that it seemed to provide a way to bridge the gap created between surface structures of particular languages and an underlying logical, propositional core of meaning. His rivals, of course, are the behaviorists who continue to try to ground language in perception.

8. There are remarkable similarities between Stoic teaching and the association of ideas usually seen as an innovation of British empiricists such as Locke or Hume.

9. Benson Mates, in *Stoic Logic* (Berkeley: University of California Press, 1961), credits the Stoics with discovering Frege's distinction between sense and reference. There are some similarities. The Stoics had a simple insight: logic does not study the symbols of a language, but what they stand for. Barbarians hear the sounds of Greek, but they don't understand. It is what they don't understand that the logician studies. Frege, on the other hand, was concerned with a

technical problem as he attempted to construct a logical language, modelled after mathematics. Ordinary sentences would not behave truth-functionally in certain contexts. In order to solve the problem Frege distinguished two aspects of meaning: reference and sense. If used only for a sense, or an idea or presentation we have of something, a term with the same reference might not be substitutable. The deep problem may be the same: logic requires some stable unitary reference, but in spoken language these references are always obscured by the intentions and desires of particular speakers.

10.   For example, to use the Stoic terminology, "If the first [proposition] then the second, and the first, then the second." Although this first of the Stoic "undemonstrable statements" might seem trivial, some of the others are less immediately grasped: "If the first, then the second, but not the second, therefore not the first" (Diogenes, 72ff.). Introductory students of logic still regularly get this wrong, and in a similar fashion, other of the Stoics' undemonstrables might not seem immediately self-evident to opponents in debate who are less than logically quick-witted.

11.   This makes Philo's conditional the same as contemporary logic's material conditional. Quine, for example, distinguishes between the truth-functional conditional which is a compound of two statements, and implication, in which we mention the names of statements in talking about the logical connection between them: *Methods of Logic* (New York: Henry Holt, 1955), 37–38.

12.   Thus foreshadowing the truth-tables of propositional truth-functional logic.

13.   See Sextus's critical account of the Stoics' Wise Man, or Sage. If we settle on some wise man's view as the standard of truth, how will we know he is stating what he believes? Being wise, he is dialectically adept, and he may be defending what is really false in order to prove how intelligent he is by showing that we can't refute him even when he states falsehoods (Sextus, *Outlines of Pyrrhonism* V, 42).

14.   The Sceptic's position is that there can be no absolute criterion of truth. Although provisional knowledge may be possible, one must always be suspicious of any dogma and resigned to the fact that one may be wrong.

15.   Φαντασία, literally a spectacle or show, must be distinguished from φάντασμα, an appearance or apparition, as well as from sensation (αἴσθησις), which we share with the animals. Presentations can be sensory, but can also be internal of ideas. Again the Stoic distinction is similar to Locke's between ideas of sensation and reflection: *Essay Concerning Human Understanding* (Oxford: Clarendon Press, 1924), Book II, 2.

16.   Traditional concepts of soul were inadequate for Stoic purposes, whether of the soul as the seat of emotion and impulse, or as a functional harmony of the bodily parts. The Stoics refer to the ἡγεμονικόν, or ruling part of the soul, to be distinguished from appetite and emotion. "What is fit for rule is the master of the soul in which are the the the perceptions and impulses. From the ruling part comes logic" (Diogenes, 159).

17.   There was considerable dispute among the Stoics over the ontological status of

the *lekton*. Given their view that all existents were bodies, a higher category was needed above undifferentiated substance (τὸ ὑποκείμενον) and particular qualified being (τὸ ποῖον), "the what" (τὸ τί), for non-bodily beings such as meanings.

18. Greek is not the only language that would play this role. Later French, and then English, as the language of an imperial power, also became an international language of diplomacy, learning, and law, necessary as the second language for anyone who wished to make a way in the "civilized" world.

19. The Greek gymnasium, especially as revived by Alexander, was not only recreational. In Aristotle's *Constitution of Athens*, as in Alexander's military governments, it played a primary role in preparing young male citizens for compulsory military service and for the later responsibilities of citizens.

20. Although Cicero was critical of some aspects of Stoicism, for example of the spareness of their rhetoric, his doctrine of natural law and right reason is typically Stoic.

21. Zeno separated men into those who were wise (σοφός) and those who are foolish (φαῦλος). There were considerably more of the latter, and the good state was ruled by the few.

22. Cicero's politics were Republican, that is, he supported a oligarchic aristocratic republic against the rule of one emperor. An advocate by profession, his first mention of natural law is as a useful forensic tactic to defeat claims based written law. Later in the fully developed discussion of *De Legibus* and *De Republica*, he claims natural law as a universal principle conveniently congruent with the laws of the beleaguered Roman Republic.

23. In the addition of an all-powerful creator God some commentators have seen a Semitic influence traceable to the Phoenician ancestry of Zeno. Certainly, Zeno's innovation recommended Stoic logic to later Christian theology, based on the absolute sovereignty of the creator father god of the Old Testament.

24. Antigonus visited Zeno in Athens and invited him to court. On the occasion of Zeno's death, he commanded the Athenians to give him a state burial and to pass a decree in his honor. In Sparta the Stoics were on the side of reaction. King Cleomenes, with Stoic advice, reinstituted the austerity that prevented the rising class of wealthy merchants and tradespeople from claiming political power as they had in Athens.

25. The Stoics' recommendation that slaves should be treated less harshly was consistent with later Roman imperial policy. In the early days of the Republic, when there were abundant numbers of slaves from Rome's many conquests, efficient economy dictated that, slaves being cheap and replaceable, they be worked to death to spare the expense of their reproduction. Later, with fewer conquests and fewer slaves, a different imperial policy was required. Slaves, as the basis of the Roman economy, were valuable and so were protected by Roman law. In the name of the Stoic principle of *humanitas* there were legal restraints on an owner's treatment of his slaves.

Part II
Medieval Logic

5

An Arsenal of Reasons: Abelard's Dialectic

> Because the Word of God, the Lord Jesus Christ, is named Logos in Greek, as well as the Wisdom of the Father, it would seem to be very close to him, this science, neighbor to him in name, which by derivation from the word Logos is called logic. Just as Christians draw their name from that of Christ, logic is named after the Logos Christ (Abelard, *Invective*).

> Many, stupified by logic's subtlety, retreat before its threshold like those who are made to vomit by just a hint of an unfamiliar flavor; because they can't, in tasting it, discern the quality of the flavor, they blame its subtlety instead of praising it, excusing the very real weakness of their stomachs by the fictitious reproach they make to science (Abelard, *Dialectica* IV: Prologue).[1]

So Peter Abelard praises logic and ridicules its enemies. Logic may be too "strong" for most palates, but those with weaker, less virile spirits should refrain from vilifying this divine "treasure," "as difficult as it is subtle, as rare as it is difficult, as precious as it is rare, as much worthy of great study as it is precious" (*Invective*, 133). Abelard attributed the ill will directed toward his logical skills to envy, especially since, he points out, logic is not something that can necessarily be mastered even with the most diligent of study. It is a divine gift, a capacity of soul given only to the few, a special act of benevolence bestowed on a few men by God. Those who are not strong enough to lift themselves up to pluck the sweet "raisons" of knowledge should not cry "sour grapes" (Ibid.). Logic is a legacy from the God-man Christ who promised his apostles an "arsenal" of reasons. "I will give you," Abelard quotes Jesus from Luke 21:15, "a mouth and a wisdom which your adversaries cannot resist" (*Invective*, 136).[2]

Highly as Abelard may have rated logic, by the twelfth century there had been considerable regression in logical knowledge. Abelard, historians of logic complain, no longer seems to have a clear idea of the difference between propositional logic and term logic; he implies that the force of a conditional is dependent on terms; his concept of truth is not purely semantic but relies on relations in the world.[3] One reason for these logical "mistakes" that even Abelard's God-given gift would not have been able to overcome was the fragmentary state of the classical sources available to him: only the *Categories* and *On Interpretation* from Aristotle and only hints of Stoic teaching filtered through Boethius.[4] In the thirteen hundred years since Zeno, much had been lost.

But there were other than textual reasons why logic had been arrested in what looked like progress toward greater formality and "subtlety." A momentous event had intervened. Zeno's divine Logos-Zeus, who provided the logical grammar of the cosmos, had spoken. Not metaphorically in a primeval dissemination of logical objects, but directly through his son, the Logos-Christ. Now there was no need to intuit the spermal order of the universe; instead truth came first-hand in the word of God, and any tampering with that truth by the human mind could only be a distortion. Therefore, all that was needed was repetition. The word of God must be passed down intact from Biblical patriarchs to the apostles, to the Church fathers, to faithful copyists working to reproduce manuscripts in monastery libraries, to teachers in monastic schools, to diligent Bible students who listen and memorize. The correct approach to knowledge was to read authorities, repeat their teaching, and, for the very few, to perform whatever exercises might lead to renewed revelation. At first, this seemed to leave little room for logic.

As authorities were complied, however, some of Abelard's predecessors had gently begun to propose the usefulness of logic to the faith. Anselm of Canterbury urged rational reflection as a divine element in human life and as the means to a deeper understanding of the faith. Lanfranc argued that logic, though subsidiary to revelation, could make dogma intelligible. Abelard was less cautious. His slashing refutations of respected theological positions were neither quiet nor contemplative, nor were they made in the sportsmanlike spirit that, at least sometimes, seemed to prevail in aristocratic Athens. Logic, for Abelard, was a weapon, and he was ready to use it in a fight to the death, if not of actual bodies, certainly of reputations and honor. He freely exercised his agressive art in front of enthusiastic audiences of students who, often humiliated themselves, took great pleasure in seeing their masters made fools of by Abelard's subtleties.

Abelard told the story of his many dialectical triumphs with bitter relish in his autobiographical Letter, *Historica Calamitatum* (A History of Misfortune). He described himself, armed like his soldier father but this time with the "weapons of dialectic," engaging in "conflicts of disputation" (*Letters,* 58). He "attacked" his teacher William of Champeaux with the result, according to Abelard, that William's lectures were held in contempt by his students and William was forced to retire from teaching. He took on the aged and respected Anselm of Laon, ridiculing him to the other students and luring them away from their master's lectures to his own presentations. He angered the powerful Bernard of Clairvaux and was called twice before church councils on charges of heresy. The resentment he aroused as he applied logic to questions of theology was, he claimed, always due to jealousy. His lectures were popular; he had no problem attracting students away from other teachers; he was famous throughout France. But, in the end, his humiliation was complete; he died a broken man, humbled in his confrontation with Bernard's Inquisition, prevented from exercising the dialectical feints that he believed would have vindicated him.

If Abelard was a failure, the dialectic was not. Fortified by the discovery of the rest of Aristotle's logical writings in the mid-twelfth century, logic replaced grammar as the core of the curriculum of the medieval University. In the "trivium" of grammar, rhetoric, and dialectic required as preparation for the higher studies of theology, law, and medicine, dialectic now played a central role as the form of all knowledge and learning. Students at the Cathedral School of Notre Dame, where Abelard had made his reputation, and at the University of Paris that developed out of it, studied logic eagerly, reading Abelard and poring over the sophisms and puzzles of the newly discovered *Sophistical Refutations* of Aristotle. No longer was the *lectio*—a reading, dissection, and gloss of the text of some recognized authority—the only medium for learning; the logical *disputatio* was added, a lively dialectical contest, something like an academic cockfight, often ill-tempered, pugilistic, and with little regard for truth.[5] The students looked forward to these popular events, took sides, bet on their favorite masters, and cheered the unpopular on to defeat. Even in the old *lectio* logic established itself, as masters now found it necessary to defend their interpretations of authoritative texts against other interpretations. Finally the student himself, in the last rite of passage as he entered the rank of master, was required for the completion of his degree to enter the fray and "defend a thesis" against hostile arguments.[6]

Even Abelard's admirers had some doubt about the value of these debates. John of Salisbury, for example, a logician in his own right, who studied under Abelard in Paris and was impressed by his brilliance, returned twelve years later to find students and masters debating the same questions with more rancor but with no progress in understanding. This suggests, John concluded, that logic, although it might aid in the study of certain subjects, in itself is "barren and bloodless."[7] John went on in his later work to criticize the moral corruption of the new learning structured according to the dialectic, citing power, money, and ambition as the major motives in academic dispute, and pointing out disputation's connection with arrogant bureaucratic power.

But for its champion, Abelard, logic was the science of truth, the ruler of other disciplines, not a mere tool in their study. If theology or any other body of knowledge was true then there could be no contradiction between it and logic. This view accounts for much of controversy that surrounded logic in the twelfth century. Although Abelard made no claim that logic could refute dogma, that seemed nevertheless to be an unwelcome possibility. If there was a conflict between theology and logic, which would yield? Abelard's rational reconstructions of theological doctrines such as the Trinity, the Eucharist, and the Resurrection brought down on him Bernard's charges of heresy. He had tampered with the faith in order to make dogma intelligible. The high mysteries of the Church did not need to be brought within the grasp of human intellect, argued monastics like Bernard. They remain mysteries and objects of faith. Theological understanding does not come from the arrogance of human thought but from the love of Christ.

Rationalization of mystery was not the only danger that logic presented to the Church. As Aristotle pointed out in *On Interpretion,* the logician must separate statements into true and false propositions in order to generate the inconsistencies and identities that are the substance of logical argument; but when the doctrines of faith are sorted out into propositions with attention to oppositions, it is clear that authorities can conflict. In his tour de force, *Sic et Non,* which became the classic statement of method for scholastic philosophy, Abelard listed page after page of such inconsistencies. Not only had the corpus of authorities steadily grown as more sources were recovered and saints added to the roster, insuring that there would be differing conceptions of ethics and faith, but also mistakes in hand–copying of manuscripts had compounded these inconsistencies.

Inconsistencies, Abelard argued in the preface to *Sic et Non,* were inevitable and need not be detrimental to faith if logic is used to help sort out the truth. Spoken and written words are used in different ways, for different audiences, for different rhetorical purposes; mistakes can occur in copying; dicta can be meant as a strict rules or only suggestions. In all these cases a choice between authorities may be necessary. Even the Bible can have inconsistencies which, although they cannot be due to mistake, can still be due to misunderstanding or wrong translations. Here, Abelard argued, the logician's skill in setting out opposing propositions and disambiguating words is crucial. In its human testimonies the Word of God is a language like any other language, never completely transparent and requiring logical analysis to make clear what is meant. Without attempting any reconciliation, in *Sic et Non* Abelard presented a staggering list of contradictions, in order, he said, to prod the reader to deeper thought and reflection.[8]

The very number of discrepancies were alarming to the orthodox. In these opposing pairs, Abelard seemed to have discovered the form of dialectical conflict in the sacred body of dogma itself. The body of the faith was marked with the pros and cons of logical debate. It is not hard to sympathize with Bernard's position. Wasn't there a grave danger that the substance of faith would be lost in this collection of contradictions on which the logicians would proceed to operate? Might not theological meaning and truth instead depend on depth, nuance, metaphor, continuity of interpretation, all of which were abstracted out of Abelard's opposing propositions? Didn't logic threaten to take away the content of faith and leave only empty forms to be bandied back and forth in a profane contest of wits?

Abelard, like his predecessors, struggled to defend logic against the charge of contentlessness. Logic was more than an repertoire of verbal tricks that reduced a subject–matter to vacuity. In order to show what its proper content is, Abelard became involved in the most divisive, heated, and long-lived controversy of Medieval philosophy: the question of universals. Agreeing with the Stoics that any attempt to establish superphysical essences as logical objects would fail, but unwilling to adopt the heretical nominalism of Roselin, Abelard tried to negotiate a narrow course between formalism and essentialism that would vindicate logic's successes on some basis other than ambition and rancor. Again the key to the grounding of logic could not be thought or perception in any psychological sense because such thought or perception could always be mistaken. Nor could it be any actual spoken language. It would have to be found in that great middle ground of semantic meaning already marked out by the Stoics. Logical relations, whether between propositions or terms, are neither relations between words (*vocibus*) nor relations between thoughts (*intellectibus*), they are relations between meaning, argued Abelard.

As Abelard attempted to reformulate this Stoic insight, the remnants of Aristotelian logic to which he had access often got in the way. He had continued problems, for example, with the status of conditionals or *consequentia*. Although he agreed that in a conditional statement the whole proposition is denied or asserted, Abelard persisted in thinking that the force of the conditional was in the terms and not a relation between true or false propositions. (*Dialectica,* 485–486). In a perfect conditional the antecedent would include the consequent, and in others the relation between species and genus might be involved, but in many cases the connection between terms of a conditional, he argued, would have to be determined by some sort of natural science. The truth of, "If he is a man, he is not a stone," for example, could not be determined, Abelard argued, by definition. We might know the definition of "man" and "stone" and still not see the incompatibility of stone and man. Here, Abelard regressed to a term logic, forfeited the useful independence of Stoic semantics, and seemed to require that the logician must also be a physicist or scientist in order to establish the relations between things that support his inferences (*Dialectica,* 284).

In the words of one historian of logic, Abelard "did not understand properly how to overcome the difficulty" by distinguishing between "*a priori* and empirical studies" (Kneale, *Development,* 218, n. 2). He had lost the Stoic's insight into the truth–functional nature of conditionals that allowed complete systemic rules for the manipulation of if-then connectives to be generated. But this "mistake" was not just a result of the fragmentary state of the propositional logic bequeathed to him by Boethius. Abelard, accustomed to thinking in terms of a theology of substantive doctrines, is understandably reluctant to formulate logical relations in terms of a "material conditional" that is only a calculation of previously determined truths.

If it is true that "If Socrates is a man, he is an animal," then there must be some relation between "man" and "animal," a connection that is not just a verbal connection or a connection in someone's mind, but a natural relation. Somehow, our categories must be made to depend on reality.[9] At the same time as he sees that some such connection is necessary to ground logical truth, Abelard also is unwilling to fall back on either Platonic Form or Aristotelian "substance." In their admiration for the ancient writers, in their attempt to make sure that all authority was Christian authority, the Church fathers had allowed pagan metaphysics to distort their view of truth. Abelard's old rival William of Champeaux, for example, argued that a substantial human essence was present in all men, making himself vulnerable to Abelard's refutation: if humanity is all men then all men are the same. But Abelard also saw the threat to the authority of logic in the extreme view of his old teacher, the nominalist Roscelin, who argued that universals were only words or names (*nomina*) used for convenience in human interactions. It was not that radical nominalism entailed religious scepticism; more often, it was used to found a return to faith and revelation as the only way to knowledge. But nominalism also could be used to call into question the claim of logic to truth.

Somehow logic and the Word of God would have to speak as one. Although nominalism might seem an attractive alternative because it could turn theology away from a dangerous colision-course with logic, its segregation of reason and faith could also lead to a final schism between science and theology and the discreditation of all rational thought. Those of Abelard's contemporaries who continued to cling to what seemed to be an archaic and untenable Neoplatonism may have had sound instincts. What would happen if a secular science based in logic was allowed to separate itself from theology and claimed all knowledge for itself? Abelard, however, attempted a subtle compromise between nominalism and essentialism that would relocate logic in God's world.

Faithful to what he takes to be Aristotle's definition of universals in the *Categories,* Abelard begins with the thesis that a universal cannot be any kind of thing.[10] There were two current views, he argued.[11] Either a universal is an essential substance found in all the individuals of which it is true, or a universal is a collection of individuals. In both cases there had been a radical misunderstanding of how universal terms function. The first view is that there is some material substance that is each man, although each man is distinguished in form from other men by way of nonessential qualities. If this is true, Abelard points out, fallacies result. If Socrates and the mule Buncellus are both the same universal, i.e., animal, then the same thing is both rational and irrational. Material essence cannot account for the relation between universals but inevitably reduces all to the most general categories. In the end there can be only substance itself, and the logician is reduced to the Parmenidean autism of "substance is substance."[12]

If a universal is not a material essence, neither is it a collection of individuals. Again fallacies result. If a universal were a collection defined by its parts, in the same way a football field is made up of two halves, then, if you take away one member you would have a new universal, just as you would have a new field if you took away one half, or no field at all if you took away both. But this is not the case with universals. "Man" does not change because one man dies. There are universals which are true of nothing. A universal precedes what it is true of, in a way that a collection or a whole made up of parts does not. A football field is not a universal because it can be divided into parts, any more than Socrates is a universal because he can be divided into arms, legs, torso. What must be understood, Abelard argued, is the linguistic–logical function of universals; they do not refer to objects in the same way "Socrates" refers to an object. Instead what makes a universal a universal is the way it is used: it is predicated of several subjects. A universal cannot be a thing, nor can it refer to a universal thing. In fact, it does not refer to any*thing,* even a resemblance between things. A resemblance is not predicatable of many things any more than a collection is predicatable of many things. A universal does not refer at all, either to a thing or to anything else.

This would seem to leave Abelard with radical nominalism. If universals do not refer, then they are *nothing:* only arbitary relations between words in a language. There is no way to establish their truth, or avoid the possibility that different languages might have different relations between words. This would mean the destruction of logic. Although universals do not refer to resemblances between things, they must be somehow based on real resemblances between things. In this subtle negotiation of a reference that is not a reference, and a cause that is not a thing, Abelard takes up again the problem of locating the substance of logical truth. Again the problem is to avoid the stasis of Parmenidean Being. If logic only concerns itself with identities, then nothing can be said of anything else. We are back to a pure formalism which must amount to either Parmenidean silence or the refutation of all positions. Instead a predication such as "Socrates is a man" must be understood some other way than as a connection between two terms which refer to the same thing, Socrates and man.[13] At the same time its truth cannot be only a matter of grammar, of a purely linguistic construction. Grammar is insufficient to found any kind of knowledge. If it was sufficient, we could reason from "Socrates is a stone," which is grammatically correct but untrue. Logic must concern the nature of things. But how is it to engage the nature of things if general terms do not refer to things? Somehow the truth of logic must be established on some other basis than reference. A universal, Abelard concludes in his master stroke, is a use of words, an "institution."[14]

But how can the merely human institution of a use of words carry logical authority? The answer cannot be in the spoken words or in the objects to which they refer, both of which have natural not human causes, but again in meanings. These meanings, Abelard argued, are written on sounds in the same way an imprint is engraved on the metal of a seal. Although a meaning does not add another thing to the speech sounds that carry it, it has a different cause, just as the seal and the imprint are the same thing, but have different causes. The seal is a natural object and has a natural cause, but the cause of the imprint and/or meaning is not natural but human. And in each case the cause is not a thing.[15] How can something that is no thing be a cause? It is a cause, Abelard argued ingeniously, in the same way a wish can be a cause of something that we do or fail to do (*Logica Ingredientibus*, 20). A universal is not a thing, nor does it refer to a thing; it is a human institution which is caused by something like a wish or a decision or an intention. The Stoics' rational presentation has a new gloss, but one that may prove embarassingly thin.

How are these rational "wishes" that are the source of the institution of our use of general terms formed? Abelard certainly did not want to admit that universals are "wishful thinking" with no necessary connection to reality. What is their relation to perception which can always be confused or distorted? In order to answer these questions Abelard makes a distinction between imagination and reason.[16] Again, what distinguishes a man is his rationality, his ability to pay attention to and reflect on an object as *being something:* a substance, a thing, a body, colored. Sense, which men share with animals, is passive, but reason is active, we "*intelligeons*" when we think, we do not just receive an impression. But reason must also be distinguished from imagination in which we construct a kind of figment or phantom of an absent or fictitious object. These images are not the source of general terms which refer directly to things. Sense and imagination are only preparation for thinking, as when a painter roughly sketches in the forms he will paint. When we move to "intellection," there is nothing tentative or indistinct; a thing is understood clearly, as a substance, body, or man. If sense touches only the surface of things and an image only fixes our attention on a thing, in intellection we see the truth of a substance, what it is, as having a certain nature or property. The institution of a universal, then, is based on a certain intellectual way of seeing, in which a man is able to direct his attention not to the object itself or to its qualities, but to a given property. It is a special kind of inattention to the diverse, blurred concrete and individual qualities of a thing. It is this *act* of attending peculiar to man that founds the "institution" of the use of universal terms. Although the common use of a word is caused by something like a wish or decision, this is a cognitive wish that sees rationally what a thing "really" is.

But how are the objects of these cognitive intuitions fixed? And how can we be sure that our intellections will be consistent with the Word of God? One solution, tentitively suggested by Abelard, is to attempt to connect intellections with ideas in the mind of God. It is according to "both authority and reason," says Abelard, that ideas in the divine mind correspond to general notions. When we see a thing truly our logic recovers its closeness with its divine neighbor the Logos (*Logica*, 22–23). Such a closeness is particularly appropriate in the case of "man," the universal that continues to be Abelard's prefered example. Why do we call men "men"? It cannot be because they are one thing, which clearly they are not (*Logica*, 19). It must be because such a concept was "instituted" by men. But even though some similarity may be cited as the "reason" why such a common notion is "possible," other similarities and differences, and therefore other "institutions," would also seem to be possible. Why is it "man" that is what a man is, why not "animal," or "biological organism," or something else altogether? And what about women? How are they to be classed, are they men or something else? Do they have the rational soul that is so often the supposed similarity that makes possible the institution of "man"?

But if it is understood that men are created in the image of God, in the image of God's understanding of himself, "man" has a special kind of unity and substance to it. An example of how an identification between God, the "image of God," and the universal "man," buttressed by the arsenal of reasons provided by the dialectic, would later help to answer questions about the essence of man can be found in St. Thomas Aquinas ("On the First Man," Question XCII).[17] Thomas, using the format of Abelard's *Sic et Non* and the tools of the new logic, struggles to reconcile Biblical passages on the creation of men and women with logical consistency. If women are misbegotten males as Aristotle argued, then why were women made in the first creation? Is a woman created in the image of God? If God knew that woman was going to sin, why would he have created her? Why was she subordinate even before she sinned? Aquinas's solution is to make clear the close connection between men and the "image of God." This allows Aquinas to circumvent the differences between men and women that threaten to blur the concept of "man." The image of God is in every *man,* but women are only human; men are the beginning and end of woman, so women are not men and are not in the image of God. If the idea of "man" is a necessary institution for logical argument, the idea of a God in whose image man has been formed can be used to validate and clarify that institution.

Even Abelard, however, seemed to have doubts about the wisdom of attempting to ground the "institutions" that are the foundation of logic in the mind of God, or specific "institutions" such as the concept "man" in the image of God. If logic could be used, as it soon would be by Aquinas and others to smooth apparent inconsistencies in doctrine, this alone might be justification enough. And it is on this pragmatic basis that Abelard's logic, after his death, played a major role in political and church affairs. Regardless of metaphysical questions as to the nature of universals or the nature of man and God, the "institution" of rational concepts and their use to codify doctrine according to logical rule was valuable in the most literal sense. Not only could Abelard's logic provide a tool by which theology could be made into a coherent body of dogma which the faithful could be commanded to believe, but also logical consistency could become a new principle of legal order in the relations between rulers and subjects, Pope and believers. In the politics of papal supremacy, and later absolute Christian monarchy, puzzles as to the metaphysical underpinning for logically ordered directives were less pressing than the coherence and univocality of those directives. If emperors and popes and kings continued to proclaim a theology that cast their power "in the image of God," they also found in the institutions of logic a powerful technique for exercising that power. Logic could be used to make theology a self-consistent body of forced belief, it could rationalize the conflicting ordinances of canon law into the decree of a universal Church, and it could order an effective system of administration over diverse social orders based on codified canon law.

Regardless of Abelard's death in disgrace, it quickly became evident to secular and religious authorities that law and doctrine codified and made consistent on logical principles was the administrative tool necessary if emerging state governments and the absolutist Catholic Church were to consolidate their power. The newly rediscovered Justinian Code, with roots in classical Roman law and the Stoics' rational grammar, provided a model.[18] In the Justinian Code, the emperor proclaimed the law of the state; the judiciary, the enforcement agencies, the minsters were instruments of his will. In order to insure this rule, consistency and unequivocable expression were necessary: where but in logic could such rigor be found? A new rule of law would solidify the power of the Church, unify the Christian community, and be the basis for the policing of faith and morals. Both the local, community-based Germanic legal traditions and a developing English common law based on precedent interfered with this stabilization and rationalization of control over large territories and heterogeneous peoples.[19] On the other hand, a law structured by logic, in a rational system of self-consistent propositions issuing from one central authority, embodied the very principle of effective rule.

The textbook for the Church's codification of canon law was Abelard's *Sic et Non*. The old canon law, just as the theological authorities that Abelard collected in *Sic et Non,* was an inefficacious and disparate collection of pronouncements from the Bible, from Church fathers, from popes, bishops, saints, and church councils. Scholars, commissioned by the Pope, proceded to follow Abelard's instructions for rationalization. Propositions, or "sentences," were set out in logical order. Inconsistencies were discovered and rationalized. All tangles were combed from the Logos of law where ordered concepts would reliably regulate the lives of the faithful. Following Abelard's instructions, dissonant authorities were reconciled or rejected, and discrepancies explained by local circumstance, miscopying, or mistranslation, and eliminated. All disputes were resolved in favor of the decree of the Pope.

In 1140, the year of Abelard's death, Gratian's *Decretum: The Concordance of Discordant Canons* again followed the example of *Sic et Non,* laying out contradictory theses and using logical arguments to declare a winner. It was clear to both popes and emperors that a logically articulated law would perform the function of exercising and rationalizing power more efficiently than any ad hoc use of physical force. An identification of the source of the law—whether emperor, pope, or king—with divine power continued to be useful. All continued to claim to be speaking by divine right, which resulted predictably in wars and uneasy alliances between competing spokesmen for God. But in the mean time, relations in a new legalistic church and state between believers and priests, heretics and Inquisition, rebellious abbesses and bishops, popes and rebel monastic orders were restructured. In the thirteenth century the Church was able to launch a crusade against heretics, sorceresses, and unbelievers that unified Christendom under the rule of the Pope and of Christian emperors and kings. Dialectic in the form of codified and rationalized law was the concrete substance of an exercise of power for which the claim to speak for God was only symbolic. Just as it might not be necessary to ground logic in any formal or substantial reality, it might soon no longer be necessary to invoke any divine Logos to support semantically ordered laws that govern the universe. Logic, in the form of law, might stand by itself as the self-evident structure of thought and the self-evident form of human behavior.[20]

The edges of this dialectical weapon in the fight for the faith were sharpened in new educational institutions. The great secular universities at Paris, Oxford, Bologna, and elsewhere, began to turn out lawyers, bureaucrats, ministers, and bishops necessary to the new central governments of church and monarchy. Abelard's dialectic structured the curriculum and the relationships of the university. The new learning did not completely break with the past; the old *lectio* with its reading and gloss on an authoritative text remained, but Abelard's *Sic et Non* inaugurated new methods of historical and textual scholarship that changed the character of learned research and swelled the ranks of professors, lecturers, masters, and students. First, the techniques of logical analysis and disambiguation greatly inflated what could be said about an authority. If no authority could be found that had not been fully glossed, glosses themselves became new authorities to be glossed in turn, as scholars commented on Abelard's gloss on Poryphry's gloss on Aristotle. Scholastic practice, armed with the dialectic, developed its own rules, its own hierarchies, its own subject divisions disciplined by logic.

But Abelard's dialectic contributed to the university and to scholarly disputation more than a method of augmenting exegesis. Even more important was the training universities offered in the reduction of unwelcome inconsistencies and the adversarial techniques necessary to put down dissent. If logic, as Abelard had claimed, was the queen of all knowledge, it was because, no matter what the subject, the dialectic demanded that when all methods of exegesis failed, one of the two opposing statements must necessarily be declared false and eliminated. Academic training could no longer involve only a faithful and peaceful repetition of authorities, as had been the rule in the old monastic schools. Although authorities would continue to serve as the material on which dialectical inquiry operated, interpretations of authority, and even authority itself, must sometimes be refuted, and those refutations answered, and the answers rebutted. A scholar's reputation was no longer made by how well he could explain a text, it was made by how well he could refute a position or an interpretation of a text. Abelard's viciousness, shocking though it may have been to his contemporaries, became the approved demeanor of the successful academic, who sallied into the fray, who fought in the lists, who returned crowing with victory at the humiliation of his rival or with feathers ruffled and stained with the blood of defeat. This would also be the acquired manner of the universities' successful students as they graduated into the world of monarchial, imperial, and papal politics. If Abelard's ego seemed too big to his contemporaries, it would become the only means to survive in academic life, just as it was the only means to insure success in the ruthless competition between men for honors and wealth in papal or royal courts. If Abelard's competitiveness seemed out of place in a community of monkish scholars, as preparation for scramble up the hierarchy of secular and church power it was essential.

The point of the dialectical training offered in the new universities was not to produce substantive knowledge, scientific, historical, or moral. Just as logicians had isolated a language of meanings apart from things and ordinary speech, so the university carved out a world of intellectual meanings and produced its own hierarchy, patronage system, and mechanisms of defeat and success based on those meanings. But the scholastic logic-splitting, empty of substantive content, that critics like John of Salisbury so deplored, was at the same time practical. These students were not being trained as the Stoic's wise advisor in tune with the cosmic order of Zeus, but as the servants of those who ruled. Their teachers were busy producing the legal and theological techniques by which that rule was perpetuated. The wise no longer searched for the truth; they prepared the syntax of truth for those who would proclaim it. This claim to produce an unassailable truth independent of all contingencies is the very substance of logic. A pattern such as "If x F and G, it is F" is a form stripped of meaning, from which consistent patterns of belief, and action, can be generated from one originary center.

Again the key to this logical achievement was the establishment of the independence of propositional meaning. The Christian insistence on scriptural authority was already well suited to the idea of a proposition. If knowledge came from authority, what else could be its idiom but "sentences," citations taken as true or, if conflicting with authority, as false? Furthermore, if hierarchical relations between speakers in which one is an authority and the other a listener are to be established, those propositions must not appear to be subject to the wishes or intentions of individuals or the prejudices of any particular culture. Instead there must be a realm of meanings to sustain a unitary wish and intention independent of any speaker and of any particular reality. Many of Abelard's "logical" achievements, imperfect though they may seem from the point of view of a completely formalized logic, depend on this seminal logical insight. What is true, he argues, is not an utterance at a particular time and place; instead a utterance is only true if it posits what in reality is (*proposit id quod en re est: Dialectica,* 53). This *dictum,* like the Stoics' *lekton,* is not a thing but a thing as existing in a certain way, a *modus rerum,* an abstract entity that corresponds to the logical form of an utterance, and which can be understood rationally (*Dialectica,* 160).

The distinction that both Abelard and the Stoics made between signs and things grounds a new way of talking to others that is the communicative substance of universal law. "Things" such as particular acts of speaking or particular judgments cannot be regularized; they are thick and resistant with the physicality of gesture, expression, and tone, and cannot be ordered dogmatically in any system of rules. Nor is it possible to derive from them the identities and binary contradictions necessary for a unquestionable validity.[21] "Things" such as objects in the world also resist such an ordering, having individual, experiential, cultural, symbolic presences that interrupt the regularities of logical law.

If logical relations are to be established between speakers, some other basis for communication must be fixed that is not an object of mutual concern, not a thing, and yet still *something*. This can only be the logician's propositional contents, meanings that are elements in a universal discourse that can be infinitely articulated and referable to all situations because they are not bound to what anyone says but only to a central authority who must not be contradicted. Abelard's logic is the form of that implacable will, infallible, absolute, self-consistent, immune from all of the weaknesses of the flesh: the Word of a God, the Word of a Pope, the Word of an Emperor, the Word of Reason.

But what of Abelard? What did he mean? Aren't his, the logician's, motives pure, however kings, popes, or ambitious academics may have used or misused his logic. Didn't he struggle with the problem of universals, realizing that there must be some basis in reality for logical institutions because otherwise they are arbitrary stipulations? Can't he be absolved of the political uses made of his logic? For Abelard, fortunately, we have a way of answering these questions. In his account of his own "unfortunate history," Abelard unflinchingly laid bare his own desires and intentions: he was ambitious, he had a talent that others did not have, he used it to make a name for himself; he even used it to win the love of a woman. These motives, freely admitted by Abelard, can be examined more closely in an actual dialectical exchange from the famous series of letters between him and his lover, Heloise. Their story is well-known and the subject of much myth and romance. Abelard, already wearied by easy academic triumphs, decided to try the battle of the sexes. For his victim, he settled on Heloise, the young niece and ward of a canon, known for her learning. He gained entrance to the canon's house by becoming Heloise's tutor, seduced her, got her with child, forced her into a secret mariage, and was eventually castrated by her uncle in retaliation. On his command, Heloise reluctantly took orders and became a respected abbess, administrator, and spiritual counselor. Many years later she read Abelard's autobiographical letter. Troubled by his attitude and his distorted account of their affair, she initiated a correspondence.

This questioning of the great logician by a woman who was not a logician, and who was concerned with reaching an interpersonal and truthful understanding of a catastropic series of events, brings out clearly the intent of Abelard's logic. His first response to Heloise's letters is to refuse to address her concerns at all. Instead he makes a pious and self-interested plea that she remember her spiritual and wifely duties to pray for him constantly and bury him if he dies, and asks that otherwise she leave him alone. This is consistent with his general view of women's logical powers as expressed in his autobiography: it is not appropriate for women to take part in logical debate, which is the only kind worth having. He agrees with St. Paul that women are meant to be under the rule of men. He deplores the practice of allowing abbesses to be in charge of convents, or worse allowing them to rule over affiliated communities of monks (*Letters*, 101).

In her next letter, however, Heloise forces the issue. She charges, among other things, that Abelard was and is incapable of love and only had lust for her, that he miserably failed to fulfill the obligations of concern and mutual presence that arise from human relationships, that he has forced her into a religious life for which she has no vocation, that he has misunderstood her radical criticism of the institution of marriage and misinterpreted it as a flattering concern for his honor as a philosopher. Inherent in Heloise's reproaches are positions on the meaning of love, the economic basis of social institutions, the source and nature of moral responsibility, and the substance of spirituality that are sharply at odds with twelfth-century orthodoxy.

When Abelard finally, although still reluctantly, responds to her criticism both of himself and the institutional beliefs of his Church, he responds as a logician. He explains clearly the terms of that response.

> I have decided to answer you on each point in turn, not so much
> in self-justification as for your own enlightenment and encourage-
> ment, so that you will more willingly grant my own requests when
> you understand that they have a basis of reason, listen to me more
> attentively on the subject of your own pleas as you find me less to
> blame in my own, and be less ready to refuse me when you see me
> less deserving of reproach (*Letters,* 137).

The purpose of Abelard's logical response is not to respond to Heloise's substantive points, or to attempt to grasp with her the truth of what has happened to them. His response is not a response to what she has said at all. Instead he speaks to "enlighten" her, so that she will do what he wants, what the Church wants, what God wants, in other words that she should listen attentively and obey. He makes clear the purpose of his logic: it is meant to regain his and the Church's power and control over Heloise.

One passage from his argument, which has often been praised by com-mentators for its rationality in contrast to Heloise's emotionality, illustrates some of the ways in which this can be done. Abelard tries an argument based on the story of the Ethiopian woman in the Biblical Song of Solomon. Although not in deductive form, the paradigm of the Ethiopian woman that Abelard presents for Heloise's edification is structured by a network of those related "universals" or "modes of being" or "institutions" which are the basis for logical inference. Heloise should emulate, Abelard argues, the Ethiopian woman and accept the marriage-bed of Christ in the same way the Ethiopian woman accepted the marriage-bed of Solomon the King. Being black, the Ethiopian woman is less lovely than other women, just as any woman is black compared to a man. But in her association with what is white a black woman can find that she is white within. In the same way a woman can be enobled in her intercourse with a man. The flesh is not lovely and therefore it is black, but inside are hidden the white bones, just as the evil body hides the white purity of the soul, and the man hides the woman hidden in his bedchamber.

The "institutions," or meanings, that order Abelard's "rational" argument are symmetrical identities between paired concepts—man/woman, white/black, good/evil, soul/body; they are also a notation for racist, sexist, and body-phobic attitudes and practises. The logical institution of these concepts corresponds to actual institutions that place nonwhite, non-Christian cul-tures as inferior to white Christian ones and women as inferior to men. In Abelard's response to Heloise it is clear that the institution of these concepts serves a practical purpose. Abelard does not simply subscribe to the sexism or racism of his time, or approve the exploitative genital gratification that is the only form of sexual love he or his church recognize. With the help of logic, he writes these practices into thought itself. Heloise is to be made to think "rationally" about her situation by way of these concepts. She is to order her opinions and behavior with the principles of logic. Instead of her "unformed" questioning of his motives and behavior, her thought about their situation will be regularized and she will assent to his and the Church's wishes and rule in the same way that the supreme law of the Church makes believers into willing subjects.

Fortunately, Abelard's logic was not powerful enough to convince Heloise, although it seems to have been sufficient to convince her contemporaries that nothing of her writings should survive except her letters to Abelard. Heloise refused Abelard's logic, refused to duel on Abelard's terms with his weapons. In her other letters, under the pretext of asking Abelard to propose rules for a women's monastic order, she manages to continue her thinking outside of the institution of logical categories, raising substantive questions about the limited and perverted view of love that results from the Church's separation of body and soul, about the prostitutive nature of twelfth-century marriage, about the weakness of a religious ethics whose only substance is obedience to rule, about the incoherence of a monastic spirituality that is to go beyond this-worldly virtue of Christ and his apostles.

Abelard's logic was never meant to probe these weak points in medieval thought; it was meant for the opposite task, to buttress and armor them into law against the kind of criticisms that Heloise and others might press. The enmity that he aroused he was sure was due to envy. This also was consistent with his logic. In Abelard's dialectic, there are no substantive universals, only a battleground of male wills, competing in hierarchial social structures for advancement, reputation, power, women. Abelard's logic is the discourse of that world, structured by antagonistic adversarial positions that open opportunities for political and canonical victories. His final capitulation to the authority of the Church takes the only form of salvation possible in such a world, submission to a supreme Will, sovereign over all. His repentance adopts the only possible moral in such a world, unquestioned obedience to the commandments of God embodied in the law of the authority that speaks for him.

Notes

1. References are to the following works of Abelard: the *Invective* against someone who understands nothing about the dialectic and who nevertheless finds it evil that it is studied, and thinks that its teachings are only sophisms and deceptions, reprinted in Jean Jolivet, *Abelard: Commentary and Choice of Texts* (Paris: Seghers,

1969); *Dialectica,* ed. L. M. Rijk (Assen: Van Gorcum, 1970); *The Letters of Abelard and Heloise,* trans. Betty Radice (Harmondworth: Penguin, 1974); *Logica Ingredientibus,* in *Philosophische Schriften,* ed. B. Geyer (Munster, 1933).

2. If Abelard is right and it is a Christian "logic" that is meant here, the verse immediately proceeding might throw some light on the nature of that logic: "Settle it therefore in your hearts not to think before you will answer" (Luke 21:14).

3. Complaints about Abelard's backsliding are common in the standard histories of logic, e.g., William Kneale and Martha Kneale, *The Development of Logic* (Oxford: Clarendon Press, 1962), 203ff., or I. M. Bochenski, *A History of Formal Logic,* trans. Ivo Thomas (New York: Chelsea Publishing, 1970), viii–xiii.

4. The logic of the Stoics was not available until Sextus Empiricus was translated in the mid-fourteenth century.

5. Gabriel Compayre, *Abelard and the Early History of the Universities* (New York: Scribners, 1893), 188–189. This was the judgment of Renaissance critics.

6. This survives in the institution of the defense of the doctoral thesis, still an ordeal necessary for a higher university degree.

7. Quoted in Kneale, *Development,* 225–226.

8. The challenge was taken up by Peter Lombard in his *Sentences,* which becomes the orthodox text that resolves all contradictions, referred to as the theological authority throughout the Middle Ages.

9. Modern quantification theory also goes inside the proposition to exhibit logical relations between propositions, but sidesteps the problem by focusing not on terms, but on which terms are true of which individuals. The subject of the status of general terms is deferred as a subject for a metalogical set theory which then takes logical objects as its reference.

10. Abelard attributes his view to Aristotle in the *Categories:* "the universal is that which, by nature, is attributed to several subjects." Aristotle's *Metaphysics* was not published until the second half of the twelth century, so Abelard did not have Aristotle's full theory of substance, but he was aware of his criticism of Platonic universals.

11. The following argument is taken from Abelard, *Glosses on Porphyry* from *Logica Ingredientibus,* in Geyer, ed., *Philosophische Schriften,* repr. in Jolivet, ed., *Abelard,* 111ff.

12. The material essence view is in some respects similar to contemporary scientific realism in which reference is to natural kinds. As Abelard charges, this eventually must lead to a kind of monism (in the case of scientific realism, atomism).

13. Aristotle's sentence, for example, is a combination of two referring terms, a subject term and a predicate term.

14. In *Logica Ingredientibus,* Abelard says a universal is *voces,* a sound (Geyer, ed., 16). But later in the *Logica Nostorum petitioni nostrorum,* a universal is neither a

voces or a *res,* but a *sermo* or term. (Geyer, ed., 522; repr. in Jolivet, ed., 122–123). Later, he revised his view again and called it an "institution."

15. Abelard got into trouble for using the same metaphor of the seal to explain the Trinity: God the Father, Christ, and the Holy Ghost are all the same thing, but differ in the same way the metal of a seal, the imprint on the seal, and its use to make a mark differ.

16. The following argument is from *Logica Ingredientibus* (Geyer, ed., 312–318, repr. in Joviet, ed., 126–133).

17. In *Basic Writings of Saint Thomas Aquinas,* ed. A. Pegis (New York: Random House, 1973), repr. in *The Philosophy of Woman,* ed. M. B. Mahowald (Indianapolis: Hackett, 1983), Aquinas considers the pros and cons of questions such as: Whether woman should have been made in the first production of things? Whether woman should have been made from man? Whether the image of God is found in every man? Whether the image of God is found in every man? Whether the state of innocence men (including women) should have been equal? Aquinas then tries to reconcile these seeming logical mistakes on God's part.

18. In the early Roman Republic, priests interpreted the law. As the Roman military state became an empire, professional jurists began to give advice. In the late classical period, the jurists came under control of the Emperor and eventually his personal spokesmen. The process was continued in the Codes of Theadosus and Justinian, where law becomes the will of the Emperor.

19. Before the twelfth century there was a diversity of law that might be applied in each case. In the southern Mediterranean, for example, Roman codes existed along with Germanic and other "barbarian" traditions. Germanic law itself was diverse, comprising different laws for manor, city, village, or state.

20. This further development is described in the work of Michel Foucault. The legislative dicates of the King are replaced by the authority of knowledge itself which, in the rationalized discourses of medicine, criminology, and psychology, objectify and regulate human behaviors.

21. This was also Ferdinand de Saussure's insight as he invents the science of structuralist linguistics:

> But what is language (*langue*)? It is not to be confused with human speech (*langage*), of which it is only a definite part, though certainly an essential one. . . . Taken as a whole speech is many-sided and heterogeneous; straddling several areas simultaneously—physical, physiological, psychological—it belongs only to the individual and to society; we cannot put it into any category of human facts, for we cannot discover its identity.

Course in General Linguistics, trans. Wade Baskin (New York: McGraw-Hill, 1966).

6

The Antinomies of Power: Ockham's Razor

> Logic is distinguished from the real sciences in the following manner. The real sciences are about mental contents, since they are about mental contents that stand for things . . . Logic, on the other hand, is about mental contents that stand for mental contents (Prologue to the Expositio super viii libros Physicorum, *Philosophical Writings*, 13).[1]

The terminist logic initiated in the thirteenth century and popularized by William of Ockham in the fourteenth is the crowning achievement of medieval logic. There is a long interim before significant advances are made again. Even twentieth-century innovations in logic fail to adequately acknowledge the groundwork laid six hundred years before as Ockham and his colleagues took up the study of the mental contents that stand for mental contents which are the proper subject matter of logic. Ockham's interest in purging language of metaphysical assumptions and reforming language as a device for drawing correct inferences has striking parallels with the logical analysis and linguistic philosophy inspired by the Vienna Circle in the 1930s. There are also socioeconomic parrallels; both the first half of the twentieth century and the fourteenth century were periods of catastrophe: war, economic upheaval, extremist religious and political views.

In the chaos and uncertainty that had overtaken the *City of God,* Ockham certainly had reason to believe that some reform was needed. The peace and unanimity of the high Middle Ages had disappeared. The Church's universal law had not restored order. Doctrinal purity enforced by the terror of the Inquisition had not eliminated heresy. Rebel monastic orders buttressed with the authority of saints defied the rule of an institutional church. Franciscan monks adopted an apostolic poverty which was a direct criticism of the worldiness and wealth of the Papacy. Women, declaring their independence from Church rule, formed religious communities and "beguines" which challenged orthodox conceptions of the pious life. Emperors meant to be the arm of God ordained by the Church refused to obey Church dictates and ruled without the benefit of ordination. Canon law, purged of inconsistency with the tools of Abelard's dialectic, was often a dead issue as papal courts lacked the military and police power that more and more enforced the decrees of secular rulers. An emerging capitalist economy faltered with uncontrolled inflation and bank failures. Crop harvests caused famine and disease. Workers, both agricultural and urban, staged strikes and sometimes openly revolted. In the cities, with populations doubling and tripling, poor sanitation, poverty, and plague took a daily toll of life, and institutional piety was often rejected for ecstatic experiences induced by spellbinding but unauthorized preachers.

Ockham, like the positivists of the twentieth century, thought the reforms of language he urged could help to restore order to human affairs. Denied his degree at Oxford on charges of heresy, Ockham was called to answer before the Papal court.[2] Embroiled in political and doctrinal controversy, he wrote his *Summa Logicae* in Avignon, where the Pope sat, some said, a captive of the French King. Also in Avignon, where he mixed with radicals critical of the absolute power of the Pope, Ockham began to develop the political views that would eventually cause him to be expelled from the Church. Finally convinced that the Pope was a heretic and no longer competent to decide his case, he was forced to flee to Germany where he took refuge along with the renegade Franciscan Michael Ceasena at the court of the apostate Emperor Ludwig of Bavaria. The rest of his life he spent justifying in his writings the Franciscans' vow of poverty denounced by the popes at Avignon, and the independence of secular power from papal rule.

The question of the relation between Ockham's logical writings, especially the formidable *Summa,* and his later political writings has been posed as a puzzle. What is a logician doing getting involved in politics? What connection can there be between logic and politics? Some commentators find none, deplore the waste of Ockham's philosophical talents in the messy business of politics, or regret that he abandoned his logical insights to return to traditional doctrines in his politics.[3] Others have attempted to find some *logical* connective between logic and politics, arguing, for example, that Ockham's nominalism committed him to a universe of bare particulars from which he *inferred* a radical individualism in politics.[4] But there is a closer connection between Ockham's politics and logic than entailment. It is not that his politics was deduced from a politically neutral and technical logical ontology. The problems that his logic was devised to solve as well as the motivations behind its distinctions were from the beginning theological and political. The reform of language that Ockham proposes in his logic is a reform of theological discourse that will rework relations between popes and scholars, theologians and scientists, priests and believers. In the process, theological language would be purged of the last vestiges of pagan philosophy, and the terms of a truly Christian logic established.

The central innovation of the terminists and the one that Ockham develops most completely is the final rejection of the naive view that all elements of language are referential to objects in the world. For a long time it had been understood that there were "syncategorematic" terms, such as "all" and "some," that could not be supposed to refer to objects (*SL* I.4), but with these exceptions, most philosophers and theologians still assumed that "categorematical" terms were intimately connected with reality. Words like "humanity," "animality," "tallness," and "being," it was argued, must refer to something just as "this man" or "Socrates" do, otherwise it was not clear how general words could have any meaning. The nominalists' view that universals are empty sounds was no solution; it left unexplained the linguistic functioning of general terms and simply proclaimed either their conventionality or their subjectivity.

For the majority realists, who inherited from Neoplatonism and Aristotelianism a view of a natural world permeated with essence, language was transparent, the means of access to an illuminated substantive reality which it was the philosopher's or theologican's business to grasp. Ockham's terminism, focusing on the uses of words rather than any substance, brought a darkening of the light. Language was no longer transparent. The clear linguistic glass through which the philosopher thought he viewed the eternal forms of reality was an opaque medium which is the real object of the logician's study. The logician's business is with terms, that is, with the texture of language itself, and he must understand that wayward uses of words often obscure the view of any reality.

The first step, Ockham argued, was to make clear the proper subject matter of logic. Logic treats not of terms of "first intention" that name things in the world, but of terms of "second intention" that refer to other terms (*SL* I.12). In this way, Ockham marked out a new terrain for logic. Logic is a metalanguage. Its job is not to represent reality correctly but to order correctly the concepts which various disciplines use to represent reality. Logic has its own subject matter. No longer will it be confused with science, or philosophy, or metaphysics, or even with theology. The logician's job is not to represent reality but to indicate the correct uses of language.

This is not to argue that logic has no objects, but to argue that it has its proper objects. These objects are not things but the concepts we use to represent things. The point of logic is not so much to produce arguments in theology or elsewhere but to clarify the use of terms, exhibit the general formulae in which truths can be stated, and lay out the proper form of arguments. An "intention" is something that naturally signifies something else, and a first intention, or first-order sign, signifies what is not a sign, as "soul" signifies what is common to all men. But a second intention or second-order sign signifies a sign or a kind of sign. These, then, are the objects of study of logic: species, genera, properties, etc. (*SL* I.12).

Once this subject matter is made clear and the logician examines language itself, Ockham argued, it is clear that many uses of words are not directly referential to objects in the world. A word can refer in different ways: it may have a "personal" reference or "supposition" to a particular thing or things in the world,[5] but it may also refer to the concept or "intention of the soul" which is its correlate, or to itself as a word. "Man" in "A man is running," does not refer to the same thing as in "Man is a species." Confusing these different uses has caused equivocation and therefore fallacies in argument, as in: Socrates is a man, Man is a species, therefore Socrates is a species, or: Socrates is a man, Man is a word, therefore Socrates is a word.

Again the naive mistake that all discourse must have "personal" reference to things is avoided. Even when actual usage confuses the issue by allowing the same word to stand for a thing, its conceptual correlate, or itself as a word, logic can disambiguate these references and avoid fallacy. Propositions such as "Man is a rational being," or "Color is the first object of sight" do not require that there be mysterious essences, "man" or "color," to which we refer. Either they refer simply to a concept and are false, or are generalizations about actual objects that will require a clarifying gloss (*SL* I.66). Again the distinction brings out the proper scope of logical studies. The logician is not to discover what may be true of this man or that man, or even of what might be necessary features of men. He will lay out the various confusions in reference that lead to the incorrect use of words like "man" and therefore to fallacies in arguments, and elucidate the proper logical form of propositions.

The problem of universals, which Ockham did so much to resolve for the next centuries of Christian thought, was not only a technical matter. The degree of transparency of language and the connection between language and world was related to an issue of crucial theological concern: the nature and the authority of God. This question was particularly pressing when the rest of Aristotle's corpus of writings finally became available through Arab translations in the thirteenth century. The Philosopher— Aristotle's honorary title in the Middle Ages—had too long been considered an authority of equal weight with the Church fathers to be dismissed.[6] In addition, his qualitative physics proved invaluable in rationalizing some Christian mysteries, the most important of which was the Eucharist's miraculous change from bread to the physical body of Christ essential in maintaining the exclusive authority of the priesthood. Nevertheless, many of his metaphysical writings deviated radically from the orthodox Christian view of divine nature. Aristotle's Prime Mover was no creator father–god shaping the world, laying down commandments, punishing, rewarding, and justly monitoring the affairs of his people through his earthly agent the Pope. Aristotle's God was a distant intelligence who set the world into motion like a giant clock which ticks on eternally regulated by the heavenly bodies.

To make it worse, in *De Anima,* Aristotle's theory of human intelligence was not coherent with Christian ideas of the immortal soul. We have, Aristotle argued, both a passive and an active intellect. The passive intellect is only the form of our body; it receives the marks of our life experience and dies with the body. Although Aristotle's active intelligence, the faculty that allows us to grasp essences and form the syllogisms that demonstrate knowledge, is separable from the body at death, such an intelligence cannot have the kind of personal immortality that is one of the main attractions of Christianity. Aristotle's immortal soul is not individual. "Bearing no marks of memory or of love," released from the corruption of the body, at death it becomes perfectly itself, a pure knower unmarked by any time and place. The dilemma was painful. Either human reason was passive, a transitory record of one individual's experience that must die with the body, or it was active and immaterial, the manifestation of a divine universal intelligence that transcended any individual. The survival of such an intelligence could hardly be equated with the personal immortality promised in Christian eschatology, nor could it be made consistent with freedom of the will or accountability for failure to believe in God.

Thomas Aquinas had struggled to synthesize and reconcile the dissonant authorities in Christian thought, attempting to weave together Biblical authority, the Platonism of the church fathers, Aristotle's metaphysics, and patristic doctrines of the supreme power of the Church into a homogeneous fabric of faith. In Ockham's view there should be no more equivocation. The God of the Church must be the Christian God whose primary characteristics are absolute power and the will that his creatures obey his commandments. This is the choice, in Ockham's view, that Thomas was not quite able to make. Thomas's view that there is an essential connection between linguistic categories and existence and that there are fixed universals and necessary connections in an "intelligible" world challenged the absolute power of God's will essential to Christian worship.[7] Ockham's Christian god, who is not the Truth but the Law, cannot be in the world or bound by the world, nor can his workings in the world be in a way limited.

Ockham's logic redressed the antimonies generated when this Christian view of divine power was confronted with Aristotelian logic. Claiming loyalty to the spirit of Aristotle, but disagreeing with or interpreting the master when necessary, he reframed Aristotelian essence as uses of language. No longer would language be allowed to fix necessary relations on the world which bound even God. Terminist logic proposed a new view of language and knowledge consistent with God's infinite power. Language is not a transparent map of the essential substances, but only a way to represent things in a world which remains wholly God's creation.

If Ockham's examples were theological, this was because it was the language of the Church that was to be reworked. Whatever his logic might foreshadow for the idiom of a future experimental natural science, this was not Ockham's concern. He was not interested in original research in science; his physics was Aristotelian with few innovations. It was theological discourse that he hoped to reform in the new terminist logic. When the categories with which we speak are themselves made into things, theological argument tripped itself up and ideas inconsistent with dogma were allowed to mingle with doctrine. Arab ideas of a universal intellect, for example, or Aristotle's Prime Mover, were allowed to compete with correct Christian doctrines of God's omnipotence. Theology cannot be a science in the Aristotelian mode that begins with self-evident conceptual truths and leads to necessary conclusions. The starting points of faith cannot be self-evident because they are the will of God as revealed to men. Not even the conclusions drawn from them are strictly necessary when God's freedom demands that he could have commanded differently. Boldly Ockham proposed a logic that would protect theology from fallacies committed by believers as well as by leaders of the Church, including the Pope himself. Ockham's doctrine of second intentions and his distinction between personal and impersonal supposition prepared the way for a reform in which the confining universals which restricted the freedom of God were relegated to their proper status as terms that referred to particular objects created by God.

First, Ockham mapped out the proper use of abstractions that had so often been taken as metaphysical essences. Such terms as "humanity" and "fatherhood" had encouraged philosophers to manufacture vast ontologies of abstract entities. Ockham begins characteristically by carefully mapping out the linguistic uses of different kinds of abstract terms. Some abstract terms refer to an actual quality in the object which the corresponding concrete term indicates: "This is hot" indicates an object which has heat in it. Does "humanity" then indicate a quality in an object, or a separate object from its concrete term, "man"? Ockham's answer is no. "Humanity" does not refer to anything but men. "Humanity" and "Socrates" stand for the same thing—Socrates—although "humanity" also stands for other men as well (*SL* I.7). Ockham deplores the verbal tangles and "volumes" wasted when this simple truth is not recognized (*SL* I.8). Although for theological reasons Ockham cannot quite allow the complete synomomy of Man and humanity,[8] he is clearly attracted to the view he attributes to Aristotle that many abstractions formed from substantive terms are empty embellishments of style which have led "saints and philosophers" away from the clarity of ordinary language (*SL* I.6).

Ockham's distinction between connotative and absolute terms completes his analysis of abstractions. The mistake of the realists was to think that all terms are absolute, that is that they have a single unequivocable intention or reference to a substantial thing. In fact there are many terms that do not indicate things directly but only connotatively or indirectly, either by way of certain qualities, or their relations with other things, or their location in time and space. These are not "things" but only contingent facts about objects, which may or may not hold at different times and places. There are, on the other hand, absolute terms such as "Socrates" or "man," which do refer directly to objects. "Socrates is a man" is true because both "Socrates" and "man" represent the same thing. This is to be compared to a connotative term such as "white"; "Socrates is white" does not mean that "Socrates is a color." "White" indicates Socrates indirectly by pointing to his color. Although some of the abstract terms corresponding to connotative terms are absolute (Ockham was still willing to include physical qualities as substantives, such as individual whitenesses or sweetnesses), most are not. Instead the abstract term is either a synonym for the concrete term or a shorthand way to indicate predicates that can be necessarily attributed to the individuals to which the concrete term refers.

Here Ockham further qualifies his analysis of how different terms function. Not only do they sometimes have impersonal rather than personal supposition, but even when they do refer to things, the ways in which they refer are different. Objects in the world can be referred to directly or absolutely as complete entities, or by way of some contingent aspect of their condition or situation. In the latter case, it is a mistake to equate the quality or situation by which we indicate something, e.g., its tallness or its nearness, with any object. To call someone "tall" is only to connote him by way of some contingent fact about him. Although some connotative terms do indicate an object by way of the contingent presence in it of some substantial quality such as heat or whiteness, others only indicate an object which is located somewhere or is in a given relation to other objects. Again, Ockham is able to show why certain kinds of argument are fallacious. If Socrates is white, that does not mean that Socrates is a color. The Parmenidean puzzle of how something can be what it is not cannot be solved by conjuring up an artificial universe of interlocking Platonic forms; instead the explanation is found in language, in the differing ways in which words are used to refer to objects in the world.

Ockham's attack on metaphysical realism draws on these distinctions between kinds of terms. A common noun does not name a single substance that can be found in all the individuals to which it can apply. This is to miss the correct linguistic status of common names, and to make the naive assumption that each word must apply to some unique substance. It is to take away the very generality that makes a universal universal. The distinctive feature of a universal noun is that it is common, that it can be applied to more than one individual. "Man," which continues to be Ockham's preferred example of a universal, can stand for Socrates, Plato, Ockham, etc. Any attempt to make it stand for some indwelling substance is to turn it into a name for one thing and take away its generality.

Like Abelard, Ockham saw the necessity for giving some account of how general uses of words are possible—his is that there are similarities between things—but the epistemological basis of universal terms is of less importance to him than their correct linguistic determination. Even as he relates the word established by "convention" for a universal to a "natural" concept in the mind, it is still the linguistic function of that concept that makes it general. Like the word, the natural sign or mental concept stands for several things; it is an act of understanding capable of being predicated of many objects (*SL* I.15).

So Ockham maps out against the turgid speculative subtleties of metaphysicians such as Duns Scotus the literal workings of words in a logical syntax consistent with God's power. Medieval philosophers attempting to express what they saw as the metaphysical reality behind ordinary experience had taken many liberties with language: horses were "equinizing of prime matter." God was "his existence and his divinity." Literate was "literacy." But with the correct uses of abstract, concrete, and universal words spelled out, Ockham was able to say simply that such abuses of grammar were false, thus rescuing theological language from inaccessible, arcane tangles caused by uncontrolled metaphysical speculation.

But his concern was not only with theological confusion and lack of communicability. The deeper issue is made clear throughout his *Summa Logica*. If universals are the primary data of knowledge, there can be no divine creation. Something, in this case humanity, would always pre-exist each individual man. God could not destroy a man without at the same time destroying all men, because if "man" is in individual men, He would destroy the universal humanity by destroying one individual (*SL*, I.15). For Ockham, who translates his adherence to the creed "I believe in God the Father Almighty" as the belief that God can do anything not logically impossible, this was an intolerable diminution of God's power.

The theory of universals was to solve the difficulty. There are no universal forms or models for God's creation. What there are in the world are God's creatures, individual things that are as God made them. What we speak and think and reason about, he argued, are not universals but these individuals. Individuals are not composite substances of form and matter, or of individual and universal substance, but only *supposita,* naked of any universal clothing, identified simply as those things that our words stand for. If these are the referents that Ockham's logic requires, it is because they are the referents that God's power requires. These are the individuals that can be created and destroyed at God's will, the "creatures" which must populate God's universe, the subjects over which He has absolute sovereignty. As Ockham cuts away essence, even the impenetrable mystery of God's creation of the God-man Christ can be expressed. If we think in terms of universals, then a universal damnable humanity must be in both Judas and Christ, but this cannot be true of Christ who, as God, must have nothing damnable in him. In Ockham's new ontology, the difficulty is avoided. Christ is one of those singulars to whom the term "man" can be applied. Because there is no separable universal sinful "humanity," this means that we do not have to posit in him human sin (*SL* I.15).

The doctrine of universals that Christian philosophers inherited from pagan philosophy was inconsistent with God's absolute power. Whether Aristotle's God was bound by necessary forms and relations in the natural world, or by the necessary ideas in his own intellect,[9] only his immanence or position as first cause preserved his omnipotence. But this is not the kind of power claimed by Ockham's Christian God. The Christian Father-God, inherited from patriarchal Semitic sources, was identified with transcendent law and commandment and required an absolute autonomy of will. This generated many puzzles. Could God command something evil? Could God create men who didn't sin? Could God cause a sinner to be saved? Could God make a black thing white? In his new logic, Ockham was able to resolve many of these paradoxes. By rejecting any universal, immanent, natural, regulating order, and purging theology of the last remnants of Aristotle's prime Being, he cleared the way for a God who could do anything he willed. The relations between a god who admits of no necessity but his own will, and his creatures is marked out by Ockham as he puts the "terms"—God, man, Christ, humanity—in logical order.

The kind of world that results is spelled out in Ockham's treatment of necessity and impossibility. Not only were these words in common use, but necessity was a standard notion in the logic and metaphysics inherited from Aristotle. In Aristotle's view, the very possibility of knowledge depended on the existence of necessary relations and properties, and even Ockham was unwilling to give up the possibility of an Aristotelian demonstrative science that begins from premises that are necessary truths. Such a science, however, would have to be reconciled with the Christian dogma of God's omnipotence. Logical necessity seemed to indicate that there are things that God cannot do, such as make a man who cannot sin or laugh,[10] or perform a meritorious action by himself without the human agency that makes it meritorious, or make a white thing black. But if God is omnipotent, this is an intolerable restraint on his power.

Ockham cures this defect with subtle distinctions in modal logic that draw on his analyses of universals, supposition, and absolute and connotative terms. The important distinction to be made is between the necessity of natural essences and relations as they have in fact been made by God and the absolute contingency of that creation. Once God creates things, they are necessarily as they are, they must necessarily be that way. Nevertheless no creation can be seen as necessary. Ockham demonstrates this with careful attention to how the logic of modality should be formulated. "All men are necessarily animals" is true in the sense that if you have a man, he will be an animal. But it is not convertible into the proposition, "This man is necessarily an animal," because God might not have created any men at all.[11] Ockham can now apply this insight directly to the problem of God's omnipotence. Although it is necessarily true that a being which creates must be God, this does not burden God's freedom with the necessity of any creation. He might not have created anything or might have created a different world without men or any other existing species. No creation of an omnipotent God can be seen as necessary though he may choose to create substances which have particular substantial essences (*SL* II.10).[12]

Ockham can make a similar analysis of impossibility. It is logically impossible that God could perform a meritorious act alone or make a white thing not white. But although God cannot perform a meritorious act alone, a meritorious act can be performed by God alone. This seemingly impossibility is accommodated once we have the idea of supposition. That act which is referred to in the former statement as meritorious could have been performed by God alone. Presumably it would no longer be meritorious because no human agency is involved, but the sense that there is some act God cannot perform is removed. In a similar way although God cannot make a black thing white, a black thing can be made white by God. That thing which we are referring to as black could have been made white by God, or could be made white by God in the future. It is a matter of contingency not necessity that this or that act be meritorious or white, a contingency which God absolutely controls (*SL* II.10). The result is that what is not dictated by dogma can only be known empirically. In such a world, the only way to knowledge is through revelation direct from God, or failing that a direct sensuous cognition of the objects of his creation.

This resolution of the problem of necessity is accomplished through an analysis that converts propositions to their logical equivalents. That analysis depends on the understanding of universal terms as referring not to a universal substance but to more than one particular, the view that only terms for individual substances and their substantive qualities are absolute, and on the theory of supposition that creates an ontology consistent with God's power. The act of a created thing could have been meritorious or caused by God. A created thing could have had in it the quality white or black.

When Ockham comes to the problem of the central mystery of Christianity, the God-made-man, Christ, the problem is more challenging, but he stretches the theory of supposition to accommodate. In his theory of abstraction, Ockham had already singled out the very special universal, "man," for special treatment. Whereas a genus like "animal" requires abstraction—we must experience and note a similarity between a number of examples before we have the concept—we can get the idea of a man from one instance. Although Ockham may partly be suffering a regression to Aristotelian secondary substances,[13] he has his own Christian reasons for noting the uniqueness of "man." Man is not just the name of another species but also figures centrally in dogma as the incarnation of Christ. The Christian God becomes a Man, and so Man cannot be synonomous with any ordinary humanity (*SL* I.7). Again supposition is to do the work of showing how this is logically possible. Although it is impossible that God become a man, Ockham argues, it is not impossible that a man become God. The thing that man "supposits" for could be the God Christ (*SL* II.20). Words supposit for substances which may or may not have certain qualities, or perform certain actions, or be in certain relations to other substances. Apparently they also can supposit for things independently of their substantive identity.[14] Here Ockham stretches supposition to its breaking point. Dogma does not require that a thing be black and white at one time in the same way as it seems to require that Christ be a man and God at the same time. Ockham defends the apparent impossibility with an additional analysis, this time an equivocation on the word "man." "Man" supposits for ordinary men; it also supposits for the super-special man who is Christ. Not only is man the special species man, it is also the unique God-man. How that can be has to be left to mystery, and Ockham reverts to scripture: "Before Abraham came to be I am" (*SL* II.20).

The new terminist logic was not meant to eliminate mystery. Unlike Abelard, Ockham did not strain to find metaphors that make mystery intelligible. The point of his logic is not to perform the impossible task of making all the elements of the Word of God accessible to human understanding. Many doctrines, he admits freely, such as the Trinity, cannot be understood. Instead logic is meant to remove a metaphysics inconsistent with Christian belief and to map out clearly the logical features of the world ruled by an omnipotent Christian God. All necessity in such a world must be contingent; everything might have been different. White things could have been black, voluntary actions could have been performed by God alone, a man can turn out to have been God. Nothing can necessarily be deduced, even from God's essence; even to be bound by his own nature would be an inadmissible restraint on God's power. The world is an absolutely free creation of will.

This logical doctrine is also political doctrine. It is not surprising that Ockham's logical and theological writings came under suspicion even before he framed his radical politics of separation of church and state. Neither philosophers nor the authorities of the institutional Church can interrupt the authority of dogma some of which is unintelligible and must remain so. This unintelligibility is no defect in the terms of Ockham's logic. Logic is the idiom of mystery just as it is the idiom of faith. One of Ockham's frequent complaints against the metaphysicians is that they think that dogmas of faith can be rationally proven. His treatment of propositions embedded in belief statements is an attempt to correct this mistake. "I believe that God who is three and one is immortal" is a central statement of Christian faith. But, Ockham argues, we cannot *know* that a thing is three and one, because that is a contradiction. Again the doctrine of supposition allows us to express this intelligibility logically. What we are claiming is that we know that that thing (which a Three-in-One God supposits for) is immortal (*SL*

II.29). The reference to a particular and the bracketing of its substantive identification allows belief in a central Christian dogma to be expressed without distortion. The mystery of the Trinity cannot be understood, nor should it be "rationalized" so it can be understood. Ockham's logic is an idiom in which we can profess a Christian belief consistent with an omnipotent God: an idiom in which we can believe without question in the immortality of a God identified by way of a mystery we cannot understand.

The consequences for both Christian faith and logic of this solution are far-reaching. It has been popular to read Ockham as a man ahead of his time, claiming that his logic is a brilliant foreshadowing of the physical science of the seventeenth century. He is often portrayed as someone who set theology aside to investigate the purity of logical truth. Ockham makes clear in his examples, however, that it is theology, not science, that is his main concern. Although he uses illustrative nontheological examples such as, "A white thing cannot be black," they are placed to prepare the way for the theological clarifications that follow. Over and over again, he points to the "fallacies" to which believers have been tempted by an ill-applied rationality.

Many false or confused statements have been "conceded" by "saints and philosophers": these authorities however, cannot be accused of making mistakes. Instead Ockham proposes that what they say be restated in the correct form of terminist logic.

> When such propositions or ones like them are posited by authors, they should be glossed—even though they are, properly speaking, false. In the same way, authentic words are often false in the sense which they convey, i.e. in their literal and proper sense, and yet they are true in the sense in which they were uttered or written. The reason for this is that authors frequently speak equivocally and improperly and metaphorically. And thus in exposing philosophical authorities one ought mainly to penetrate their underlying meaning and thought processes and intention rather than to take the words as they sound, i.e. literally (SL II.4).

Instead of struggling to reconcile rationally metaphysical concepts which may or may not be appropriate to Christian belief, Ockham proposes a new solution. When what authorities say seems to be literally false or confused, it must be assumed that their intention does not match the strict sense of the words. Therefore what they say must be "glossed": analyzed or converted into an idiom consistent with the nature of God that we can assume corresponds to what the saint or philosopher must really have meant. When this is done, sophisms, puzzles, and antinomies either disappear or are bracketed. Ockham proposes a reform of theological language, a new idiom in which the mysteries of the faith can be accommodated intact without contradiction.

Two logical innovations were foundational for this change. First was the doctrine of reference or supposition. Although Ockham is still too much influenced by Aristotle to entertain the idea of a purely logical object, supposition moves in that direction. Words refer to things in a variety of ways; the characterization of these things is removed to language to make way for the contingency that divine power demands. This is not to say that Ockham imagines a bare substratum or matter which bears Aristotlian form. Even matter is gone; what is left are the anonymous "things" that words supposit for. The wedge has now been more securely driven between language and the world. No longer is language permeated with reference because it is intimately involved with material interactions; no longer do things bear the meanings by which we speak of them. Language, detached from ordinary intercourse, has a new foundation. Its only business is deduction, either from the recorded Word of God or, where nothing has been said, from whatever sensory experience we may have of the objects created by God. The motive for this move toward a logic in which "x's" may be men, or mortal, or white, or Socrates, or God is theological. This is the language consistent with a world totally subject to the will of God.

Semantic structure is no longer to be read onto reality, so that the forms of speech become metaphysical entities. The Logos is no longer in the world. Ockham's terminist interpretation of Aristotle's logic replaces the Platonic doctrine that the Forms of speech exist substantively. At the same time, there is no question of returning language to either passionate experience or its role in human communication. Either logic begins with propositions which are transcriptions from the received word of God or it is anchored to the world at the points of intuitive cognition of the contingent particulars which are his free creation. The natural signs or concepts that are the necessarily veridical results of these cognitions are the basis of abstraction to the general ideas with which we think. Using the example which continues to be a paradigm, in an intuitive cognition we grasp a man; we then go on to isolate his rationality, his color, his ability to laugh. We also abstract his animality, his humanity, his semantic kinship to God as Christ. At the same time it is understood that this is only man as God made him and that God could have made no men, or made a different species with different qualities. Loosened from metaphysical categories, logic can now be used without hinderance or contradiction for inferences from dogma necessary to Christian belief, as well as for the common-sense deductions from experience that guide us in our practical or political lives. The question to which Ockham turns in his politics is predictable: what are the proper spheres of these two projects? Because Ockham's interest in logic is already theological, there is no need to explain his active involvement in the politics of church and state.

A logic founded on Scripture is not likely to accept without question the institutional authority of the Church. Instead, the scriptures can serve, just as they did for Ockham's allies, the rebellious Franciscans in their defense of apostolic poverty, as authority for arguments that no Pope can overrule.[15] The institutional interests of a Church that had become a center of administration and commercial power were irrelevant to such a fundamentalist logic. Even without the excesses of the "heretic" Pope, John XXII, Ockham would have been in conflict with the papacy. Aristotelian metaphysics might have supported the idea of a *City of God,* but strict adherence to the letter of Biblical Christian belief did not. Dogmatics, if it was not to be amplified and distorted with metaphysics, was concerned with specific tenets of belief and morality dealing with worship and salvation and based on the authority of scripture. Even the authority of saints and Church fathers, as Ockham notes, might have to be glossed to bring their teachings into line with doctrine. It can only follow that the sphere of Church power should be limited to these otherworldly concerns.

Even in the case of religious doctrine, the officials of the Church were not infallible. If the Pope ignored the obvious testimony of scripture on the poverty of Christ's apostles with arguments drawn from property law in order to justify the wealth of the Church, then the Pope himself would have to be declared a heretic.[16] Nor was this a question that could be decided by individual conscience; there was a fact of the matter and it should be decided by expert exegesis, including the Pope's when he was not a heretic, in formulations that appealed to each believer's understanding.[17] Other matters that did not have to do with Christian belief should be left to the secular authorities. The maintenance of civil order, which Ockham took as the main purpose of monarchy, was not governed by dogma but by expediency. In this area, natural law deduced from the nature of man or inferred from similarities in different secular law codes was the proper guide for the regulation of practical affairs. This natural law is in no way binding on God and must not interfere with Christian belief in any way; but it is appropriately administered by sovereigns and not Popes. Ockham's division of the spheres of church and state is not a result of his nominalism, but like his nominalism is a result of his adherence to doctrine. It is as impermissible to expand the Word of God past its literal meaning as it is to contradict it. Ockham's apparent liberalism as he denied the absolute infallibility of the Pope or the Pope's right to control secular affairs in fact supported a new fundamentalism that would serve the Protestant reformers of the next centuries.

Already in Ockham's thought there were elements of the militant Protestantism that would soon rival Catholicism in many parts of Europe. In Ockham's logic, only the will of God sustained the world: any reference to necessity or immanence identified with natural order or cycles was inconsistent with divine omnipotence. It followed that the business of Christian teaching was faith, and in parts of a man's life unrelated to faith, he could make his way in a world unmarked by moral absolutes. It also would seem to follow that if God in his omnipotence can save a sinner and condemn a good man, he cannot be subjected to the necessity of paying any debt, so there should be no selling of indulgences or penances. Priests have no monopoly on salvation; every man with a Bible is a priest. If the will of one God rules the world, threefold though he may be, that God cannot coexist with any other divinity. The saint worship and Mariology with which Catholic practice had been contaminated were regressions to paganism.

Nowhere in the hundreds of theological questions raised and answered throughout Ockham's logic is there any mention of Christ's mother, whose popular worship in Catholicism often pre-empted her son's. Ockham's Christian logic demanded that there be only one God and one divine will paramount over all. If something of the Spirit-at-the-center-of-the-world of mortal opinion had lingered in Parmenides's Being, or in Plato's Form of the Good, or even in Aristotle's Prime Mover, now she had disappeared altogether. Certainly there had been little left of her in the mind-bending subtleties of Scholastic metaphysics that Ockham rejected. In Catholic practice she lingered, her spiritual power diverted to Mary, humble mother, chaste virgin, handmaiden of God, faithful spouse, dispenser of the will of God. Legitimated with a thin veneer of Christian theology, the Goddess was still worshipped in rituals and rites that survived both the Hellenic invasions and Christianity.[18] Regardless of theology, in popular songs and poetry, in the daily devotions of women, surrounded by Aphrodite's doves and roses, identified with love and childbirth, Mary the Spirit of mortal opinion was still the Queen of Heaven, reflected in the stained glass windows of the great cathedrals. If her worship provoked sharp disagreement in the fourteenth century as to her divine status, in the Ockhamist logic of Protestantism there would be no more debate.[19] In the new churches of Luther and Calvin, the dying Christ and his all-powerful Father had no rival.

This final rejection of the last traces of divinity associated with generation and fertility, as well as of the essences and substances that had replaced her natural cycles, was coherent with much of the experience of fourteenth-century life. In fact, as well as in theology, divinity had been banished from the world. In the economic, political, and spiritual upheavals that made daily life increasingly difficult, any benevolent natural order was seriously compromised. The ravages of the plague resulted from hunger and poor living conditions imposed on an exploited populace; the Hundred Years' War made Europe a perpetual battleground for men defending rival sovereigns; Church fathers who claimed to be the spiritual leaders of the world devoted themselves to political intrigue and the marketing of indulgences, dispensations, and offices. The degraded standard of life in overpopulated cities caused dispair and crime; the new boom in commerce and finance inspired greed and cynicism. In fact as well as in logic, the great chain of being was gone, and in its place was a new contingency in which the most unthinkable of disasters could and did occur in a world in which God's purposes remained obscure. Fanaticism, horror, hatred, violence, were the order of the day and burst out in trances, flagellations, killing of Jews, persecution of women, massacres, and rebellion. Neither the Church's retreat from the doctrines of Aristotle back to the Neo-Platonism of the Church fathers which prompted the accusations against Ockham, nor the Franciscans' celebration of God's love over his intellect was sufficient to contain the panic. In such a world, a new Christian logic was needed. Logic could no longer depend on any natural order of things, but must return to the literal Word of God. The new Protestant doctrines of salvation through faith alone and predestination were coherent with such a logic. Christian thought should focus not on natural philosophy but on sin, redemption, evil, and the unpredictable gratuitous exercise of God's grace in a world that had irreparably fallen.

Metaphysical notions of the nature of men, women, and slaves may have rationalized the oppression of women and barbarians in classical Greece, conceptions of male/female or body/soul embedded in canon law may have kept women and heretics under the control of the Church, but the new logic would not improve their situations. The Protestant reformation which Ockham's logic helped to free from Papist metaphysics would lead to oppression as deadly as that of the universal Church. The Catholic Church continued its legalistic institutional oppression. Independent convents of rebellious women had been gradually eliminated by the thirteenth century or had submitted to strict rule by monastic orders. Beguines, the lay sisterhoods in which women were able to work and live outside of the rule of a husband in marriage, were outlawed. Female mystics such as St. Catherine of Siena and Julian of Norwich were kept under close scrutiny and censorship by male religious advisors and confessors to be sure that their female natures did not lead them into heresy. Lay religious groups like the Deventer brotherhood in Holland, which accepted women on an equal basis, were suppressed. In 1430 Joan of Arc was brought to trial. In 1487 *The Hammer of Witches* was published.

At first the teaching of the Ockhamist Martin Luther might have seemed a respite. Convinced like Ockham of the absolute freedom and omnipotence of God, driven by the sense that sin was permanently embedded in his and other men's souls, he turned the logic that God could save even a sinner, if he wished, into dogma. We are not saved by our works. God does not have to save those who are good or damn those who are bad: this would be an intolerable restraint on His power. Instead God's grace decides who will be saved. The only way to this grace is through faith, and for faith, only the Word of God is necessary, not the Church, or the Pope. Like Ockham, Luther deplored the excesses and moral decay of the papacy and argued for the separation of church and state.

At first, some of his teaching might have seemed liberatory. He argued against the celibacy of the clergy and denied that Eve need take all the blame for the Fall. He praised women as playing an honorable if subordinate role in marriage as housekeepers and mothers. Although logic made it clear that it had been a grave mistake to think that divinity could be shared or that a woman could be divine, especially given the role of Eve in the Fall of Man, women were conceded a domestic role as the helpmates of men. They were doctrinally required, however, to maintain that role. Luther, Calvin, and other Protestants rested on Scripture, reading there the correct God-ordained role of women in social life. Women were naturally weaker than men even before the Fall; Eve's rebellion was also against the proper rule of Adam.[20] If the serpent had tempted Adam, Adam would not have given in.[21] Now, after her sin, woman is more than ever a "nail driven into the wall," that is, she is confined irrevocably to her duties in the home.[22] Calvin in his *Commentary on Genesis* agreed; women were weak and should play a restricted role in human affairs.[23]

Cheap Bibles from the new printing presses and the popularization of colorful Biblical narratives such as the Adam and Eve story, gave immediacy to the new Christian teaching. Picking and choosing among the scriptures the most central and "useful" to the faith, Luther and Calvin were able to draw necessary conclusions for a wide audience. These arguments could now be addressed to the faithful from the pulpit, where scripture could provide the basis for an accessible argument that metaphysics could not. Illustrated simply for children in Sunday schools and in regular schools, Bible studies would be required. No more was the Word of God a province of a few monks or prelates; increased literacy meant that every man could refer to the text as ministers pointed out the relevant passages. The punishments for adultery and fornication were luridly described, moral depravity such as dancing or drinking condemned, the evils of female rule exposed, queens denounced, midwives, healers, and anyone who was a heretic declared doctrinally unclean and eliminated. *The Hammer of Witches,* the witch-hunter's bible, was printed in new Protestant editions.

The renewed Protestant campaign against witches was expressed in a fundamentalist logic. Beginning with doctrine from the scriptures that needed no exegesis or analysis, witch-hunters inferred the proper methods for the identification and punishment of witches. Supported by such arguments, by the mid-fifteenth century the great witch-hunt had securely focused on women and would not relent until a century and a half later. Both Luther and Calvin approved. Protestant theology, free from Papist metaphysics, would rest on the Word of God alone, which meant that there would have to be even stricter doctrinal insistence on the evil to be destroyed. For the salvation of men, for the greater glory of God, abominations and blasphemies must be exterminated. Any woman not firmly under the control of a man as wife or daughter was suspect. If that for which the term "man" supposits can be God, that for which the term "woman" supposits can be a devil.

This is not to say that terminist logic caused either the witch hunts or the Protestant reformation. The causes were material: economic collapse, misogyny, natural disaster, and abuse of priviledge. But Ockham's logic provided a model for a new way of talking and thinking in which the attitudes and policies of persecution could be perpetuated. Natural language in which the actual experiences, hopes, desires of women and men are expressed and communicated had become a way of referring to the objects and events willed by God. Beginning from a Word of God not rationally analyzable without blasphemy, beginning from mysteries that were to be taken on faith and that were not intelligible, beginning from selected sentences taken from scripture, the theologian escaped the burden of thought and drew the conclusions that logic demanded. He was not to concentrate on his "works," not to attempt to think how he or his world was or should be morally ordered. The doctrine of predestination that followed from God's omnipotence did not mean that he would live in fear of damnation; it meant that he could be certain of his status as one of the elect. Although it was incumbent on him to try to deserve salvation, it was understood that this would never be possible; his failures—traffic with prostitutes, adulteries, domestic cruelties—were therefore inevitable. His only virtue was faith, his only certain commitment was to do God's will in a contingent world in which no essences: no natural community, no natural law, no natural sympathy between women and men could get in the way of God's commandment. As for what was not covered in scripture, what was not a matter of faith, what involved men's political and economic life, there expediency and secular powers could rule.

The theological applications of Ockham's logic were more immediate than any contribution Ockham is supposed to have made to the experimental science of the seventeenth century. The science of Descartes or Galileo was inspired by advances in mathematical thinking and by the necessity for a physics that could explain the mechanics of cannon balls for a world perpetually at war and guide efficient machine production for a developing capitalist economy. Ockham's retention of the view that physical knowledge is based on sense experience was characteristic of medieval science, not the new mathematical science of Descartes's dream. The residual Aristotelianism of Ockham's reliance on an intuitive sensory apprehension of necessary characteristics was inconsistent with such a physics.

If there is a connection between seventeenth century science and Ockham's logic, it is through theology. Ockham's Christian cosmos was ruled by a contingency totally dependent on God's will. It was not so far to a further inference. If God can rule a contingent world, then so can his surrogate, Man, rule under him. There is no natural order that is necessary or that man in the image of God cannot interrupt, there is no natural law he cannot manipulate. He can create industrial complexes where women and men are worked to death. He can mobilize weapons that destroy whole populations. Language refers to only contingent events, free from any intersubjective meaning; all are subject to the will of God or his agent man. If Ockham's logic is the logic of a world in which God's will is supreme, it can also become the logic of a world willed by men. The functional science purged of value and quality that begins to develop in the seventeenth and eighteenth centuries makes possible the realization of that possibility. It would be the twentieth century before logic is fully adapted and a logical idiom formulated in which the last vestiges of spoken words have disappeared, leaving only the formulae of manipulation.

Notes

1. References to Ockham are to *Philosophical Writings,* trans. P. Boehner (Indianapolis: Bobbs-Merrill, 1957); *Summa Logicae (SL)*, Part I trans. M. Loux (Notre Dame: University of Notre Dame Press, 1974); Part II trans. A. J. Freddoso and N. Schuurman (Notre Dame: University of Notre Dame Press, 1980).

2. The charges against Ockham were multiple and included issues such as the inconsistency of his account of quality with the doctrine of the Eucharist. See, e.g., G. N. Buescher *The Eucharist Teaching of William of Ockham* (New York: St. Bonaventure, 1950).

3. For the former position see, e.g., F. C. Copleston, *A History of Medieval Philosophy* (New York: Harper and Row, 1972), 236. For the latter, see P. Boehner, "Ockham's Political Ideas," in *Collected Articles on Ockham* (New York: St. Bonaventure, 1958).

4. See, e.g., George de Lagarde, *La naissance de l'éspirit laîque au declin du moyen age* (Paris: 1962, 1963), where Ockham's "anarchism" is supposed to have followed from his nominalism. This view, however, simplifies and distorts Ockham's complex view of politics as well as his nominalism. See the discussion of A. S. McGrade, *The Political Thought of William of Ockham* (Cambridge: Cambridge University Press, 1974), 29–35.

5. Ockham uses both "signify" and "suppose." Signification, however, is the property of a term that it can stand for one or more things. Supposition is also a property of a term, but only when it is in a proposition (*SL* I.63). Therefore "supposition" is closest to the contemporary use of "reference."

6. Although attempts were made to prohibit Aristotle's writings (e.g., by the council of Paris 1210 and by the Bishop of Paris 1277), given Aristotle's authority ar i his acceptance as the Logician, this was not a comfortable solution. Ockham's indictment in 1323 was part of a second wave of reaction which also included some of the theses of Thomas.

7. For Thomas, the intelligibility of the world depends on *ens,* intelligible being,

those geni and species created by God as forms in which substances may participate. There are also necessary truths about the natural world, such as the Principle of Efficient Causality, that everything which begins to exist does so through the agency of an already existent extrinsic thing. One implication might be that God is not all-powerful: is God unable to create something without a cause?

8. Ockham gets into some tangles of his own when, "for theological reasons," he must deny that "humanity" and "man" are synonomous. The problem is that "man" can mean "Son of Man," but "humanity" cannot. Christ was the Son of Man but he was not part of humanity. In order to solve this problem, Ockham adds a rider to his definition of man: "man" can also be a Godly being. Christ was a man that was not human but God (SL I.7).

9. Ockham rejects the idea that there could be ideas in God's mind on the grounds that this would be inconsistent with the "unity" of God. God as will, not knowledge, can admit no internal diversity.

10. Ockham's inclusion of "risibility" (the ability to laugh) as one of the necessary features of man is a refreshing addition to the usual "rationality" and "mortality."

11. Ockham's illustrative example: that every truth is true is necessary, but it is not the case that every truth is necessarily true, because some truths are only contingently true; that is they might not be true in the future, or not have been true in the past. Here again God's absolute power conflicts with the idea of a proposition as a timeless entity, true for all time.

12. Probably Ockham did not include logical principles such as the law of noncontradiction and of excluded middle which would be necessary creations. God cannot make a thing that is black and white at the same time.

13. See my discussion of Aristotle's secondary substances in ch. 3 of Part I.

14. Even if we admit that the suppositum that is Socrates could keep its identity through a color-change, it is not so clear that it could be maintained through a change in substance.

15. The main objection of Ockham's allies the Franciscans was to the materialism of the Papacy. Money poured into the Avignon Church in its role as tax-collector, banker, and landowner. What angered Ockham, the theologican-logician, was also the way in which the Pope was willing to twist doctrine in order to promote the institutional interests of the Church.

16. John used the, to Ockham, specious argument that regardless of scripture, poverty was contrary to reason. No right to use can be established apart from ownership. Therefore the Papacy could not own the things the Franciscans used, but the Franciscans had to take back the ownership that they had ceded to the Church. In 1323, the Pope declared it heretical to deny that Christ or the apostles owned anything. See McGrade, *Political Thought of Ockham,* 10.

17. Ockham's position on the settlement of doctrinal disputes is complex. Learned men, or doctors, are often in a better position to decide than pontifs, but even their decision is not completely conclusive, especially if their credentials are in

question and they have reached their position through patronage rather than merit.

18. See, for example, Maria Warner's discussion of the incorporation of pagan fertility rites into Christian ritual, "Growth in Every Thing," ch. 18 of her *Alone of Her Sex* (New York: Wallaby Books, 1976).

19. Especially controversial was the proper formulation of the Immaculate Conception. Mary must not contaminate Christ with sin, but nor should she be elevated to full divine status. Exactly when did she become sinless? Was it before or after conception, before or after birth? Authorities hotly debated different answers: Peter Lombard, Thomas Aquinas, and Dun Scotus worked their usual subtleties, Dominicans and Franciscans took rival positions.

20. Martin Luther, *Lectures on Genesis* in J. Pelikan ed., *Luther's Works* Vol. I (St. Louis, Mo: Concordia, 1958), p. 115.

21. Ibid, p. 151.

22. Ibid, p. 116.

23. John Calvin, *Commentary on Genesis* (Grand Rapids, Mich.: Eerdmans, 1948), chapt. 2, v.8.

Part III
Reading Frege

Prologue

For a long time, it seemed to me that with Frege logic was finally unreadable, that this "name," Gottlob Frege, was so deeply hidden, so barricaded behind correct technique, that it could never be revealed. The consensus among logicians is that Frege's is the most important achievement in the history of logic. Was this because Frege had finally managed to close all the openings where I, as a reader, might intervene? Had logic finally become what it had aspired to be all along, a pure artifact beyond understanding, to be examined, used, contemplated, admired, even discarded, but without response?

For a reader, an opening must be given, to condemn, correct, regret, sympathize, but in Frege's texts I could see none at all. Criticism of Frege's work by his disgruntled colleagues, logicians themselves, seemed to me, as it did to Frege, to be only a willful refusal to see what he had been able to do. If they had seen, they would have realized that there was no place where any response, critical or approving, could take hold. It was this closure that Frege intended to create, a closure that would reduce any would-be reader to exegesis.

It was only reluctantly that Frege answered his critics, and when he did, their unfairness, their interested attempt to protect their logically vested interests, was so evident that he could only retell again in ever simpler terms, patiently, wearily, in the tone one takes with inattentive students, what it was he was trying to do. The revisions he was willing to make in his notation were always internal, a refining and shaping of the idiom itself, not a response to criticism. Let someone else cut his diamond in another way, said Frege, although he was sure enough of his mastery, sure enough that the thought he exhibited was not some clumsy human design but shaped after the hard stone of reality. Although his thought could not literally be put in the hands of his audience, they were to examine it like a diamond, from all sides. It was something like this that he expected them to do, and all that it would have been appropriate for them to do.

If Frege's *Begriffsschrift*[1] is the delineation of a thought beyond which nothing can be thought and nothing said, then to read or to comment, for which a certain thinking outside and beyond is necessary, is not to think at all. Reading is superfluous. One spins out notes so voluminous that they cannot be brought into any order, or becomes reduced to small insignificant carping at detail each time cured in the increasing complexity of the notation.

I surrendered to repetition, painfully, one step after another, following Frege the master, following the argument as one does the voice of an irrefutable didact who will not be interrupted or contradicted. Frege's final failure, the antinomy in the formalization of number pointed out to him by Bertrand Russell, was so difficult to believe. How could he have failed? How could there have been a flaw in this seamless construction? How could paradox or inconsistency survive in an idiom from which everything human has been erased, in a notation in which facts are to be presented with no distortion of personal prejudice, interestedness, desire, in expressions in which truths are stated so as to elicit no concern, love, anger, horror? If once there was horror or love, it had hardened into stone, the gesture that might have initiated that stern monument not even a memory, the gesture it would have been possible to read.

Notes

1.   References to Frege are to the following English translations of his works.

    Begriffsschrift, 1879: "Conceptual Notation" (CN), in *Translations from the Philosophical Works of Gottlob Frege,* ed. Peter Geach and Max Black (Oxford: Basil Blackwell, 1970).

    "On the Aim of the Conceptual Notation" (ACN), "On the Scientific Justification of a Conceptual Notation" (JCN), and "On the Law of Inertia" (LI), all reprinted in *Conceptual Notation and Related Articles,* trans. and ed. by Terrell Ward Bynum (Oxford: Clarendon Press, 1972). In these articles written after the *Begriffsschrift,* Frege tries to explain in simpler language the point of the new conceptual notation.

    Die Grundlagen der Aritmetik, 1884: *The Foundations of Arithmetic* (FA), trans. J. L. Austin (Oxford: Basil Blackwell, 1959), in which Frege uses the new notation to explain number.

    "Function and Concept" (FC), "Concept and Object" (CO), "Sense and Reference" (SR), and "What is Function?" (WF), in *Translations,* ed. Geach and Black. In these articles Frege works out in more detail the semantic adjustments necessary for the complete formalization of number in his *Die Grundgesetze.*

    Die Grundgesetze der Aritmetik 1893, 1903: "The Basic Laws of Arithmetic" (LA), in *Translations* ed. Geach and Black.

    "Thoughts" (T), "Compound Thoughts" (CT) and "Negation" (N) in *Logical Investigations,* 1918 – 1919, ed. P. T. Geach, trans. Geach and R. H. Stoothoff (New Haven: Yale University Press, 1977): Frege's last reflections on language and judgment.

    Posthumous Writings (PW), ed. H. Hermes, F. Kambartel, F. Kaulbach, trans. P. Long, R. White (Chicago: University of Chicago Press, 1979).

7

Breaking the Power of the Word

> If it is a task of philosophy to break the power of the word over the human mind, uncovering illusions which through the use of language often almost unavoidably arise concerning the relations of concepts, freeing thought from that which only the nature of the linguistic means of expression attaches to it, then my "conceptual notation" further developed for these purposes can become a useful tool for philosophy (ACN, 106).

Platonic and Aristotelian logics were generated out of natural language. The classical logician claimed to discover *in* language the conceptual relations necessary for formal relations or the grammatical regularities allowing syllogistic manipulations. It is this dependence on the Word that Frege saw as the major impediment to the proper development of logic. As long as categories such as subject and predicate, substance and quality, essence and accident determine logical form, logic would always remain unintegrated into the mathematical scientific thought which the nineteenth century had accepted as the paradigm of knowledge, and scientific-mathematical thought would be unintegrated into logic (ACN, 107). The result is that both suffer: logic because it is separated from accepted scientific epistemologies, and mathematics and science because they are denied logical rigor and universality. Classical logic, even when algebraicized by logicians such as Boole, retained a linguistic analysis of sentence structure which would always resist mathematical thought; Frege's new notation exhibited in the *Begriffsschrift* was to show how mathematics is at its source logical, and how thought or logic when properly analyzed is mathematical.

In order to find a logic in which mathematical and scientific truth can be expressed, it is necessary to be critical not only of the formal relations insisted upon by logicians and grammarians, but also of language itself. Natural language is ambiguous, unsystematic, and uneconomical. Either there are gaps in reasoning or intolerable prolixity. Metaphorical expressions combine with a shifting multiplicity of meaning to produce concepts that can never be delineated sharply.[1] Furthermore, even when linguistic concepts are rigorously redefined in a science or in mathematics they still may retain their old grammatical status and introduce unwarranted assumptions. These deficiencies make natural language unsuitable for expressing truth. Logic, which has stayed too faithful in the past to linguistic syntax, must find its own idiom, in which truth can be expressed without the intervention of language (WF, 116). In such a notation the distortions inevitable in all representation are minimized and a standard provided to which any language, insofar as it professes to express truths, can be compared.[2]

In order to discover the conceptual notation true to logical form, a new analysis of the sentence is necessary. A sentence, in Aristotelian logic and in traditional grammar, contains a subject and a predicate, a subject that stands for a substance and a predicate that stands for accidental or necessary properties of that substance. These elements are then combined in a sentence that, if true, reflects their relation in fact. Not only has this linguistic analysis initiated endless and futile controversy over the status of universals, it can never account for predication or generality. No logic that depends on forms or concepts can capture what is most characteristic of a proposition: that it says something true of, or not true of something. In a logic consisting only of relations between concepts, the relation of a thing to what is true of it is lost and what is left is only a string of items out of which no judgment can be made (CO, 54). It then becomes impossible either to account for the origins of forms or universals or to explain how forms can ever be connected with particulars.

In mathematics, however, it is possible to express generality.[3] Functional mathematical expressions mark constant relations holding between quantities. For this to be possible in logic, all that is necessary is to analyze a sentence in a new way, one in which one part of the sentence is seen as remaining the same and the other as variable (FA, 11–13). In this way it is possible to replace the subject-predicate analysis (A is B) true to grammatical form, with a functional analysis $(f(x))$ true to mathematical form. In this functional analysis all the mystery that historically surrounded the status of universals disappears. A universal is a general numerical relationship holding between all particulars of a given kind. Such regularities, in fact, are the only kind of knowledge possible, because no knowledge can be had of particulars (FA, 4). When a functional notation is used in logic, a law showing how one quantity (the value) varies as another quantity (the argument) can be expressed. If logical generality can be seen in terms of mathematical generality, then linguistic predication can achieve the clarity and precision of the mathematical function, and mathematical thought the general applicability of logical truth.

But before this can happen, changes are necessary both in the linguistic concept and in the mathematical function. First, the notion of a function must be extended. If functions are to be the form of logical analysis, then objects other than numbers need to be substitutable in the argument-places of functions. Second, if sentences are to be seen as functions, mathematical equations $(x^2 = 2)$ as well as mathematical quantities (x^2) must be seen as representing functions. Only in this way, can the truth or falsity of sentences be accomodated.[4] If an equation can be seen as a function of a special kind, whose value is not numerical but "the True" or "the False,"[5] then the correctness of an equation can be seen as analogous to the truth of a sentence and a sentence can be analyzed as a function.[6]

To say that an equation is true for a certain argument is to say that that argument has the property that the functional expression represents.[7] Seen this way, a concept is only a special kind of function whose value is always a truth value. This becomes clear in the functional analysis of a sentence (FC, 2–4). The unchanging part may be the grammatical subject, or the grammatical predicate, just as 'Socrates is mortal' can be exchanged with 'Mortality is a characteristic of Socrates.'[8] In this, sentences are similar to mathematical equations in which it is also possible to see either one element or another as function or argument and a particular choice may have only a communicative value.[9]

In this way, the seemingly irreducible distance between the notation of arithmetic and notation of logic is closed. It is not subject and predicate standing alone that are linked in the sentence, requiring that one locate the separate objects they represent. Instead a sentence, like an equation, expresses a constant relation between two varying or unvarying quantities without recourse to ontologically suspect entities such as substances or universals. The Aristotelian universal sentence ('All men are mortal') now can be understood as, 'If anything is a man it is mortal,' a function that always has the value True no matter what is the argument.[10] In this functional notation any truth can be expressed, whether logical, mathematical, scientific, or philosophical. The exact value of each functional expression, no matter what is its content, can be represented by a truth-table indicating a range of values, just as in mathematics a table may be made of a mathematical function that illustrates a numerical relationship. The result is that thought will be unified and logical errors in science, mathematics, and philosophy exposed.

The very scope of a logical notation contributes to its initial incomprehensibility because we are used to either an easy formalism or a fuzzy logic of ideas. The *Begriffsschrift* is neither. It is a discovery only realized by a great labor of revision and rethinking.[11] This is not an empty construction, and must be accompanied by deep semantical-philosophical investigations into meaning and reference.[12] The functional structure of the sentence is not arbitrary, but dictated by what it represents.[13] The sentence is only the name for something more important: "the structure of the sentence serves as an image of the structure of the thought" (CT, 54). It is only because it expresses a thought that it can be understood. This content must not, however, be confused with sensations or emotions. "Ideas" are subjective and transitory, and can never be the content of a logical notation. The content must be a thought which is the "same everywhere." "Mankind, in fact, has a common store of thoughts which it transmits from one generation to another"

(SR, 59). Neither personal or subjective, thoughts are what they are regardless of any human intention, both in structure and in truth or falsity.

Thought occupies a middle ground between the outer world of events and the inner world of ideas (T, 13–14). If one takes, for example, the Moon as an object of knowledge, it is clear that it cannot be "grasped" by an individual's eye whose transitory visions have no stability or certainty. "Such an idea is often saturated with feeling, the clarity of its parts varies and oscillates" (SR, 59). On the other hand, the "sense" of the Moon, a necessary component of any thought about the Moon, is public property. It is there when when we take our eyes away, the same each time we look again. It is there not just for ourselves but for others to whom we might want to show it. Thoughts do not need to be thought by anyone to exist, and they are true or false whether anyone believes them or not, true or false whether there is anyone to believe them or not. It is not minds that the logician is interested in, but "the mind" (T, 25).

There must be such a mind. If it did not exist there could be no communication. It is only when we grasp something that exists independently of our several understandings that we are able to speak and be understood. "The very being of a thought may also be taken to be in the possibility of different thinkers' grasping the thought and one and the same thought" (N, 35). It is impossible to feel another's pain or to have another's vision. This is because we can never be someone else, never can be literally identical with another person (T, 13ff). Logic offers the only approximation of understanding: a thought from which personal differences are erased, a thought which exists apart from any individual and which is graspable by all. Logic makes possible the only kind of communication possible, a communication in which what is to be said is fixed beforehand. Individuals communicate when they indicate this truth, when they are able to reach the out–of–themselves vantage point at which they must come together if any understanding is possible.

It is to delineate more clearly this being–of–one–mind that Frege turns to semantics to show the content of that thought which the signs of the conceptual notation are to represent and which is the content of the functional sentence.[14] The content of a thought cannot be just a sense but also must include a reference. A thought must be about something, it must have an object. If a thought is to be true or false, it is necessary to pass from the sense, from the mere grasp of a concept, to the complete thought that something is true of something. The problem will be to specify these two parts of the thought: the object and the predicate or concept. Here, where the connection between logic and mathematics is particularly sensitive, there must be a particularly resolute analysis.[15]

We cannot expect to find the distinction in existing linguistic surface structure. There is no sure linguistic sign that an object is named or a concept expressed. Criteria, such as that an object–name takes a definite article, are generally reliable but there are exceptions (CO, 65). Furthermore, a functional analysis reduces even more radically the difference between the subject which might be thought to represent an object and the predicate which might be thought to represent a concept, as it is often permissible to analyze a thought in different ways (CO, 49).[16] So it cannot be only the role of function or argument that produces a concept or object. Empty formalism would result if concept and object are defined only contextually as the content of what functions as a predicate or the reference of what functions as a name. The difference would be only notational.[17]

A function is a relation between two quantities, between an argument and a value; for a function to have a value there must be an argument that is insertable; a place for it in the notation is not enough. Concepts or functions, even if they have argument places, are not true or false, and they are true or false only when a name with reference is inserted. A concept or a definition can be arbitrarily devised, just as two symbols ($\sqrt{}$, -2) can be artibrarily written down together ($\sqrt{-2}$). But this does not mean that such an object exists. It is one thing to generate definitions, it is another thing to discover truths. Whether a concept can be part of a thought, or is only meaningless marks, depends on whether that concept can be realized (LA, 195). If there is nothing of which a predicate is true, there is only a "construction."[18]

A name must be defined as what has a reference. If a functional expression is different from a name, this must be because there exists objectively a difference between what the functional definition represents, i.e., a function, and what the name represents, i.e., an object. This difference must be indicated. A function is incomplete: it has blanks where arguments are to be inserted. Similarly, a concept is "unsaturated," in contrast with the completeness and "boundedness" of an object (inter alia, WF, 115; CO, 65).[19] What must be added to these metaphorical "hints," which must take the place of definition for the most basic notions, is the specification of an object, a mathematical object. If mathematics or any other science is truth-yielding, such objects must exist.

As with any object, mathematical objects may be defined contextually as what functions as an object. We say, '4 is an even number'; therefore numbers exist in the context of a judgment. But it is also necessary to show that mathematical objects are logical objects. This must be proven. It must be made clear that if the content of mathematics is not psychological or practical, it is not formal either. The kind of object a number is can be discovered by thinking more deeply about the nature of a concept and more specifically about the functional nature of a concept. A number only occurs in conjunction with a concept. It is never 12 simply, but always twelve somethings of which we speak. Therefore, it is not an object to which a number attaches but a concept. What its exact relation to concept is must be made clear.

To say that a concept is a function is to say that it has reference to a relation between an argument and a truth value. This is its substance. A concept has a sense in that the relation may be "presented" in different ways, but the reference to the functional correlation between arguments and truth values is its referential content. This correlation is the extension of the concept, or in more functional terms, its value-range. To say that one concept is equal to another—and here we are close to the problem of number—is to say that their value-ranges are equal. (Their sense, strictly speaking, can never be the same.) Given that the universe of discourse must include every object, concepts are equal when they carve out of that totality correlatable sets of objects. To say that a bachelor is an unmarried man is to say that there is a one-to-one correlation between bachelors and unmarried men. To say that two concepts are equal is to say that they have the same number. To say that two concepts are equivalent is to assert a numerical equivalence.

Now the nature of the mathematical object can be made clear. If to say that the extensions of concepts are equal is to say that the numbers of the concepts are equal, then a number must be the same thing as the extension of a concept. Furthermore, once the nature of a number in general is understood, it is possible to explicate particular numbers by finding a concept that necessarily has a given extension. O is the number which belongs to the concept "not identical with itself" because that concept's extension must be zero; 1 can then be defined as the number which belongs to the concept "identical with O" and so on with each of the numbers in turn (FA, 90). Numbers are given objective existence as the extensions of given concepts.[20]

Puzzles in the theory of number are now solved. It is now possible to explain why it is that different numbers can apply in the same situation without sacrificing objectivity. The number applicable depends on the concept under which a judgment is made: 'How many cards?' or 'How many decks?' Nor does counting seem to involve the contradiction that the objects counted are both the same and different. They are the same in that they fall under the same concept but are different because they are different objects. In addition, it is clear that fifty-two cards are not an aggregate of intuitable items, nor only a subjective idea. Mathematics is not a contingent order that we impose on the world. Nor is it empirical. Numbers are given to reason (FA, 156). The definition of number requires no recourse to experience.

Judging something true or false, once the functional nature of the concept is understood, always means that numerable items are correlated with truth values. Such is the nature of judgment because such is the nature of reality. A grasp of a concept is a grasp of the number of objects of which the concept is true. Numbers are logical objects in the sense that their existence is assumed in any thought about reality. Thought is quantified and that quantification is not to be seen as a particular form of judgment among others but as the necessary form of all judgment. When we talk we necessarily talk of numbers of things. This is why to say that a number exists is not to say only that a number functions grammatically as a name or is insertable in an argument place, it is to say that a number has a reference.

This way we avoid a "physical view of number without slipping into a psychological view of it" (FA, 116). A number is not a physical thing or an idea. In fact, no object is a simply intuitable physical thing. It is always *as* something that we experience an object. Without a concept it is impossible to say how many of any object there are. Sets of correlatable items between which identity statements can hold are the objects of mathematics as they are the objects of thought. Now numbers are given objective status at the same time as concepts are given a content that is not subjective or ideal. To show that numbers are objects is to show that numbers are the missing content of thought. The missing reference of a concept is the countable set of objects that, when correlated with truth values, make up its extension. That we are able to correlate the instances of a concept with the instances of another concept shows that we have grasped the concept and that we can make a judgment. In this way, the reference of a concept is an objective fact: once an argument is inserted in a function, one cannot invent its value. Truth and falsity follow automatically, just as a mathematical function yields arithmetic values. Even when a concept is not true of anything, there is an object of thought, the value-range with all arguments correlated with the False. In fact, it is from exactly such a void extension that the reconstruction of mathematics and of thought can take place.

The only number originally specifiable is O; by articulating O in successive folds in self-reference (what is identical with O, etc.) it is possible to generate numbers. Once one sees that nothing is an object, and that nothing's identity with itself is also an object, one can begin to see how mathematics has content and therefore how thought has content. If self-subsistent objects do not exist, the value-range of a concept exists, and it exists most surely when the concept is not true of anything at all. The content of logic as of mathematics is impossibility.

One can think about nothing and about nothing's identity with nothing. One can think also about that thought, whose sense is an object, and about its truth and falsity. As for the ordinary things one might need to think about—politics, friends, family, war, birth, death—it is impossible to think about them except in this way. 'Mary is a battered woman' is meaningless unless we mean that 'There exists someone who is a woman, whose name is Mary, and who is battered.' It is only by way of correlatable sets of countable objects that anything can be talked about. The objects that fall under a concept exist because the concept exists. A concept picks out the objects of which it is true. When an argument is inserted and a judgment made, the argument or objects already have their places, the value is already determined in the value-range of the concept. Only in this way can things be understood, can things be made clear.

Frege has touched an emptiness, a silence at the heart of language, a silence that can make thought wander and mistake itself. He has made that silence, that nothingness, into a presence. And what is more appropriate to silence than the presence of impossibility, than the self-cancelling of contradiction? In this way, the nothingness can spread, break the power of the word, subdue the Babel of talk. Frege has taken the self-silencing that begins as a perversion, as a tiny tear in the texture of thinking, and turned it inside out, painstakingly, meticulously—because the operation is delicate—until it has become the very regulating boundary of thought itself. Now ordinary talk, with its noisy ungovernableness, is an unassimilable tear in a continuous and homogeneous science of truth.

Notes

1. Some typical examples: a) gaps or prolixity: we say, "This card is blank," leaving it to context to determine which card, whereas to make too specific would require an intolerable number of words; b) grammatical confusion: predicate words like 'horse' can be used both as names and as concept words; c) ambiguity: names can fail to refer to anything, and/or have more than one sense.

2. The connection between natural language and logical notation cannot be completely severed. Even natural language, imperfect as it is, aims at truth. When, therefore, surface linguistic structures are true to logical form, they can be cited as proof: "It is very much to my advantage that there is such a good accord between the linguistic distinction and the real one" (CO, 45).

3. A functional expression in mathematics represents a common form among mathematical expressions. What is common, for example, between 3^2 and 4^2 may be expressed by the functional expression $(\ )^2$. What is not common may be conveniently marked by a place-holder variable that will facilitate mathematical operations (x^2). A function then takes on a specific "value" depending on what "argument" is substituted in the space held by the variable.

4. '2^2' cannot be true in the way that 'Socrates is mortal' is true, and to resort to the introduction of a special mathematical sign, $=$, linking an expression to other expressions would be to undermine the project of the logicizing of arithmetic. If mathematics is truly logical, then it is continuously logical, and the introduction of a specifically mathematical symbol at this point should not be necessary (FC, 30).

5. The analogy must be further extended to include the true and the false as objects which the sentence names in the same way an equation indicates a numerical value or number. If the functional analysis is to hold, equations and sentences must have values. Since the truth is what gives a sentence its "value," truth is the logical choice. This conflation of two senses of "value," mathematical quantity and normative value, is consistent with Frege's view of logical laws as both objective and normative. See SR, 63–64, where Frege seems to express

some doubts himself about these objects. True and False, that he has been "driven into accepting."

6. The similarity is only close between the "correctness" of an equation and the "truth" of a sentence; however, applying "true" to an equation is also necessary in order to show how mathematics corresponds to some reality just as a sentence does.

7. To say that $2^2 = 4$ is to say that 2 has the property ($x^2 = 4$). It is to say that ($x^2 = 4$) is true of 2 in a way similar to that in which being mortal is true of Socrates (FC, 30).

8. Some adjustments are again necessary. That the two sentences mean the same thing may not be immediately apparent, especially when it is in very different contexts that one would imagine them used. What is preserved is "cognitive content," a concept that allows one to disregard elements that are not properly speaking functional. Frege explains: "If the the inadmissibility of such transformations were recognized then any profound logical investigations would be hindered" (T, 10).

9. "All such aspects of language are merely the results of the reciprocal action of speaker and hearer; e.g., the speaker who takes account of what the hearer expects, and rises to set him upon the right track before actually uttering the judgment. In my formalized language there is nothing that corresponds" (CN, 3).

10. A similar clarification may be introduced into existential statements such as 'Some men are mortal.' This is to say that the function $A_x \supset M_x$ is not false for all arguments, $(\exists_x) (A_x \supset M_x)$. Given this functional notation, one is now able to express serial generalities not representable at all in spoken language because only the use of the quantifier allows the indication of the precise scope of the quantifier.

11. In the introduction to the *Grundgesetze,* Frege explains the many changes that were necessary in the course of his investigations as well as the paradox that results from these advances. Just what constitutes progress may be the very "obstacle in the way of the circulation and effectiveness of my book" (LA, 142).

12. This combination of mathematical and philosophical research was another reason given by Frege for the poor reception given his work. Mathematicians were uninterested in conceptual and semantic questions, and philosophers turned away at the sight of a formula, (LA, 143).

13. Frege admitted that the *Begriffsschrift* could function as a formal system, but to have treated it as such would have had no interest. No one is content with words alone (LA, 188).

14. The uneven "genesis" of this semantic analysis, from the *Begriffsschrift,* through the revisions and reworkings of "Concept and Object," "Sense and Reference," etc., to the final presentation of the *Grundgesetze* is for logical purposes irrelevant. The adjustments necessary for a completed functional analysis were bound to be many, but to dwell on them would be misleading. We would be supposing

that concepts sprout in the individual mind like leaves on a tree and we think to discover their nature by studying their birth: we seek to define them psychologically in terms of the human mind but this account makes everything subjective and if we follow it to the end, does away with truth. (FA, VII)

Therefore, it is appropriate to look immediately at the finished theory.

15.   It would be tempting, especially given the contextualism of the *Begriffsschrift,* to give up the attempt to define concept and object. Frege never gives in to that temptation. If this is the point at which the conceptual notation could slip back into a naive view of subject and predicate, it is also the point at which mathematics and language could be most securely joined.

16.   In addition, not only can an object be part of a concept or a function, as in 'belongs to Mary,' but a concept can be "turned into" or at least "represented by" an object, as when one says "the concept 'horse' is easily learned" (CO, 45).

17.   Again some have regretted that Frege did not avoid the disappointment to come by contenting himself with a contextual definition: see Michael Resnik, *Frege and the Philosophy of Mathematics* (Ithaca, NY: Cornell University Press, 1980), 193, or Ignacio Angelli, *Studies on Gottlob Frege and Traditional Philosophy* (Dordrecht: D. Reidel, 1967), 160.

18.   For truth, in addition to horizontal relations holding between concepts (a concept falling under a concept) there must be vertical relations that link concepts to objects. Frege's contemporary, Ferdinand Saussure, the founder of structural linguistics, also insists on the existence of a "signified" in addition to syntagmatic relations between relations between signifiers. Given the view that the link between signifier and signified is arbitrary, the signified as "object" is as problematic as Frege's numerical object.

19.   A concept in its incompeteness is so different from an object that it is almost impossible to talk about a concept without misleadingly making it seem to be an object. The minute one says 'the concept horse,' its status as a concept is lost.

20.   It is for this that the "extension" of a concept is necessary. The problem is to move from conceptual equivalence to the specification of an object. That two lines are parallel or that two concepts are equal does not yet give the specification of either a direction or a number as an object, because there is still no way to set up identity conditions.

8

The Marriage of Mathematics and Language

> One can count everything which can be a subject of thought: ideals as well as reals, concepts as well as objects, temporal entities as well as spatial, events as well as bodies, methods as well as theorems (LI, 32).

The problem began with mathematics. The nineteenth century had seen a flurry of mathematical innovation: the discovery of irrational, imaginary, and negative numbers, the invention of new calculating devices, the development of non–Euclidian geometries. But, in Frege's view, there had been no showing that these innovations were not based on promiscuous, unlicensed invention, incomplete induction, or unfounded intuition. There had been no showing that the new numbers and new techniques were consistent or that they corresponded to any reality. No stable foundations had been discovered for mathematics that could have decided the question. How can it be possible to prove the existence of irrational numbers when mathematicians could not show what a simple number is? How can advanced operations be justified when you cannot logically justify the simplest of arithmetical processes?

The two most common ways of founding arithmetic Frege rejected: formalism made mathematics empty and of no interest; idealism made it a matter of ideas and thus subjective. Both allowed fashions in mathematics to come and go, and resulted in the confusion and incoherence that Frege deplored in so much of the work of his contemporaries.[1] For Frege the problem could not be solved by simply restoring rigor to mathematics, which might amount to only a new formalism or a new useful technique. In order to show what was a "construction" and what was based on reality, it was necessary to go beyond the (strictly speaking) mathematical to the deep source of mathematics. Gaps in mathematical reasoning, inductive presentation of new concepts, the unwarranted extension of definitions were only symptoms of a deeper disorder: an inadequate and demeaning image which mathematics had of itself as only a tool useful in practical matters, a mere calculating device. This compromised the generality of mathematics. If there is to be any adequate science, mathematics must be the necessary basis of any grasp on reality. And if this is true, then mathematics must be shown to have its source in the most general of truths, truths which mark the limits of the knowable. Mathematics must be based on the logic that underlies all truth-asserting language. But if arithmetic, the most basic of mathematics, is to be made healthy again, it is not only its health that must be in question, but also language, that natural language which had excluded mathematics and made it an outcast.[2]

The problem was not in mathematics alone. If there was an estrangement between language and mathematics, the fault had to be on both sides. Gaps in mathematical reasoning are defects, but also defective is what had been solicited to fill those gaps: a thought and language essentially unclear. The blame must be shared. If mathematics is to be "reformed," so must language. When that happens philosophers and mathematicians, indeed all thinkers, can come together in the realization that their researches are not incompatible. Isolation was unhealthy for both, and had encouraged both, Frege charged, to promiscuous speculation. But once it is seen that truth and mathematics have a "single source" (ACN, 32), and that mathematical truth can be generated from truth in general, both would require a stabilizing content.

Frege's attention, from the *Begriffsschrift* on, was always divided between mathematical confusion on the one hand and linguistic confusion on the other. It was not only mathematics that needed repair, it was also a language that could not accommodate itself to mathematics and so had left it to frivolous, transitory experimentation. Somehow these two must be brought together in a stable alliance to the advantage of both. Then all areas of human knowledge could expand under the good auspices of science: the physical sciences, as well as philosophy, logic, and the social sciences. All had suffered, as mathematics had, from the weakness and imprecision of language, but once language was joined with mathematics all knowledge would achieve new substance and accuracy. Logic would have a content, not an empty formal content, but a content constitutive of the very nature of reality (LI, 32). Mathematics, in providing that content, would acquire a grounding in the most basic of truths. Language would achieve new power and precision. It is this possibility that the mathematical formalists were too shortsighted to see. A consistent system of relations might describe mathematical operations, but it could never give mathematical objects the authority of logical objects. You can construct a calculating machine, but only if it can be established that there is something to count will its calculation have content.[3] It is for this that the reconciliation between natural language in which human interests are expressed and the calculations in which truth can be represented is absolutely necessary.

Frege's task as matchmaker would not be easy. These two were so different: language, a discursive flow of words—fluid, pictorial, sensual, personal—and mathematics, whose nondiscoursive graphic formulae, in their rigid inexpressiveness, were the very antithesis of linguistic expression. The mediator would be logic, not the old logic too much under the influence of language, but a new logic, with a new insistence on clarity and consistency, that could serve as the institution that would unite them. Governed by logic, each would give up their idiosyncracies, including the peculiarities that made philosophers suspicious of mathematicians and mathematicians suspicious of philosophers. And logic would officiate because the authority of logic comes from the "laws of truth" themselves. These laws, to which both language and mathematics, in their union, would submit, are neither contingent like laws of nature nor conventional like laws of justice. They have both the objectivity of laws of nature and the normative force of laws of justice.[4] Everything that these two, language and mathematics, would do, all aspects of their relationship, would be regulated and regularized in logic.

It was clear that such a union could not be accomplished without some forceful persuasion. Both mathematics and language would have to be made to change. In the *Begriffsschrift,* Frege takes up his role as patient negotiator. Always with the end of final union in mind, he works through changes, hesitations, revisions. It is this that made the work so hard, harder than anyone with a formalist view of mathematics as a construction could understand. The very "characters" of logic and language had to be recovered and reconciled. The early system of subject and predicate had to be discarded for the functional notation. The too-simple "content" of a thought had to be replaced by "sense and reference." The contextual definition of concept and object had to be supplemented. And so on. Even after the final failure of the *Grundgesetze's* Axiom V, a last attempt had to be made to find another, more suitable mathematical mate for language in geometry.

If the nature of mathematics went deep, so did that of language, and Frege demanded that each compromise would have to be a real and not a token acquiescence. As he struggled to bring them together, it was language that caused the most difficulty, language that he always found himself fighting against.[5] It was the loose shape of talk that twarted him, its indulgence in poetry, in emotional expression, in rhetorical effects. Not that Frege did not sometimes express admiration for language, as unredeemed, as "virgin." Language, he sometimes acknowledged, has its own power, a "softness and instability . . . necessary for its versatility and potentiality for development" (JCN, 86). Spoken language with its poetic coloring, play of words, and nuance appealing to subjective sensibilities had an advantage over written in that it can express inner processes and "do justice to even the most delicate combinations and variations of feelings" (ibid). Nevertheless, in view of truth, all this was "trivial" (T, 10). Even writing, which is the first step in the reform of language in that it escapes the temporal succession of speech and can represent several relationships at once, retained some of the fluidity of speech that would always be resistant to mathematical expression.

The way of representing truth described by Frege in the *Begriffsschrift* might lack flexibility, but it had the much more important virtue of stability. The sensations expressible in language are fleeting. They can be "blown away" by an opposing sensation (JCN, 83); joy can at any moment be interrupted by pain, love by hate. Certainly Frege's life was evidence enough, filled as it was with tragedy—the early death of his father, the death of his wife and then of his children— lived out against a background in Bismarck's Germany of political upheaval, extremist views, and eventually war. From the threatened, and to Frege senseless, movements of liberal reform, to the pollution in German character represented to him by the Jews, to the incomprehension and even ridicule that met his work, there was no stability. On the other hand, in a conceptual notation it would be possible to avoid error in others and also in oneself. Not only would the truth be represented but it would be represented so clearly that no one could fail to agree. The world of sensation was puerile, effeminiate. Sensation, being private, was meant to stay private, just as Frege's racist, conservative politics confessed in his diary, were meant to stay private.[6] Truth was a different matter. Truth was public. And for such a truth, language that sensitively expresses bitterness, invective, love, and hate would have to harden into fact.

Nevertheless, in the negotiation that is opened between language and mathematics in the *Begriffsschrift,* it is mathematics that is made chivalrously to offer the initial gestures of accommodation. If a sentence is to be seen as functional, a change is necessary in the notion of a mathematical function. It must be able to take all objects as arguments, and to have a truth value it must encompass equations. These changes in deference to language give a new scope to mathematics, which can now be concerned with things other than numbers, and can have a truth value that represents a reference to an independently existing reality. Mathematics, in its new relationship with language, achieves generality and substance.

But the adjustments required of language were even more profound. A functional sentence is a reduced sentence. All the "psychological fat" has been trimmed away (FC, 3). Universals and forms, "puffed out" and "unhealthy," appeal to a taste for fleshy substance that Frege deplored. Once logicians allow themselves to be distracted by this "psychological peep show" (LA, 147), they can no longer appreciate the slimmer, purer beauty of logical form. No matter what elegant mathematical or logical construction is used to dress up the too abundant flesh of language, it is still in bad taste. "Fashion can give the cachet of beauty to the most detestable mode" (LA, 162). What is needed is not the ripple of soft, flexible, unreliable expression, but purity of form. Logic must penetrate to the bone, to the skeleton of language. To achieve this anorexic ideal, poeticism, tone, gesture, any intentions the speaker has, any attempt to speak for the understanding of the listener must be pared away (CN, 3).

The prescribed reduction goes deeper than the elimination of superfluous connotation; the very form of language will be altered in a functional interpretation. To state a mathematical equation such as $2 \times 2 = 4$ is to say that it is true of 2 that if you double it you will get the value 4. It is to say that if you perform a given operation on 2, you will get a particular result. To say that an equation states a law is to say that it gives a direction of a certain kind: if one intervenes in this way such and such will happen. For the union to hold, Frege's functional sentence must take the same form; it must become a sentence in which one tells someone how to act on an object with a predictable result. If the scope of mathematics has been widened to accomodate language, the scope of language has been drastically curtailed.

Already mathematics and language have changed and, at least in the case of language, the change has been substantial. But although the groundwork of their interaction has been laid, they are far from united. Mathematics has gained generality and truth, language has been reduced to fit the representations that exhibit truth, but the functional notation can take them no further. The change must go deeper than surface structure. The imposition of functional form must be more than a flattering costume, more than the imposition of a notation. The nature of language, what it really is, must change; what is expressed in a sentence, the thought, must also become functional.

Again the problem, as initially posed in "Sense and Reference," is with mathematics. One must explain how it is that mathematics is nontautological, how it is that if '2×2' is just another name for '4,' '$2 \times 2 = 4$' can be interesting and informative. Here it is mathematics that is in danger of triviality and again borrowing from language cures the defect. Frege explains: it must be understood that, like linguistic expressions, mathematical expressions have a "sense." They are not just names of quantities, do not just "refer," but, like words, include a "mode of presentation." Once this sense is taken into consideration it can be seen how mathematical expressions have content: they have content because the senses of '2×2' and '4' differ. With this analysis mathematics is again enriched, and given substance in its association with language.

This is, however, the very "sense" that gets in the way of the functional analysis of the sentence. A characteristic of a mathematical function and the one that makes possible the majority of mathematical operations is substitutivity: equals can be substituted for equals without change of value. But here the linguistic sentence with sense resists functional analysis. Even when the variety of human attitudes—imagining, thinking, wondering, knowing—are reduced by removing all expression of emotion, leaving only the logically permissible "entertaining a thought" and "judging that it is true" (T, 7), there remains in the sentence a stubborn intensionality. Words do not stand alone like formulae in an account book, they also express what is thought and believed even when that thought is limited to the simple yes or no of bivalent logic. But when this intensionality is made explicit as it is in 'I believe that Frege is the greatest logician to date,' the substitutivity necessary for functionality fails. Although I may know that Frege is the greatest logician, I may not know that his "equal," the author of the unpublished diary in which Frege confessed his conservativism and racism, for example, is the greatest logician. The sense of words in language will not stay still, cannot be fixed or counted on, or counted in the way that mathematical quantities can be counted. Therefore, that offending linguistic content, the sense that is to give mathematics content but that disturbs substitutivity in linguistic contexts, must somehow be neutralized.

With great subtlety, Frege proceeds to try to alter the uncooperative character of language with the distinction between sense and reference. Ordinarily when we speak, our words have their ordinary references to objects or states of affairs, but in sentences such as, 'I know that . . . ,' or 'I believe that . . . ,'' this is no longer true. To say that someone believes something is to say something not about the object of that belief but about the "sense" of the expression of the belief. With this distinction, intensional expressions are explained and are no longer an exception to the rule of substitutivity. Sense has been gotten out of the way so that a functional analysis will hold. If intensionality cannot be completely eliminated because we must maintain the difference, for example, between entertaining a thought and judging it to be true, still sense can be made to stand aside.[7] It is still essential as the understood but unstatable presupposition that words are to be taken seriously, but also it must be made to acknowledge that in serious matters, when truth is in question, reference must play the leading role. In every judgement, the step from the level of thought to the level of reference must already have been taken (SR, 64).

Again both mathematics and language have changed. Mathematics has acquired sense, a sense that, even though it is not involved in mathematical operations, still is present in the background to give support and substance to mathematical truth. But language has changed much more radically. There too sense and reference are distinguished. Not only are emotions, connotation, rhetorical effect to be laid aside, but also sense. The sense of a sentence, distinguished from reference, can then be prevented from disturbing its truth-functioning. The truth of a sentence may be detached from its sense.

It is at this point that Frege's negotiation reaches toward the final intimacy. In the master-stroke that is the distinction between sense and reference, Frege has shown how mathematics is nontrivial. That same sense subtracted from language produces a functional mechanism that will operate with the predictability of a mathematical function. Almost, now, are the two one as Frege delicately lays out the relationship between semantic elements. In language one reference may have several senses; there may be several different characteristics through which an object can be grasped. Furthermore, each sense may be expressible in different signs. But this is not the ideal; in a perfected language there will be a single sign for each sense. Moreover, if we were to have complete knowledge of a referent, we should know all its senses; there should be a composite sense that is exactly coterminous with a reference. The trouble is, and this is a trouble quite evident in the synonyms and overlapping references of ordinary language, "To such a [comprehensive] knowledge we never attain" (SR, 58). In language, the sense or senses, those imperfect ideas through which we understand, are diverse and multiple. They cannot be eliminated because our knowledge is never complete. Our grasp of an object or state of affairs is always particular, always only through a "mode of presentation." But it is this partiality, this imperfection, that mathematical functioning cannot tolerate.

It was the surmounting of this incompatibility that the distinction between sense and reference was supposed to cure. Once the sense, abstracted from the sentence, is set aside, the referential functioning of the sentence can proceed uninterrupted. It can proceed as if we did have comprehensive knowledge. It allows us to talk as if the partiality of our understanding were not a fact; it allows us to ignore, insofar as the value or the truth of a sentence is concerned, the partial, interested "mode of presentation" of our references. It allows a language in which truth may be separated from the way in which that truth is presented. In such a reformed language, a science with mathematical precision can be represented because, in such a language, truth can be stated without the impediment of the necessarily imperfect grasp with which it begins. If the functional sentence is a sentence in which we can give instructions for precise operations, now with the distinguishing of sense from reference, it is a sentence in which the acceptability, the "truth value" of those instructions, can be thought apart from the derivation of the terms in which they are stated. Truth then can be a function of the references of the sentences. How those references are presented, determined, or indicated can be disregarded, but not done away with completely, and here the negotiation requires the utmost in diplomacy.

Sense is necessary if the functioning of the sentence and of mathematics is to have content. If sense is done away with, there is nothing left of language's contribution to the union, and that contribution is necessary. Not only is sense needed to give nontriviality to mathematics, it is also necessary to give an interpretation to the mediating institution of logic. The sense/reference distinction, therefore, cannot eliminate sense; it can only hold it out of the way of a discourse that can get on with the business of stating truths. Therefore, sense plays an increasingly token role. It is needed, but as a figure to which only lip-service is paid with no real homage. We cannot, Frege says in "Thoughts," ever recognize a property of something, or grasp a sense, without at the same time making the judgement that something has that property. The sense of a sentence is only what certain kinds of sentences have in common (T, 7). In the case of assertorial sentences the variety of possible senses is an embarrassment: sentences that have the same truth value should not seem to be different judgments. Therefore, it would be better if "for every proper name there shall be just one associated manner of presentation of the object so designated" (CT, 11). With this stipulation, sense becomes only the projected outline of reference, its standing aside, its supporting role, its necessary presence, only the undisturbing duplication of reference and the truth-conditions that mirror truth values.[8] Almost the marriage has been consumated.

Now only one thing stands in the way. It must be made clear that the linguistic concept, the element where one is most likely to find sense, also has a reference and so may participate freely in the truth functional sentence. It is in this crucial last adjustment that the definition of number is necessary. Not just so that there may be mathematical objects and therefore mathematical objectivity, but also so that the referential functioning of the sentence may be complete. It is here that the two reluctant lovers will finally merge, where language will become numbering, and numbering language. With the reference of a concept, number will be defined; with the number of a concept reference will be defined.

But two things must still be settled: what a number is, and how a concept, seemingly so saturated with sense, can have a reference. Again there is initial deference on the part of mathematics, an admission of weakness. No one had defined number; no one could be sure that such a thing existed. Here language is again of assistance because it is only in connection with a linguistic concept that a number can be defined. This alone, however, does not make numbers objects, and if there are to be identity statements in mathematics and existential judgments—e.g., irrational numbers exist or do not exist—there must be objects. For this, language must change. Somehow, from linguistic concepts must be generated numbers.

This will be the most difficult reconciliation of all because at the same time the distinction between concept and object must always be maintained. But, Frege proposes, there is a sense in which concepts, like objects, can be identical: their extensions or value-ranges may be the same. To say that one concept is the same as another concept is to say that they are equal or that they apply to the same number of objects. In this subtle move from 'same' to 'equal,' the extensions of concepts finally emerge as objects. These are the references needed for a concept, and although a concept is not a mathematical object, its reference or value range is. Seen as referring to a value-range or number of objects, the resistant concept has finally been quantified, its truth value a product of its arguments in the same way a mathematical product is the result of the quantities multiplied.

The distinction between sense and reference was necessary for this final rapprochement. For the delineation of an object, sense had to stay out of the way; its too-close presence blurs identity. The value-range of a concept had to be distinguished clearly from any mode of presentation; only that way can it become the object with which a number can be identified. The definition of 0 as the value-range of the concept 'non-identical with itself' requires that all sense be removed. To say that 0 is the same as 'non-identical with itself' is senseless. It is only in terms of value-ranges, not sense, that there is any rapport between the two. In order to make the mechanism of this definition work, sense must not enter in.

But again sense must not disappear altogether. Even here it is not dispensible. A concept cannot be a bare collection of particulars; something must hold its extension together. Even the functional correlation with truth values is not enough, if there is no way of knowing how the correlations with truth values are to be established. Sense is needed for the definition of number; it is needed to delineate 0, without which number would be indefinable, but, and here is where the final and tragic collapse of all the Frege's efforts threatens, it must be there and not there at the same time. It must be a sense and an object at the same time, enough of a sense to hold an extension together, but senseless enough to be a number.

Language, no matter how tractable she has become, now finds herself in an impossible situation.[9] She cannot bring to mathematics what mathematics needs, because the terms on which the contribution must be made nullify that contribution. The demands on her are incompatible. Either she goes through the motions only of mathematical functioning and so brings no substance or content, or she asserts itself and interrupts truth-functional relationships. Frege realizes at once the difficulty, if not the hopelessness, of the situation. It is no longer clear how a marriage of mathematics and language is possible. There is Frege's attempt to patch the logic that was to bring them together, to reformulate the definition of number; there is his final rejection of arithmetic and the substitution of geometry as the source of mathematical truth, but all through these desparate maneuvers, there is the realization that all the work of reconciliation advanced step by step from the *Begriffsschrift* to the *Grundgesetze* has been a failure.

Frege ends his life in disappointment. Whether or not language and mathematics can in fact be made compatible, for others the match had been made. There were necessary adjustments to be made,[10] but in major currents of twentieth-century philosophical thought—logical positivism, logical atomism, structural grammar, generative semantics, analytic philosophy, cognitive psychology—the functional statement was taken as the logical form of sentences.[11] The sentence that is the subject of linguistic and logical research is the sentence as it was prepared by Frege for its marriage with mathematics. It is not surprising that the effect of Frege's negotiations on mathematics was less profound. It was clear enough that mathematics could make no real concessions. Each time that it deferred to language by opening a space for linguistic meaning to give content to mathematical thought, that meaning, to be acceptable, had to empty itself of linguistic content. After Frege, mathematics goes on as before, replacing Frege's conceptual definition of number with isomorphic mathematical structures that have no need for linguistic foundations.[12]

Language, however, continued to be forced, in linguistic and philosophical research, to play the role that logic demanded of it. The marriage between language and mathematics would survive even if the relationship on which it was based had failed. The problem which had occasioned Frege's matchmaking had not gone away, and it was not just a problem in German philosophy. In all of the West, there was the same uncertainty and fragmentation. Unity based on common Aristotelian essences or scriptural authority was archaic; neither Cartesian certainty nor Kantian synthetic *a priori* judgments could any longer provide a stable point of reference. Descartes had continued to speak in terms of innate ideas reminiscent of Augustine; Kant repeated in his logic a muddled Aristotelianism. Mathematics, the source of Descartes's certainty, had lost its univocality; the synthetic *a priori* was rejected by an experimental science that measured truth not by rationality but by pragmatic success. Philosophy had failed to deliver universal truth. Mathematical logic projected a new certainty, not substantial or even judgmental, but linguistic, and in the chaos and uncertainty between two world wars, in a world suffering from what seemed to be a terminal erosion of values and social order, this was too compelling to reject.

In linguistics and in the new schools of logical analysis that began to dominate philosophy in England and the United States from the 1930s onward, language continued to be forced to conform to logical rules. Otherwise, philosophers feared as Frege feared, there would be no unity to the diverse departments of knowledge, no bridge between the language in which human concerns are expressed and the scientific research that was to solve all human problems, no connection between science's proliferating calculative techniques and truths about the world. Neurology might tell us about brain mechanisms but nothing about human thought; functionalist sociology might make senseless correlations that do nothing to explain why events occur; structural anthropologists might describe patterns in behavior divorced from the meaning of that behavior; linguists might map formal relations that have nothing to do with what anyone says. If mathematical logic marks the boundaries of thought, and if we are to think about more than numbers and calculative techniques, then somehow the alliance with language, no matter how flawed, had to be made to hold. When we speak to each other any truth, no matter with what personal tone or nuance we chose to decorate that truth, we have to assume a core of logical form. We might in our leisure vent our feelings, but insofar as we speak the truth, whether in policy decisions, in economic deliberations, in social planning, or in our understanding of ourselves, we must speak not from any personal sense of our situation or any human or limited perspective, but from those truths discovered by mathematical science. Philosophers pledged themselves to make this their only concern: to purge the last inconsistencies between the functional truths of science and the unclear opinions and beliefs expressed in natural language.[13] Nothing would interrupt a physical science structured according to mathematical logic, as it tells the truth about man, woman, society, history, the mind, in a new rigorous physics, anthropology, psychology, sociology.[14] Science must tell us about human behavior as well as about the physical world.

The deductions of the old logic had been discredited. The arguments used by Abelard were no longer persuasive. Man's rational essence contrasted with a deficient femininity no longer seemed intuitively clear. Women's nature written into canon law, or God's judgment that a wife be subject to her husband revealed in scripture, could no longer reliably found the inference to a husband's dominion over his wife or his right to punish her. Instead, a scientific sociology expressed in the terms of Frege's functional logic would reveal the objective truth of this phenomenon, as of all phenomena. All, or most, incidences (or arguments, to use Frege's terminology) of wife-beating can be discovered to be related to a concept or value-range: either a husband whose mother was overly dominating, or the smaller size of women, or the wife's tendency to provoke her husband, or a radical feminism that makes men feel unworthy, or the unemployment of the husband, or even such seemingly unrelated matters as whether the wife had premarital sex, or whether she uses birth control.[15] The danger of vacuity in such an approach was well appreciated by Frege. First, there is the danger of formalism. If the sense of phrases such as "provocation" or "domineering mother" stands back completely out of the way, then all that is established are formal relations with no claim on reality. A provoking wife is a wife that gets beaten, and a beaten wife is the wife who provokes. If, however, enough sense remains so that provocation can be independently identified, we may learn a way to control wife beating. We may find a way to prevent women from provoking their husbands, or to encourage mothers to bolster the egos of their sons, or we can improve the economy so that there are more jobs for men, or discourage feminism. In this way functional logic prepares the way for action. It tells us what to do so there will be less wife-beating.

But what cannot be part of the functional "logic" that is to help us understand abusive marriages are the institutional relations in which these words, "abuse," "marriage," "domineering," "wife," "husband," "beat-ing," have meaning. In Frege's reduced "sense," the sense that only isolates a manipulative strategy and defines a "value-range," their meaning escapes.[16] Language stands back out of the way as required, allowing the scientist to ignore the context in which the words of natural language, "wife," "mother," "husband," "son," make sense. He is then able to ignore the institution of marriage in which wife-beating occurs and its history: a mar-riage which structures relationships between a submissive accomodating wife and a demanding husband. He is able to ignore the oppressive dynamics in which a wife is meant to stand back out of the way until she can bear it no longer and then is punished and then is forgiven because she cannot be allowed to leave but must be made to stand back out of the way, be there and not there at the same time, obedient to the will of her husband but at the same time a presence that reassures him that he is not alone as he attempts time after time to discipline her and break her will, but not destroy her or allow her to leave, because without her he could not live. The functional explanation of abuse—removed from this context and so removed from the intentions and desires of husbands and wives whose relationships were formed within this context—ignores what the wife might say about why she remains in the marriage, or the husband about why he loses control. Husband and wife have been surveyed, their answers framed in pre-fixed value ranges; they have been interviewed and their answers interpreted in the terms of the object-domain of a theoretical model. This allows a social policy to be designed that returns women to the family and patches again an institution of marriage assumed to be a necessary source of social order and happiness.[17] With the discipline of functionalist logic, the institutions within which words have meaning are preserved, structured by economic and emotional inequality, coherent with a culture that plays and replays scenes of rape and violence against women.[18]

There is a new tone to this logic: no longer the patient superior authority of Plato's refutations, no longer the removed austerity of divine law, no longer the strident certainty of scripture, but, now, the cold dictates of improving experts. Scientifically based sociology, medicine, and psychology instruct women on how to get well: how to meet the demands that society makes of them, how to keep from getting beaten, how to be better wives and mothers, how to let the sense of their situation stand back out of the way of truth.[19] And if science has not yet discovered the correlations, women are urged to wait, reserve opinion, until science has reformulated the issues and made them into judgments that are true or false.

Has language really changed? Does it matter what logicians or sociologists say? Isn't it the case that the linguistic clarifications of analytic philosophers, the proofs of logicians, the theoretical models of linguists, the functional sociology that fills professional journals take only a small portion of language's actual life as women, and men, continue to talk, deliberate, discuss, converse, and decide, in boardrooms, committees, political debates, classrooms, living rooms, with all the tone, gesture, ambiguity, vagueness, and nuance that Frege put aside to make way for logical truth? Yes, but there is a difference. We still talk, privately and publically, but even there Frege's diplomacy is felt. It has convinced us that talk is powerless, can do nothing, except vent our feelings, cause a disruption, create an alternate world of fictional images; we acquiesce, as if the real power is always elsewhere in the theories and the functional truths, in the conceptual structure and generative grammars, that decide the policies that govern our lives. Fragmented, private opinions, a matter of feelings, sensations that can change from one day to the next, an exchange of preferences, a choice between indistinguishable alternatives, only cast-off flesh of a language divorced from reality and from the life force of a living community.

Notes

1. Frege often complained of the deficiency of his mathematical contemporaries. They construct new objects without observing logical laws of construction (LA, 173). They engage in "stupendous conjuring tricks" (LA, 175). They offer unrealizable "piecemeal" definitions (LA, 159). They are unclear about notions even as fundamental as "function" (WF, 107ff.). Although Frege seems to have worked more or less in isolation, his reform of language was not unique. The early nineteenth-century logician Bolzano had undertaken a similar project of rescuing mathematics from intuitionism, idealism, and psychologism, and isolating the propositional form of sentences from what is nonlogical in expression. It was primarily through Frege, however, not Bolzano, that mathematical logic became the foundation of later twentieth-century philosophy in Britain and America, as it was transmitted from Frege, already in contact with Betrand Russell in England, to Frege's pupil Rudolf Carnap, and then to the other members of the Vienna Circle and to their foreign students such as the American Willard Quine and the British A. J. Ayer, who in turn took the positivism home with them to Britain and the United States. Also, many of the German and Austrian members of the Vienna Circle, including Carnap, subsequently left Facist Europe to teach in universities in the United States.

2. Michael Dummett, for example, argues that no one could have taken, in fact, the time to practice a Fregean mathematics without gaps. What is important, he argues, is not mathematical practice but showing the terms in which such a formalization can be conceived: *Frege: Philosophy of Language* (London: Duckworth, 1973), XVII-XVIII. It is for this reason that Dummett continues to argue, against some interpreters, that the major contribution of Frege is to philosophy of language. See his lengthy answers to his critics in *The Interpretation of Frege's Philosophy* (Cambridge, MA.: Harvard University Press, 1981).

3. Jevons was able to construct a calculating machine on the basis of Boolean logic

in 1869, which he exhibited at the Royal Society: William and Martha Kneale, *The Development of Logic* (Oxford: Clarendon Press, 1962), 421.

4. Not only do logical truths faithfully represent reality, they also entail prescriptions about asserting, thinking, judging, inferring, and consequently action (T, 1).

5. "So one fights against language, and I am compelled to occupy myself with language although it is not my proper concern here" (T, 13)

6. Ironically, it was when Dummett interrupted his work on Frege—the work which more than any other acknowledges Frege's influence on twentieth-century philosophy of language—to engage in liberal political activities, that he discovered by chance the unpublished diary in which Frege expressed his personal views, views which were virulently racist and conservative: Frege was opposed to all liberalization or parliamentary reform and convinced that Jews should be deprived of all rights and expelled from Germany. Dummett hesitates briefly—this is a man he thought rational, not only rational but a genius who had grasped and expressed the essence of rationality—and then resumed his work on Frege's philosophy of language. The moment of doubt leaves only the trace of a few sentences in the introduction to his massive tract on Frege, along with his conclusion: Frege's politics cannot be relevant to the achievement of his logic: *Frege: Philosophy of Language*, XII.

7. This problem plagues Frege from the awkward judgment stroke of the *Begriffsschrift* to the unformalizable assertion form of judgment.

8. The sense of a sentence is what would make it true, the reference is its actual truth value. The elimination of sense perhaps finds its most extreme statement in the contemporary logician Saul Kripke's theory of reference, which is suggested by Hans Sluga as the proper continuation of Fregean thought. "By separating the question of the meaning of a referring expression from the way in which the reference of the expression has come to be fixed, Kripke in effect separates the notion of sense from the theory of meaning and speaks of meaning in the way in which the *Begriffsschrift* speaks of the mode of designation": *Gottlob Frege* (London: Routledge and Kegan Paul, 1980), 161.

9. Russell's antinomy, that also intrudes at this moment, is only one point where the impossibility is most logically visible. That sense necessarily seems to involve the possibility of self-reference and so generates antinomies will necessarily embarrass any reference that cannot completely break loose from linguistic meaning.

10. For example, *Principia Mathematica* by Russell and Whitehead (1910–1913) was a Fregean grounding of mathematics in logic, in a new streamlined notation.

11. Frege's work is one watershed of the schism between the Continental and the Anglo-American phenomenological tradition analytic tradition in philosophy. Although Frege had managed to convince Edmund Husserl, who was concerned like Frege with the unsure foundations of mathematics and science, of the inadequacy of psychologism in logic and mathematics, Husserl slipped back into psychologism away from linguistic formulations of meaning to intentionality. Husserl diluted sense and reference to refer to mental acts, not just judgments, and so from a Fregean viewpoint failed to accomodate the independence

of "thoughts" from anyone's ideas. For Frege, insofar as mental acts have sense and reference, they must have the form of a judgment. Logical positivism and analytic philosophy, on the other hand, following Frege, continued with a linguistic analysis of mental acts which culminates in a cognitive psychology which keeps all the linguistic machinery of reference and truth-conditions. In the mean time, Husserl inaugurated the very different study of phenomenological experience bracketed off from questions of reference and existence. Another pivotal figure is Frege's contemporary Franz Brentano who also critiqued the looseness of metaphysical language and defined a concept as the continuity of a function, but ends with the idealist view that the only ultimate reality is the representing subject.

12. See Resnik, *Frege and the Philosophy of Mathematics,* 205, where Resnik describes the "iterative conception of sets which dominates the mathematical scene today."

13. An example is the amount of energy now spent by philosophers in developing functionalist theories of mind. Terms like "mind" and "thought" in natural usage seem to have meanings inconsistent with scientific materialism. Therefore they must be analyzed in such a way as to be congruent. Research in artificial intelligence has been useful here in bridging the gap between natural language and logic. Although natural language resists the reduction of mental predicates to brain states, the grammar of our talk about computer software has been made to provide the means for a translation that assumes no unquantifiable substance.

14. Emile Durkheim, for example, generally considered to be the founder of a functional sociology, is a contemporary of Frege, and also Bronislaw Malinowski, who defined functional anthropology in his 1926 entry on "Anthropology" for the *Encyclopedia Britannica,* 13th ed., supp. I.

15. See the review of current research in R. E. Dobash and R. Dobash in *Violence Against Wives,* (New York: Macmillan, 1979), 19–26.

16. The use of "value" here is interesting. Any essential Platonic goodness can no longer be assumed. Logical positivism inspired by Frege's mathematical logic will argue that value statements are meaningless. Technocratized and neutralized value that reappears in economic theories of value and here as the value of mathematical equation is all the "value" that survives.

17. See for example the discussion of Dobash and Dobash, *Violence against Wives,* ch. 10, "The Helping Professions."

18. *Ibid.* on the history of wife-beating, 31ff.

19. An alternative approach to knowledge of wife-beating and remedial actions can be found in Maria Mies, "Towards a Methodology for Feminist Research" in *Theories of Women's Studies,* ed. G. Bowles and R. Duelli-Klein (Berkeley: University of California Women's Studies, 1981). Mies describes a feminist research strategy in which battered women themselves participate, in which the goal is not restoration of the family but recovering women's consciousness of their situations, and in which a collective understanding of the phenomenon is developed through shared self-histories.

9

Frege's Thoughts

Nor must we say that one person might communicate his thought to another and a conflict would then flare up in the latter's private world. It would be quite impossible for a thought to be so communicated that it should pass out of the private world of one person into that of another (PW, 133).

A logical language is a language without style, a language purged of the coloring, nuance, rhythm, metaphor, rhetoric that mark an individual voice. These effects, characteristic of poetic or literary language, produce a series of private idioms particular to each speaker, and must not be allowed to interrupt the commonality of a language in which truth can be expressed. It is to this conviction that Frege returned after the failure of the formalization that would have produced stable objects for logic. If language is to tell the truth, the gaps that personality leaves in logic must be filled in some other way.

This is not just a question of the personal "coloring" of words, which might be eliminated, but of a fault in the syntax of natural language. 'I' and its complement, 'you,' related adverbs and adjectives such as 'here' or 'there' or 'this,' speaker-related time specifications such as 'now' and 'then' can have no place in a logical language. Because their references are variable and context-dependent, they introduce an intolerable indeterminacy. The sentences in which they occur cannot have fixed references or, what is the same thing, determinate truth values. 'I am a woman' is true in one mouth and not in another. To cure this defect, not only must 'woman' be clearly defined as a 'person of the feminine gender' with all variable conceptual connotation removed, but the indeterminate 'I' must also be replaced by a definite description or name whose reference is fixed. 'I am a woman' must become 'Andrea Nye is a woman' so that the sentence has a determinate truth value and can play a truth-functional role.

Not only the first person must be eliminated, but all personal pronouns. 'You' is only a 'you' for a particular 'I.' 'He' and 'it' likewise depend for their references on context and must be replaced by names. This may be necessary even when there are no explicit pronouns. Seemingly objective statements such as 'The cherry blossoms are in bloom' must also be supplemented because they too carry the implicit 'now' that relates to a particular speaker situated in space and time. It is necessary to specify that time and place for the sentence to have a reference. The understood 'now' must become 'March 29, 1985' so that the complete meaning of the sentence is made clear.[1] Tenses of verbs that indicate time in respect to a speaker must be similarly replaced by time co-ordinates, and adjectives and adverbs like 'here' and 'this' replaced by specific place-references.

Completeness of reference worked into the syntax of a logical language allows the automatism necessary for science. In a language which retains person, the thought expressed must always be that of an individual speaker whose position is one possible position among others and whose view is limited by a particular perspective. In such a "personal" language, automatism is interrupted as it comes to the nonfunctional 'now' or 'I.' Once these gaps are filled, however, logical law can operate and scientists may speak and write a language understood by others. The removal of person will take the indeterminacy from references; truth will require no author, but be a calculation that can be mechanized or duplicated. Just as a computer, in its truth-telling, is incapable of using 'I' or 'you' except as a replacement for its own name, so has the scientist no use for pronouns. If he uses one at all it will be the anonymous "we," that refers not to a person but to the authority of science.[2] This impersonality Frege saw as one of the great benefits of logical language. Mechanisms could now be expected to intervene as useful aids in all areas of activity. Mechanisms could represent the scientist's thought "hardened with time.[3] Everywhere, in science, business, government, in administration, research, and record-keeping, hardened thoughts could replace communication between people so affairs can proceed with an uninterrupted order and agreement. Frege makes no pretense of describing ordinary thought or communication. His critics, Frege explained, "find that my conceptual notation does not correctly represent mental processes; and they are right, for this is not its purpose at all. If it occasions entirely new processes, this does not frustrate its purpose."[4] Whether or not Frege foresaw the specific form such a revolution would take in the development of formal systems and computer programs, he made it clear that it is a revolution in thought and behavior that he envisioned.

This revolution can only be accomplished in the objective, depersonalized language that will provide the basis of translation between science and ordinary language, and between the scientist and his own calculations. The scientist's thought must be made to correspond to the countable facts that owe nothing to him and to his situation. Given this goal, personal pronouns are appropriate only if there is doubt or uncertainty, but as these uncertainties are successively resolved, thought functions more and more without interruption. As a result, behavior can also be expected to achieve a corresponding order as we come to "put our heart into the (re)playing" of the truth.[5]

That numbers cannot not be defined as logical objects cannot be allowed to disturb the mechanization of thought. If objectivity cannot be found in arithmetic then it must be found elsewhere in a formal syntax that will guarantee objectivity. It is to this more general question of the necessity of objective thought and language that Frege turned in "Thoughts." What objectivity can replace personal pronouns so that they will not introduce indeterminacy into language? Frege discusses one particular example at some length. A Dr. Lauben (the name that he gives the "I" in his example) has been wounded. Dr. Lauben may express this thought: "I have been wounded," but others also must be able to refer to it: "He has been wounded." (T, 11) In order to make it clear that the same fact is expressed whether Dr. Lauben expresses it or someone else, the same substitutions must be made for both "I" and "he." Furthermore, if they are to be replaced by "Dr. Lauben," it must be made clear that there is one object to which "Dr. Lauben" refers no matter who uses his name. If Dr. Lauben refers to himself as "I," the same proposition must be expressible by someone else using his name. This is necessary so that Dr. Lauben may say something about himself to which others may agree. But just the replacement of "I" by "Dr. Lauben" does not remove the difficulty. The problem is that there may be a number of understandings of who Dr. Lauben is: for one person he is a stern father or cold husband, for another the brilliant discoverer of quantification theory, for another, the author of a racist diary. If the name "Dr. Lauben" has a different meaning for different people, then how can it be that they all express the same thought when they say he is ill? Especially troubling is Dr. Lauben's reference to himself, for he, argues Frege, has an understanding of himself that is unshareable with anyone else.

The name that Dr. Lauben uses for himself and that others may use for him must have a fixed reference, but even a name has sense and it is this multiple sense that again gets in the way of proper logical functioning. Sense is bound to specific, incomplete, and personal ways of seeing things; therefore, it is necessary that one such sense be chosen as proper (T, 12). This is the specification that Frege's number theory failed to provide, but in "Thoughts" Frege approaches the source of the difficulty directly; that stubborn personality that sense never seemed able to lose because the hard objective value-range which it was to have become always seemed to retain something of value, of the value to a person and of the value of a view of things that made an aggregate of objects into a class, had to be eliminated. In "Thoughts" Frege returns to the person that is the source of the indeterminacy.[6] The "I" had caused the difficulty and so the "I" itself, must be hardened into a fact, into an object. The subjectivity with which everyone begins must become the objectivity necessary for the language of truth.

As always, Frege demands a real transformation. It will not be enough for Dr. Lauben and his interlocutors to seem to agree, Dr. Lauben retaining his peculiar vision of himself and his problems and others seeing him simply as someone "who is speaking at this moment." Instead it must be made clear that the same thought is understood by both (T, 13). There must be a real understanding. Failing to find it in mathematics, Frege now finds it in his relationship to himself. There is a primitive way in which a man is presented to himself (T, 3). Before he can speak or have knowledge, he is aware of himself and of the impressions and ideas that he has of the things around him. In order to communicate, however, he must take that subjectivity and turn it into "thoughts" that others can grasp, but how is this to be done? First, he must realize that he can do nothing with the shifting world of sensation, mood, wishes, emotion, opinion; these are private and his own. He "owns" them and he cannot give them to anyone else. They cannot be thoughts, they cannot be expressed or understood as true. They are only his. But what he can do to escape this impasse is to see that what "I" denotes is different from an idea. I may have an idea of myself, but there is something else, something more substantial, which is me. There must be also, Frege agrees with Descartes, a thing that experiences my ideas, who has them. "I am not my own idea" (T, 22). I may think about myself, but this is not to be confused with thinking about my ideas of myself.[7]

Once it is shown that our subjectivity involves not only experiences and sensations, but also ourselves as "thinking things" detached from sensations, Frege can draw a number of far-reaching conclusions. Now that he is something, he may acknowledge others as independent owners of ideas. "Nothing now stops him." Before, the fear of his own insubstantiality prevented him from seeing others as objects; now this fear is removed, he may proceed (T, 24). He can conclude that there are other objective selves. He has determined his own identity, and therefore others can also be object "I"s and know themselves. Quickly Frege trades the possibility for probability, and the probability for certainty. "Once given the possibility the probability is very great that it is in my opinion no longer distinguishable from certainty (T, 24).[8]

But from where does this certainty come? It is not that there is any logical connection between the existence of Frege as a thing and the existence of others. Instead, as Frege makes clear in the next paragraph, he *must* be certain of their analogous existences because the consequences of uncertainty are too intolerable. Without common objects, science is impossible. "The material sciences too could only be assessed as fables and alchemy" (T, 24). If truth is to be possible, Frege must move from the beginning certainty of his own existence as an object to the existence of others as objects. It is this thought, or this faith—that Frege is the same object to himself as he is to others, that they are the same object to themselves as they are to him—that justifies the objectivity of thought. Once there are "other men beside himself who can make the same thing the object of their considerations" (T, 24), then he may move on to the assumption that in addition to incommunicable personal ideas and the material objects only accessible through these ideas, there are objects, objects that are the real object of thought. Once it is seen that "I" is an object, and that others are objects, there can also be all the other objects that we have in common.[9]

The solution was there in that very unformalizable "I" that had plagued Frege from the beginning: it had resurfaced in multiple senses that compromised the rigidity of reference, in the metaphors that Frege found necessary to explain primitive notions, in the intensionality that prevented substitutivity, in the assertion that made entertaining a thought different from believing it, in the antimonies of self-reference. But here in a final attempt to come to terms with the problem, Frege has turned it inside out. If subjectivity is the disruption that cannot be eliminated, then it will become the starting point of all thought. Out of an understanding of himself as an object, Frege posits the objects that are others, others who must have the same thoughts as he does because they must be like him and think like him. Frege's "I" is no longer an unassimilable anomaly, but the center around which truth-telling language turns.[10] It is the source of Frege's belief in the existence of objects of knowledge, as well as his certainty that others can grasp the same thought as he can. Instead of trying to fill the gaps where person enters into language with references that will never be determinate, Frege gathers them into a single point of self-reference. Only from such a vantage point, can the seamless texture of truth-telling language be generated. The points of personality which are the "I"s, "you"s, "now"s, and "there"s, the references to diverse personal situations, have become one *thing,* the subject that is the object of logical thought. The source and the substance of logical thought, the logical subject, is a particular person.

What kind of a person? Who is this "I" that we must take as Frege, this Dr. Lauben of his examples? Is he a happy man? Is his the world of a happy man? It is clear enough he is a solitary man, divorced and distanced from his surroundings and from other people, a university professor, who spent his whole life in the same town, teaching the same kind of students year after year, all of whom must have begun to look the same to him. When Dr. Lauben says, "I have been wounded," two colleagues "hear" what he says. It may not have been the case that he is even speaking to them. They only "hear" it. Perhaps he was speaking to someone else, or to himself. This remoteness from those who hear what he says is what provokes the confusion of reference. "Who is this Lauben who said that about being wounded in the hall?" we imagine them asking, not friends or intimates of Lauben, but strangers, who nod formally, perhaps even with hostility, to him in the hall. Each of the people who hear about Lauben knows him very slightly. Each has some tenuous bit of information: "Born on 13 Sept, 1875," or, what passes for personal acquaintance: "The doctor who is the only doctor living in a house known to both of us," or the completely anonymous "The person speaking to me at this moment" (T, 13). Given his isolation, whatever identity Lauben has must come from himself, especially since he is so sure that no knowledge of his feelings is possible by anyone else. Is Lauben then Frege, as he was described by his student Carnap: old beyond his years, introverted, always turned to write at the board? "Never did a student ask a question, or make a remark, whether during the lecture or afterwards. The possibility of discussion seemed out of the question," Carnap reported from his experiences in Frege's classroom.[11]

"When Dr. Lauben has the thought that he was wounded, he will probably be basing it on the primitive way he is presented to himself" (T, 1). When he says, "I was wounded," it is clear that he does not mean to elicit sympathy, or to get better treatment, or to excuse omissions or weakness, or explain his bitterness, all of which would only have to do with his private feelings which only he can own, only have to do with feelings such as those expressed in his diary, personal feelings not relevant to the logic. In this sense his wounding can only have to do with himself: he is not known, he is not close to anyone. And so the questioning of his colleagues follows as a matter of course. Who is this Lauben? What does he mean he was wounded? It is Lauben's isolation that makes it necessary to find something in what Lauben says that can be understood by others.

There is only one way, given the scenario as sketched by Frege, that this can be done. Dr. Lauben must make himself an object and assume that others are like him. No direct communication is possible. Dr. Lauben will not sit down with a friend and explain his hurt. He has let drop a word. No one knows why he chose to say it then or in that place. Perhaps it was an accident. It leaped out before he could stop it. He does not want sympathy or help. Perhaps the wounding is in the past—the death of his wife, his children, or more recently the cool reception given to his work and the stupidity and disrespect of the students. For such a person understanding is problematic. He will be discussed by strangers as if he was an object. His thoughts, unaerated by mutual exchange, will become increasingly narrow, incommunicable. He will write in his diary; he will keep his thoughts to himself.

The antidote cannot be communication, which has already been ruled out, but a substitute understanding that leaves behind private experience which is incommunicable. Logic will be a thought that is apart from feelings or experience and so can be the basis of a coming together that need not attempt the reconciliation of conflicting attitudes and responses: how his wife might have seen it, or his children if they had lived, or the Jews whom he wished expelled. None of this is relevant. Logical thought represents an agreement that is accessible to anyone if they will only put feelings and experiences aside. And from the grasping of such a common thought will come action, common action. Such a thought, Frege rhapsodizes at the end of "Thoughts," is a tool of great efficacy. It can be used like a "hammer" is used, to bring about the "great events of world history" (T, 29). It is stronger than any material hammer, because it is not subject to the limitations of any physical thing; although embedded in a particular hardware, or notation, or theory, it transcends any embodiment. Also better than a material hammer, it may be used by many at a time (T, 29), by a state, by a ruling party. Not being bound like a physical hammer to reciprocity with an object, it can be endlessly articulated, remaining the same no matter who thinks it, no matter whether anyone thinks it. It may, by itself, print out the derivation, the statistics, the information, the decree that brings its verities into action (T, 30).

Was I reading the neat formulae of the *Begriffsschrift* after all? In those impersonal graphisms, was there still a sense of a stern figure, never turning back to look at the students taking notes, writing on the board but only for those who already understand, ignoring the morons in the back row who laughed at the stiff way he moves, someone who goes home to an empty house and confides his private thoughts to his diary? Are the gestures there after all, the gestures that can be read? A tone, self-occupied, rigid but determined, turning each ill–considered criticism back on itself with a precision that forbids reply and will accept only silence or repetition. The tone of someone who when, he says "I am wounded", hopes for, expects, no answer but only that the fact, the object, will take its place among others. A tone that insists that, "When a thought is grasped . . . it remains untouched in its essence" (T, 29), and insures that there will be no answering putting of a thought into one's own words that seals a personal understanding. A tone that demands not accommodation but respect, respect for the common Thought that leaves understanding behind.

It was always the object that Frege looked for, the object that would make the mechanisms of language mesh with the mechanisms of the world. In the end, it is only out of his own subjectivity that such an object could come. It is not the removal of person or of style from language that is in question, but the institution of a style. Frege's object is a new common self, not the self that feels and suffers, but someone who leaves his suffering behind to establish a public identity that can be shared by others, confident that there will be others who will be persuaded to join in, other "I"s and "you"s, the followers of a rational order, convinced that whatever anyone else says is an anachronism, anyone who is not like Frege, not hardened into a thing that thinks, anyone who is changed each time she succeeds in hearing what someone else says, each time she embraces the "you"s which her "I" addresses.

Notes

1. In "Thoughts" Frege explains how this indeterminacy is further complicated by the ambiguity of the present tense which can either mean, "is timelessly

true," as mathematical truths are true, or "true here and now." Once the latter unstated meaning is "divined" then one can go on to supply the data that completes the thought (T, 10).

2. Cf. Michel Foucault's description of the "style" of a mathematical treatise in *The Archaeology of Knowledge*, trans. A. M. Sheridan Smith (New York: Harper Torchbooks, 1972), 94ff. For Foucault academic anonymity expresses the absence (for Foucault characteristic of all discourse) of any "meaningful intention which, silently anticipating words orders them like the visible body of the intention." For Foucault the gap remains a gap, a subject place ready for the insertion of any speaking subject.

3. Frege acknowledges that the mechanism cannot be total.

> Science would come to a standstill if the mechanism of formulas were to become so rampant as to stifle all thought. Yet I would not want to regard such a mechanism completely useless or harmful. On the contrary I believe that it is necessary. The natural course of events seems to me to be as follows: what was originally saturated with thought hardens in time into a mechanism which partly relieves the scientist from having to think.

Frege to Hilbert, October 1, 1895. *Philosophical and Mathematical Correspondence* ed. G. Gabriel, H. Hermes, F. Kambartel, Christian Thiel, A. Veraart (Oxford: Basil Blackwell, 1980), 33. The question of whether such mechanisms are thought becomes in later Anglo-American philosophy the insistence that intelligence can be artificial and that the mind can be seen as functionally equivalent to a computer. See among many collections of articles, *The Mind's "I"* ed. D. Hofstader and D. Dennett (New York: Basic Books, 1981).

4. Frege to Husserl, October 30, 1906, *Correspondence*, 66.

5. Frege goes on in his letter to Hilbert to compare the process of automatization to the pianist's learning and performing of a piece of music. Once the musician learns the piece so that he can play it unconsciously, he can then "put his heart into the playing" (*Correspondence*, 33). Once our thought has been automated so that the repetition of "truths" is unconscious, then we may put feeling back into it. Such a description might fit the followers of Fascism or fundamentalist religion: having diligently learned by heart a system of belief so that thought is no longer necessary, they can then infuse those beliefs with emotion.

6. In what has seemed to some followers to be a backward step, Frege leaves behind the puzzles surrounding numbers as logical objects. This prompts some philosophers, such as Wittgenstein, to call "Thoughts" a "minor" work. However, after the description of logic as excluding any "metaphysical" talk of objects in his *Tractatus Logicus-Philosophicus*, Wittgenstein himself returned to many of the questions raised in "Thoughts" in his *Philosophical Investigations* (see Geach's introduction to *Logical Investigations*).

7. Frege more or less faithfully repeats Descartes's argument in the *Meditations*, rehearsing the argument from illusion, the dreaming argument, even giving his own version of the evil demon when he talks of the stimulation of nerve fibers. For a linguistic version see also Emile Benveniste:

The subjectivity we are discussing here is the capacity of the speaker to posit himself as "subject." It is defined not by the feeling which everyone experiences of being himself (this feeling to the degree that it can be taken note of is only a reflection) but as the psychic unity that transcends the totality of actual experiences it assembles and that makes the permanence of the consciousness.

Problems in General Linguistics, trans. M. C. Meek (Coral Gables: University of Florida Press, 1971), 24.

8. Only desperation could have provoked a logician to such a non-argument. Frege, not having proof of God to use as the transition from self to things, must rely on a different kind of faith: the faith that what is necessary for logical thought will be forthcoming.

9. Although later philosophers deplored the regressiveness of Frege's solution, when they depend on atomic realism or the canonical authority of science for epistemological grounding, they make a similar commitment: what men think should correspond to what a particular man or set of men think, namely scientists; such a stipulation is necessary if science is to be possible.

10. As Wittgenstein notes in his reformulation of Frege's logic, the *Tractatus,* the "I" of logic forms the limits of the world: "The world is *my* world: this is manifest in the fact that the limits of my language (of that language which alone I understand) mean the limits of my world. . . . the self of solipsism shrinks to a point without extension and there remains the reality co-ordinated with it." *Tractatus Logico-Philosophicus* (London: Routledge & Kegan Paul, 1961), 5.62, 5.634.

11. In the silence that surrounds the biographical facts of Frege's life, Carnap's description of Frege lecturing in 1910 is one of the few glimpses of his person. Quoted by Hans Sluga, from Rudolf Carnap, "Intellectual Biography," in Paul Schilpp, ed., *The Philosophy of Rudolf Carnap* (La Salle, IL: Open Court, 1963).

10
A Thought like a Hammer:
The Logic of Totalitarianism

Nothing is possible unless one will commands, a will which has to be obeyed by others, beginning at the top ending at the very bottom (Adolph Hitler).[1]

If with Frege logic was perfected, it is because the unity it projects is finally total. Logic does not play a limited role of regulating specific relations between men of an aristocratic class, or between emperors and conquered peoples, or between Popes and Christian subjects, or theologians and believers. Logic is the form of all knowledge and, therefore, all behavior. A unitary, consistent Truth, expressed in the clear functional terms of mathematical science, regulates that behavior. For Frege, how science would be grounded and implemented was of minor importance beside the real work of forging the logical form of a thought that can be "common" to all. Putting aside questions as to the felicity of the marriage with language which was to support that commonality, post-Fregean philosophers proceeded confidently to institute logical form in all areas of knowledge. Some of the most influential of these were the Vienna Circle, a group of philosophers, logicians, and scientists who met in Austria from 1922 until the late 1930s to discuss the unification of all knowledge promised by mathematical logic.[2]

For these men, mathematical logic cleared the way for the realization of the aspiration of nineteenth-century sciences to be unified in one consistent discipline with common principles and a common language. If science was only a collection of useful calculating devices, then it could make no more claim to represent the truth about experience than a ruler, but if Frege's logic could be made to stand as the institution that joined together the mathematical formulae of science and natural language, then science could provide the ultimate authoritative answer to any human concern. Mathematical logic would vindicate the claim of science to universal applicability. Mach, Schlick, Neurath, Carnap, and others joined by many visitors from abroad who would be in the vanguard of twentieth-century philosophy— Quine, Nagel, Ryle, Ayer, and Russell—met through the crisis and chaos of the period between the wars in Germany to discuss and promote the new world-view of mathematical logic.

If Frege felt no embarrassment in expressing extremist views, at least in the privacy of his diary, the members of the Vienna Circle were critical of the wild and unfounded opinions that more and more passed for political wisdom. The outbursts of racism and antiliberalism of the last decades of the nineteenth century had been followed by a period of relative calm and economic growth,[3] but the humiliating defeat of Germany in World War I, along with the crippling terms of the armistice imposed by the allies made any lasting political stability unlikely. For the Vienna Circle, most of whom were "leftist" in their politics, the new mathematical logic was the antidote to extremism: knowledge must be established on a properly scientific basis and irresponsible opinions based on ill-founded metaphysics discredited.

As an example, Rudolf Carnap cited the work of Martin Heidegger, who was about to find the fulfillment of his metaphysics in National Socialism and become the first Nazi rector of the University of Freiburg.[4] The grammar of natural language, Carnap argued, allows meaningless sequences of words as in Heidegger's discussion of *Being and Nothingness*. The antidote is to eliminate this meaninglessness by applying the "finer" syntax of logic which separates words into categories so that meaningless sequences are impossible. Metaphysics such as Heidegger's is not false, it is unfalsifiable. Carnap acknowledges that we want to express ourselves, that man wants to tell about "his emotional volitional reactions to the environment, society, to the tasks to which he devotes himself, to the misfortunes which befall him."[5] Carnap agrees that such personal concerns come out in "all that we say," as well as in our expressions, gestures, and the way we move. The mistake is to see this as anything more than personal expression. A metaphysician makes the mistake of reifying his feelings; he makes objects out of these personal experiences. In this he is similar to an artist who makes a poem or painting out of his emotions and attitudes, but the difference is that the metaphysician makes the claim that the objects of his metaphysics are real. He makes his personal responses into something that looks like a universe of objects; he makes his personal experience into a theory that cannot be a theory because a true theory must be scientific and expressed in logical syntax. Such pseudo-theories cannot be expressed in truth-functional sentences and are therefore outside the scope of science which must attend only to questions of scientific, functional truth. Logical analysis can expose Heidegger's metaphysical pronouncements as meaningless personal expressions.

This was the therapy Carnap prescribed to discredit philosophies of the state, race, and nature which supported extremist politics. But it was a therapy of avoidance. No "personal" philosophy could be proven false or true; it was as much beyond logic as the views expressed in Frege's diary. On this, Heidegger and Carnap hardly differed. Heidegger also believed that he had transcended linear thinking and logic. Given that the new rationality of logic could not engage personal expression, it could only lay such views aside, just as later Dummett laid aside Frege's racism on the grounds that it was irrelevant to logical truth. Nothing rationally intelligible can be said about those responses that "come out in all that we say," responses to our "environment," to "society," to our "misfortunes," to "the task we are asked to perform," except that they are unfalsifiable. All of us, Carnap acknowledged, want to express our feelings. If Heidegger found in the German people the saviors of metaphysics, and in their destiny and ascendance the return of "Being," these were Heidegger's "personal" responses to his environment and to "the task to which he had been called."

Mathematical logic limited the field of rational truth-seeking so it no longer included the intersubjective discussion of interests, needs, and desires that could have challenged the truth or coherence of Heidegger's responses. Instead, the philosophical schools that took Frege as their mentor—logical positivism, logical atomism, logical analysis, linguistic philosophy, and generative linguistics that dominated English-speaking philosophy for the rest of the century—focused narrowly on logical form, ideal scientific epistemologies, and the redescription of concepts in ordinary language in terms consistent with scientific materialism. Political philosophy or ethics, unless they borrowed from logical analysis and dealt only with the use of words, were not philosophy at all. Through the continued catastrophe of twentieth-century experience, Anglo-American philosophy inspired by the Vienna Circle continued to keep a prudent silence on any "metaphysical" questions and restricted themselves to eliminating anything from philosophic thought that might stand in the way of physical science. Values expressed in political views or moral attitudes were "personal responses." Because they cannot be verified empirically, they must remain a matter of choice.

It was not, however, the view of all of the positivists of the Vienna Circle that human welfare is of no concern to science. Another alternative was to try to provide a scientific substitute for the old metaphysics. Science itself would become philosophy, leaving no opening for a metaphysics which only depends on personal will or reaction. The Marxist Otto Neurath was the spokesman for such an application of logic. Again, the language that would unify all of science and knowledge would be physics. Knowledge would be limited to what could be expressed in Frege's functional sentences where the objects and relations refer to physical entities and processes: "What cannot be expressed in terms of relations between elements cannot be expressed at all."[6] This applies to human behavior as well as to the behavior of physical things. A scientific sociology would produce human happiness by administering a rational economy in which all decisions would be made on the basis of facts. Prediction after prediction would be systematized. The reactions and responses that Carnap had put aside as personal expression would harden into facts. A scientific "felicitology" would take the place of ethics; happiness would be quantified and measured. No matter what people say or think about what they are experiencing or the task to which they are called, science would tell them whether they were happy or not, and prescribe the proper means to the end of that happiness regardless of unreliable opinion.

To Neurath, perhaps with justice, such a managed state was far preferable to Heidegger's metaphysical notions of a racial State as an "ideal order." But the totalizing claims of such a political "logic" were soon implicated in crimes of almost as great a magnitude as Hitler's. Both Fascism and Stalinism claimed to be logical; that is, in both cases the open discussion of interest and experience that could ground coherent political practice was abolished in favor of a truth superior to what any individual might think. In Stalinist Russia, Marxist necessity soon mandated forced collectivization, thought control, a terrorist police state. Detached from any communicative reality, the inexorable laws of a Marxist functionalist logic ground out terror as efficiently as the unfounded metaphysics of National Socialism.

Not all members of the Vienna Circle were Marxists. Not all believed that ethics could be replaced with a scientific sociology. The majority followed Carnap. It is enough to eliminate metaphysics, and so limit the sphere of knowledge. Only what is expressible in the functional sentence can be known; philosophers and logicians do useful work policing the borders and syntax of science, continuing to undermine the claim of any value judgment, whether ethical or political, to truth. They can interest themselves in an analysis of ethical language, exhibiting the noncognitive form of value statements.[7] Value statements, and political statements insofar as they expressed value judgments, can be analyzed as pseudo-statements, either expressing emotion,[8] or influencing people to do what we want.[9] They are no more cognitive than "Ouch," or "Do that." There can be no rational discussion of such matters and they must remain a matter of choice, subject to the preference of public opinion. Politics must rest on the principle of tolerance and maintenance of a marketplace of ideas open to all sentiments and wishes.

But was it so easy to tell what was science and what was optional opinion? Both Stalinism and Fascism claimed to be sciences. The problem was in how to be sure that what passed for science really was science, really was grounded in fact. The epistemological problems which logicians tended to neglect in favor of the elegant mechanisms of logical syntax would have to be solved. It was not enough to argue that the question of the ultimate content of functional sentences is not a logical question, but a question of application. If logic proper did not need to concern itself with the question of what the atoms of fact would be from which inferences will be constructed, or how those facts untainted by personal responses would be found that could serve as the stable bits of truth out of which truth-functional theory is constructed, then philosophers would. These questions occupied most of the energies of British and American philosophers in the twentieth century. The source of the difficulty was in the failed marriage between language and mathematics which Frege had tried to patch up with his "thoughts."

In Frege's truth-functional logic, the truth of a complex thought is seen as a function of the truth of its component thoughts. There must then be elementary thoughts that we can take as true. But Frege's attempt to describe this truth in mathematical terms had failed. The natural language in which we express our responses and concerns involves concepts or "senses" which resist a quantitative interpretation. Words do not name a number of random objects, they do this in a certain way. Therefore, it is always possible to ask: what are the terms, the intention, the motives for a particular concept? Is the concept 'man' meant to exclude certain men, does it exclude women? Is it meant to reflect the desire that certain beings be singled out as superior to the rest? Is the concept 'wife' meant to identify, or dignify, or rationalize, a particular role for women?[10] These questions cannot be resolved by the counting of objects because they have to do with the identification of any objects which can be counted. If the concept 'man' is clearly not itself a man, there is still the possibility that it is masculine, that it is an invention of men, an institution of men, an intuition of men, a perception of men. Such a possibility must always interrupt the mechanisms of logic. It is, therefore, necessary to find some way outside of logical relations to validate elementary sentences that does not regress to personal concepts of things.

To accomplish this, the Vienna Circle proposed to infuse Fregean logic with empirical content. Incorrigible factual propositions would be found so that the machine of logical deduction could begin to grind out truths. Bertrand Russell's suggestion was the most obvious: what can be taken as true is a statement of immediate sense experience, unmediated by any intuitions or essences. But immediately there were problems. Any expression of our experience involving a concept is fallible. We may be mistaken. We may see what is not there. Our own interests and desires may get in the way. Some locution had to be found that expresses only the bare experiential content of what is seen and makes no objective assertion which incorporates any wish or desire or project of ours which might distort it. But the problem with any proposition that might report such a "sense datum" is that it must be private. The artificial terminology in which a "sense datum" must be expressed is no longer language and therefore is no longer intersubjectively intelligible. As a result, we no longer have any way of knowing whether what we are expressing bears any resemblance to what anyone else might understand.

For this reason, others of the Vienna Circle, such as Carnap and Neurath, rejected "sense data" for physicalism. Elementary propositions, they argued, are statements of elementary physical fact. But this caused even greater problems. It made it impossible to determine what facts are elementary and what are not. If two facts conflict then either can be rejected. This, Schlick argued, makes a mockery of truth, and Carnap and Neurath were forced to admit that what results from physicalism is a coherence theory of truth.[11] If observations seem to refute a theory, and those observations are statements of physical fact like any statements in the theory, it is no longer clear whether the theory or the observation should be questioned. To take an example from Marxist sociology, if the Communist Party is the voice of the proletariat and the proletariat is the progressive class and therefore infallible, but there is the conflicting "fact" that some workers criticize the Party, the latter need not negate Communist theory. Since the workers' views are not coherent with Marxist theory, they can be declared false.

One response to this impasse was to reassert the irrelevance of epistemology to logic.[12] If there could be no incorrigible elementary sentences, so be it. Wittgenstein in his *Tractatus,* like Frege, made no attempt to identify what logical objects or facts might be, although this was a renunciation that the crusading empiricists of the Vienna Circle, impressed though they were by the elegance of Wittgenstein's Fregean logic, tried hard not to understand. The question of the relation of logical elements to reality, Wittgenstein argued, is logically meaningless and unrepresentible. All logic can do is exhibit the necessary logical structure of knowledge, it can never give that structure content. If it can be done at all, it is not the business of philosophy but of science. In the end, the conclusion of many of the Vienna Circle, including Carnap and Quine, was not much different: it is professional scientists accepted as experts by our culture who must decide what is true.

In the mean time, actual scientists, in Nazi Germany and elsewhere, were working on various projects of weapon design, energy physics, nuclear fission, germ warfare, industrial management, medical experimentation, behavior modification, and market research, too busy to take much interest in the philosopher's intricate investigations into logical form. Philosophers endorsed this separation: they would stay out of the way of science. As faithful helpmates, they would clear the way, develop new logical notations that would vindicate the claim of science to universal truth, place the functional forms of scientific truth at the heart of any meaningful language, reduce and eliminate any unscientific metaphysics in our ordinary talk, expose value judgments as noncognitive, insist that the final verification of any truth had to come from the community of scientific experts and from their agreed-upon methods and procedures of experimentation. The renunciation of any substantive philosophical results for the humble role of servant to science, the rejection of substantive political and ethical issues as meaningless kept the followers of Frege out of the way of a century of extremist politics.

As the Vienna Circle met to debate the relative merits of sense data and physicalism, a splintered coalition of Catholics, democratic socialists, and liberals were attempting to hold the tottering Weimar Republic together. Many Germans, unused to democratic rule, respectful of authority and social order, jealous of private perogrative, ready to blame misfortune on a scapegoat, embraced whatever theory was consistent with their prejudices. Hatred of Jews and other racial minorities, bizarre theories of Aryan superiority, fanatic nationalism, disgust with democratic institutions, all flourished in the marketplace of ideas. Hitler, isolated but brilliant in his strategies, guided by sentiments not unlike the ones expressed in Frege's diary, worked out the master-logic of National Socialism. This would be, in the most literal sense, a thought like a hammer.

National Socialist thought, like Frege's, did not concern itself with empirical content. More important than any content of Nazi ideology was the consistency that resulted from deduction from a few simple ideas. To quote from Hannah Arendt's description of such a totalizing thought in *The Origins of Totalitarianism*.[13]

> Ideological thinking orders facts into an absolutely logical procedure which starts from an axiomatically accepted premise, deducing everything else from it; that is, it proceeds with a consistency that exists nowhere in the realm of reality (471).

> The purely negative coercion of logic, the prohibition of contradictions, became "productive" so that a whole line of thought could be initiated and forced upon the mind, by drawing conclusions in the manner of mere argumentation. This argumentation could be interrupted neither by a new idea . . . nor by a new experience (p. 470).

Hitler had no problem in finding "science" to support his racial theories. That this was bad science is beside the point once it is admitted that there can be no incorrigible observations or any absolute validity to elementary sentences, and that the profession of scientists must decide on standards for truth. The inferiority of Semitic races and the superiority of the Aryan was supported by ample observations of philologists, historians, psychologists, and physicians. No personal experience could negate such a body of truth. The law of history was inexorable. If economics was logical necessity for the Marxists, the science of nature was logical necessity for the Nazis. In nature it was clear enough that the fittest and the best survived, whereas dying and degenerate races were destroyed. The applications of logic to action that Frege had promised came readily to hand. If Jews are a mongrel race, they must be exterminated. "A thought like a hammer" demanded instant obedience to the dictates of logic.

Logic, apart from the logical positivist's academic researches into logical form, had become universal practice. Although classical logicians had always claimed logic as the only true thought, they had not anticipated that everyone could or would participate in such a thought. For Plato, only discussion between philosopher-kings could be dialectical; for Abelard the language of the Church was for prelates and popes. It had never been contemplated as a possibility that women, or slaves, or foreigners, or peasants, or ordinary believers would think logically; instead they would obey the law of the *polis* or of the empire or of the church. In the part of their lives left unregulated they would continue to think illogically and emotionally. Logic was the prerogative of those in power who would use it as the tool for correct rule. In the Nazis' logic, Parmenides' dream was fully realized. Being is a unity; there is nothing outside the homogeneous whole of fascist reality. There is nothing but one Being, one thought. Those who do not think consistently with that logic do not think, do not exist, must not exist. Because there is nothing outside thought, nothing but prurient, seductive opinion, unreliable, shifting, fat with effeminate compassion that must be cut off, reduced, not allowed to pollute the white bone of thought with its blackness, with its foreign stench.

It was Frege, at the end of his life after he had abandoned the definition of number, who explained the only terms on which such a thought can be instituted. The inevitable failure to equate the truth of linguistic predication with the truths of mathematics necessitates a regression to the "I" at the center of the universe of logic. In the same way, the impossible demand for absolute empirical justification must give way to the absolute will of the Fuehrer. It is the will of the Fuehrer that creates the world of objects that can be integrated in logic. It is his sense of himself as an object, projected onto history, that creates a world with a common will. Only in this way can there be the self-consistency and the hard-edged concepts necessary for logic, only if it is spun out from one man's will, a lonely man, someone who had been wounded, someone whose family has rejected him living or dead, someone who has never felt at home in the world of objects shared by others, someone whose thoughts must replace the thoughts and the actions of others because that is the only way there can be any understanding, someone whose will has become law.

Finally even deduction is unnecessary, the decree alone is sufficient: action follows immediately. Thought is only a calculation of decrees, of sentences. Logical necessity becomes what you must think and say, and what it is necessary to think and say is what necessarily happens in the world according to logic, according to the logic of economics or the logic of race. No thought is possible outside logic. If there are such thoughts they do not exist and so may be eliminated. Each person, even in his most private thoughts when he is alone, must think the same thought again and again, compulsively, what he must think, out of all touch with reality, ignoring the terror in the streets, the disappearances, the deaths, the concentration camps, out of all touch with others whom he assumes think like him because they must, like he must, think just like him, because he is a thing, the only thing now that he can know and they must be like him. Logic in its final perfection is insane.

Notes

1. Adolph Hitler, "Obedience über Alles" (Nürnberg, Sept. 14; Völkischer Beobachter, Sept. 15, 1935).

2. In the 1929 manifesto, "The Vienna Circle—Its Scientific Outlook," written by Carnap, Neurath, and Hahn, a wide variety of precursors were named: in addition to the logicans Frege, Peano, Leibnitz, also empirical philosophers such as Hume, Mill, Bentham, philosophers of science such as Riemann, Mach, Poincaré, sociologists such as Marx and Feuerbach, and many others. The Vienna circle saw themselves as continuing the work of eighteenth- and nineteenth-positivism in promoting progress through science, but added the new rigor of mathematical logic. Although an early group met from 1907–1912 which included Hans Hahn, Philippe Frank, and Neurath and discussed political and philosophical questions as well as questions of scientific methodology inspired by Mach, later discussions were dominated by questions of logical analysis and epistemology. Those involved directly or tangentially included many of the major figures in twentieth-century philosophy: Carnap, Neurath, Schlick, Popper, Ryle, Ayer, Tarski, Quine, Russell, Wittgenstein, Meinong.

3. There are several sources for the outbreak of racism in the period in which Frege developed his conceptual notation. In 1871, the Prussian monarchy had become a nation-state and charges were revived that the Jews were involved with the state. The financial crises that erupted in 1873, in which many small investors lost their savings, fanned resentment against Jewish bankers. Anger, resentment, and frustration were directed against the convenient differentness of the Jews.

4. Carnap's argument is in "The Elimination of Metaphysics Through the Logical Analysis of Language" (1932), in *Logical Positivism*, ed. A. J. Ayer (New York: Free Press, 1959).

5. *Ibid.* 79.

6. "Sociology and Physicalism," in *Logical Positivism*, 293.

7. Schlick, unlike the others who insisted that only a linguistic analysis could be objective, also seemed to suggest that a study of what people actually did value could provide a science of ethics.

8. See Charles Stevenson's *Ethics and Language* (New Haven: Yale University Press, 1945).

9. See R. M. Hare, *The Language of Morals* (Oxford: Clarendon Press, 1952).

10. The question on which Russell's antinomy depends, "Is the class to which a

concept refers a member of itself?" is only one such question. Put simply, the antinomy was this: there are classes such as "non-man" which are members of themselves—the class of "non-men" is not a man—and classes like "man" that are not members of themselves. But now you can ask the question—is the class of classes that are not members of themselves a member of itself—which produces the paradox that if it is a member of itself it is not a member of itself. Russell's answer, which is to save logic, is his theory of types. Objects, classes or concepts, and classes of classes are different logical types. Therefore, it is impermissible to ask whether a concept is a member of itself as if it were of the same logical type as the objects that are its members. By logical fiat, it is now impossible to ask the critical questions about concepts that are part of the normal exchanges of natural language.

11. Schlick's response is that we must return to "basic statements," that use demonstratives—this, here, now—to indicate a present experience: "The Foundation of Knowledge," in *Logical Positivism*.

12. Carnap abandons the coherence theory under the influence of Alfred Tarski, who invented the semantics that finally allowed philosophers to go on with logical analysis without epistemological worry. If you project objects and relations that are the exact counterparts of logical relations and objects, you can return to a corresponding theory in which words correspond to semantic objects. Such a semantics requires no impossible reference to physical reality.

13. *The Origins of Totalitarianism* (New York: Harcourt, Brace and World, 1966).

Conclusion: Words of Power and the Power of Words

Traditional histories of logic trace an intermittent but steady progress toward logical truth. They point out where logicians in the past made mistakes and where they show their genius by correctly intuiting logical relations; they assume that the subject matter of logic is unitary, and that logicians, whether classical, medieval, or modern are motivated by the desire to find one logical truth. Historians of logic, usually logicians themselves, have been in sympathy with that project. They have accepted the logician's claim to supra-historical status for his researches; they have agreed that to do logic you must remove yourself from any concrete situation in time and space to contemplate eternal verities; they have considered politics and personal concerns only as intrusions. If logic is used for the evil purposes of politicians or dictators, it is by accident. What guides logic is logical truth and no other. There is a logic to these histories, which connects each innovation to the achievements of the past and makes a smooth transition toward a perfected logical form.

It must be clear by now that I am no logician, that I see no "logic" in the history of logic. Each story, each history has been different: different times, different concerns, different tones of voice, different ways of speaking, different men whose logics are no more commensurable than their lives. I have uncovered no progress of a universal rational World Spirit; nor have I found any materialist law of production that ultimately determines the forms of thought. Neither a materialist nor an idealist analysis could do justice to these complex movements of thought and action, to the subtle reworkings of communicative relations that position and reposition subjects, students, believers, followers, citizens in respect to those who rule them. If logicians have shown us ways to speak to each other, they have done so in a variety of ways, and these ways of speaking are not determined by any universal idealist or materialist dialectics, but by a diversity of purposes and desires.

According to the dictates of logic I have committed fallacy after fallacy. Purposes and desires can have nothing to do with logical truth. How could they, when the point of logic is to separate truth from what is subjective and to found a certainty independent of passion or intention? Logicians will be pained by these readings that compromise the purity of logic with biographical notes, relevant to an antiquarian, or a social historian, or a novelist, but never to a logician. There are logical names for the fallacies I have committed: the genetic fallacy, the *ad hominem* fallacy. It is a fallacy to think that the genesis of an idea is relevant to its truth and falsity. It is a fallacy to think that a critical understanding of the person who holds a view can count against the truth of that view. Logical truth is independent of both its genesis and of the man who speaks it. No matter its historical source, or who speaks it, or the intentions or desires with which it is spoken, truth must be judged on its own merits. Truths may be stated for the worst of reasons, and be true. Truths may have the most sordid of origins and be true. Bad men speak the truth, good men speak falsehoods. It is the business of logic to establish the laws of that truth without reference to men and without reference to the origins of ideas in specific social conditions. That a logician happens to be the certain son of a certain mother is irrelevant to the Name of the Truth. From that absolute point of reference come truths that are independent of contingent human affairs and of natural language's role in concrete human experiences of interaction and intercourse. From a logical point of view, there can be no reason to *read* logic, no reason for any account of logic that is not an analysis of its logical truth.

It must be clear by now that I have refused to accept this account, the logician's account of himself, at face value. Motivating this refusal is my own desire, my own commitment, a commitment that you, my reader, have already no doubt read. I believe that all human communication, including logic, is motivated. I believe that, although a word processor may print out truths mechanically, people when they speak or write always want something and hope for something with passion and concern, even when part of that passion and concern is to deny it. In my readings of logic I have tried to understand such a denial. I do not see how any judgment on the "truth" or "falsity," or correctness of what logicians say can be made until what logic "means" in this deeper sense is made clear. If truth is more than a sterile formality, more than a mechanical semantic matching of formulae with other formulae, we must first know the meaning of the words that we are to judge true or false. What is it that Aristotle is saying? Or Frege? And how is it possible to know without knowing the "genesis" of their words, without knowing the situation and concerns out of which logicians spoke, without hearing in their words who they were, what sort of "men" they were?

If, in the new law courts of Aristotle's city-state, the point was no longer to tell the truth but to convince judges and juries of positions that were most likely false, juries must have yearned for the return of such an understanding. Heads swimming with clever arguments of plaintiffs, how many of them must have suspected that the intricacies of forensic rhetoric only got in the way of truth? How many of them must have yearned for the old understanding of women and of men, of women's and men's situations, that would have told them what the debate was all about? Words had begun to break free from the truth; manipulated and rearranged in endless combinations, they had become only signs. But words themselves, no matter how cleverly arranged, cannot tell the truth; they must have meaning and to have meaning they must be spoken by someone somewhere on some occasion. It is only after sense has finally disappeared that it is a fallacy to argue the merits of ideas on the basis of their origins in social concerns or the personalities of those who voice them.

If I am right about this, there can be no superior logic that will show up the mistakes of logicians; there can be no feminist logic that exposes masculine logic as sexist or authoritarian. And this might be taken as weakness. Have I fallen into the old trap, an attentive listening woman who understands all and forgives all? If Dummett put aside Frege's fascism because it was irrelevant to logical truth, does my "understanding" have the same effect? The experience of a lonely man, cut off from others, bitter, concentrated on one supreme intellectual task, one obsession—such an understanding makes Frege's logic intelligible but does it also make it forgivable? If a feminist reader is to remain a reader and not turn logician at the last moment and present the feminist truth by which she will judge and legislate, how can she condemn the logic of Empire, Church, or State? Desperate, lonely, cut off from the human community which in many cases has ceased to exist, under the sentence of violent death, wracked by desires for intimacy that they do not know how to fulfill, at the same time tormented by the presence of women, men turn to logic. Doomed to fail in their Parmenidean flight out of the world, fated tragically never to realize their desire for permanence and purity, can they be condemned, or only pitied, or even admired for their nobility?

But as I read I saw little to pity or admire; instead I condemned the narrowness of the views, was angry at the tone of certainty, felt horror at the indifference to suffering caused by those whose authority was based on logic. Against the force of the authoritative relations that logic structures, a judgment of falsity is inadequate; to make such a judgment is to abdicate from judgment, to join the debate, enter in the lists to fight for a truth that can be universally applied. Even to judge Frege pitiable or admirable is to enter into the debate and make again the Sophist's dichotomous division. The old game is joined. A new philosophical position is presented, debate continues, rejected, refuted, or accepted.

The point of these readings was not to make a judgment but to respond. It was to take up the words that have fallen from logician's mouths and reshape them. So this is what you are saying, this is what I have understood you to say, this is what you meant then whether you will admit it or not. If words are always spoken from and for the mouths of others, it was to take the words of logicians and make them mine, shaping them into a response that might wound more painfully than refutation. The discussion of a man in authority with a woman who sets herself up to refute his pronouncements is always on his terms, and likely to end only in one way: with the reaffirmation of his power. But if a refutation can always be refuted, a response cuts deeper. A response might refashion the words of those in power into a serpent whose bite is exposure, the exposure that pricks inflated vanity, the exposure that weakens the resolve to continue on in ridiculous, imperious blindness to reality, the exposure that makes it impossible to continue to deny one's vulnerability and the limits of any human power, the exposure that shows all men to be mother's sons dependent on others. If logic is words of power that proclaim an authoritative unitary truth, there is another power in words, the power to respond and so to challenge another's discourse and refuse its pretensions to autonomy. The antidote to logic is no supra-logical metalanguage that will criticize and regulate the forms of logical thought, but language itself, the normality of human interchange that logic refuses, the answer that at its most effective is sensitive, penetrating, intelligent, shrewd, the answer that cuts to the quick. If I have not always succeeded in giving such a response, I am convinced that the words of power of logic and its derivatives can only be vulnerable to such a response.

Are women in a privileged position to make it? Is logic masculine? Can I put to rest the questioning which began so long ago as I tried to master the exercises in Quine's logic text? One thing is clear enough: those who have made the history of logic have in fact been men. Different kinds of explanations have been given of that fact. The simplest is to blame it on exclusion. If women had been permitted they would have been logicians, they would have been citizens, professors, pontifs, ministers, leaders? Would they? Once it is agreed that logic is equivalent to thought, this solution seems inescapable; there is no other way to defend women's equality and ability. If only they had been admitted to the Courts, the Assembly, the Church or University, women would have made great achievements in logic. Heloise would have been Abelard, Diotima Plato. If they had been included in the debate. But feminist experience would indicate that it is not so simple. Even when admitted to the Church, to the University, to public debate, to those disciplines in which logic rules, women have not felt comfortable. They have had an agonizing sense that the terms of success still escape them, that what they care about is lost in following the rules, that their experience must either be ignored or distorted to fit the conceptual scheme within which they are to think. They have the nagging suspicion that they must stop thinking and feeling to succeed, and that is hard for them, and so they don't succeed, or not as often as men succeed. And those who do continue to have the discomforting feeling of being the tokens that prove that male superiority is based on no arbitrary exclusion of women.

Logicians have been men. As men, they have spoken from a men's experience. Aristotle and Plato spoke from a masculine culture rigidly and defensively segregated from the generative life of the household. Ockham and Abelard spoke out of a commitment to a patristic Church founded on the authority of a transcendent male God, an exclusively male priesthood, and a theology that identified women with sin and evil. Frege speaks from the male preserve of the German University where masculine egos in mortal combat fight for glory and status. The arena of logic was made by men for men; it was expressly founded on the exclusion of what is not male, as well as what is not Greek, nor Christian, nor Western, not Aryan. From Plato to Ockham, until Frege finally banishes all substance from logic, the most common example of a concept which figures in logical arguments is "man," as if logic itself were only a grand articulation of one idea or obsession, the identity of man. Women must be interlopers here, because their assigned role is always outside. As the contrast that determines what a man is, their presence must at the same time threaten the institutions of logic. It is not that men are cleverer than women or that they think differently. The speech situations that logic structures are between men. At logic's very birth, Parmenides made clear this purpose: to leave the world of women, the world of sexual generation and fertility, the world of change, of the emotions, of the flesh. If this "birth" of logic must be repudiated in the name of Logic, as logicians claim descent only from the paternal name of Truth and Being, still the work of ordering and regulating relations between men in a world separate from women goes on.

If logic constitutes the words of power that ensure success in such a world, can women afford to give it up? Contemporary structuralist and poststructuralist theories of language have inscribed logical relations at the very heart of language. If this is true then the meaning of what we say is dependent on our words being in correct logical form. Women who speak illogically cannot speak truthfully, or persuasively, or cogently. They may express their pain or register their anger, they may break in and disrupt orderly discussion, but what they say cannot challenge the truth of what is said about women, or found just, nonsexist policies. If women are not content to moan inarticulately, rave hysterically, cast their eyes heavenward in ineffable ecstasy—none of which is likely to improve their situation—the only alternative, it would seem, is argument, in which logically constructed sentences allow the deduction of sound conclusions. If they do not accept these terms, they would seem to be condemned to the status of Parmenides's masses, wandering and confused, wracked by the physical sensations of their bodies, or of Aristotle's docile emotional housewives, obedient to the rule of their husbands, or of respectful Heloise's soliciting Abelard's superior wisdom.

But here be careful. Aren't these the alternatives that logicians have devised for us? If you do not speak logically, you will prattle like a woman, you will moan like a woman. Is it wise to accept the logician's account of what women's thought is or should be? Is it wise to accept so quickly the inscription of logic at the very threshold of thought? It was precisely the thought of women such as Diotima, a thought rooted in generation and change, that logic began by challenging. For the Eleatic Parmenides, mortal opinion was still very much alive and dangerous to the new order of law and the superiority of the Hellenes. Isis, Demeter, Moira, Eilethyia, Aphrodite, whichever name she was called by, was a deity with powers older and more compelling than those of Zeus; it was she who was worshipped in the towns of women and men, past which the logician rushed driven by his desire for Truth. By the time of Plato, logic had defined the public space of the city as the preserve of men; the towns were only insignificant rural outposts. In the place of the human community was founded the segregation that logic instituted, between an illogical feminine household charged with administration of slave labor and reproduction, and a male *polis* with law courts, assemblies, and magistrates in which rational discourse prevailed. Logic reinforced the boundaries of that segregation. If, as the Sophists argued, all free men may speak and be listened to no matter the form of their remarks, so might artisans, or laborers, or slaves, or feminized barbarians, or women speak and be listened to. Instead a standard of logical discourse must be maintained. Plato was willing to pay the final price for a definitive exclusion. By the terms of logic itself, if a woman passed the intellectual tests, she must be allowed to speak. Although women were generally incapable of logical thought, logic itself demanded that any exceptional woman who could master argument should rule with men. Qualified women, women who could pass as men, this "first feminist" argued, must be included. Of course their numbers will be small, and they will not reach the very heights of the philosophic truth that will rule the city. It is this invitation, visionary in the fourth century B.C., that still seems to require a positive response. Its rejection, a rejection of the logic that structures acceptable academic theorizing, or political debate, or theological dispute, would seem to return even the exceptional women who can think like men, who can master logic, to the household where their sisters subsist without power or autonomy.

But once the terms on which logic is based are understood, the choice is less clear. Is a woman to become the wealthy citizen who lives off the labor of slaves? Is she to become the administrator of an Empire that crushes ethnic identity with bureaucratic decree? Is she to be the priest who punishes heretics, the social scientist who justifies oppressive institutions in the name of truth? The relations between speakers that logic structures are alien to feminist aims. Nor is it possible to argue that these are misuses of logic which a feminist logic can correct. If the point of logic is to frame a way of speaking in which what another says does not have to be heard or understood, in which only the voice of a unitary authority is meaningful, in which we can avoid understanding even what we say to ourselves, then no application of logic can be feminist. If, for example, a feminist "logic" prevailed and a "rational" policy for welfare mothers consistent with that logic was instituted, as long as those women themselves were not heard and understood, that welfare policy would only return women to the domination of a paternal state bureaucracy more oppressive and paralyzing than the domination of a husband. If the passions and motives of policy-makers are hidden by theory and so not heard and understood, the racism and sexism of men or of women can continue to structure their directives.

But the alternative cannot be, as some contemporary feminists have urged, a woman's language. Such a language spoken between women for women cannot have the power that can challenge the authority of logic. By its very terms, it does not engage logic. It is outside logic, different from logic, other than logic, an expressive alternative that leaves thinking to the men, while women continue to speak and write for each other. Such a communication between women may be useful to build confidence and form new concepts by which women's experience can be understood and alleviated, but if logic is allowed to stand as reason, as rational thought, and as the underlying structure of public language, a woman's language will always be impotent.

An alternative is the one I have tried: to answer to the desire that motivates the claim of logicians to prescribe the rules of thought, even though the desire of logic is that there should be no answer possible; to respond that, understood in this way, logic is not thought at all but the denial of any challenge that might stimulate thought. It is only when the claim of logic to be reason and truth and knowledge is accepted that the anarchical chaos of purely personal expression is the only alternative to masculine rationality. With that claim exposed as a particular project of domination, it becomes possible to undertake a new feminist study of thought and language free from the logicist assumptions that dominate contemporary linguistics and epistemology.

But if logic is in fact the language of power, is this not a utopian project? If communication in the world in which women live is ordered by logical relations then it would seem that to refuse logic is to rule out the possibility of power and settle for an unrealizable dream of free thought in which all speak and decisions are reached through understanding and consensus. Even if such an oasis of communicative freedom could be realized, wouldn't it be infinitely vulnerable? Where could woman find a place to talk where that talk would not be fragmentary and furtive, carried on between wars, between bouts of alienated servile work, between incidents of violence? Isn't it the case that no matter what the purposes of logic, women must learn logical techniques if they are to survive, that they must take up words of power and fashion them into the same weapons as men? Women philosophers master logical analysis to establish a rational basis for women's issues. Women politicians exploit the concept of law to force consistency in the treatment of men and women. Women theologians search for scriptural inconsistencies in order to undermine Biblical authority for women's subjection. Women social scientists expose the logical weaknesses of theories that purport to prove women's inferiority.

But it is important to be aware of the dangers here. It is the very point of logic that no matter what content is substituted, logical relationships remain the same. The feminist logician speaks from a script in which the master always wins. Women professors find themselves refuting junior colleagues with the agressivity and jealousy of their own examiners. Women jurists ignore the inarticulate claims of poor women in the name of the law of property. Women theologians proclaim the superiority of Christianity over the spirituality of non-Western women. Women social scientists objectify their clients as research objects.

It is tempting with this realization to despair and find the only solace in deconstructive irony. Refusing to institute another logic, "the critic of patriarchy" resigns herself to exposing the pitiable vulnerability of disciplines ordered by logic and to disruptively tangling sexist arguments, all the time acknowledging while she ridicules the superior power of logic. Trapped in a language that has its substance not in speech but in formal relations issued from the Name of the Father, women play a futile game on the outskirts of logic, trying again and again the blind spots of reflexivity, Frege's antinomy, Ockham's mysteries, Aristotle's intuitions, Parmenides's Being.

But there is an escape from this dilemma. These fissures of nothingness from which the logician's refusal began, his refusals of the physical world of generation and change, of the thoughts of others that must be erased, of the otherness always in our thoughts that makes us doubt ourselves and question ourselves, these are not the necessary beginnings of thought and culture. This is the illusion that it is in logic's interest to maintain—that it is from nothing that this world of reason comes, like a trick of mirrors, the world of Ideas, the only world in which it seems we know how to live. In fact, it is men who have made the illusion, not all men, only some men, men who like all of us have their hopes and fears, men who have their own reasons for denying that there can be any other world than the world ruled by Rah or Yahweh or the Form of the Good, men who have their own reasons for attempting to build a world in which women can only be faithful daughters, adepts in logical technique, or rebellious protegés tolerated on the fringes of orthodoxy.

Regardless of an avante-garde of women's language and women's writing, logic remains a permanent and central part of the curriculum that represents current knowledge. It is taught in every philosophy program and is proposed as Critical Thinking for all courses of study. Women still struggle, if not with Quine with other texts, with computer programming, statistics, economic models, for there are many texts now. Logic is not in the words, she tells herself, it is somehow underneath or above the words and you must forget about the epidemic, and about Jones's peculiarities, about poverty and injustice. Forget what is *said*. Don't think. Logic will teach you to be critical, to learn not to accept an opinion as true without demanding an argument, it will teach you to defend your position with force. We must learn to think logically, learn to demand support for claims, catch incorrect inferences, search for inconsistency. Otherwise, there is no truth and clever politicians and merchandizers will deceive us. Logic is necessary because it forces us to take responsibility for what we think, to be ready to support it and defend it against counterattack. So the defense of logic continues. And even women, some of them, can learn.

But such a remedy for thoughtless conformity already assumes the language which logic has restructured. Before statements can be connected in arguments or judged consistent or inconsistent, speech has become the logician's propositions. Speech has become the campaign slogans of political ideologues, the come-ons of advertisers, the dogma of the catechism, "the proposition that can't be refused" to which Plato's Theaetetus is only to register assent or dissent. We already have lost our voices, already are only the auditors of sentences whose truth or falsity transcends any individual understanding. Our political thinking, whether democratic or Marxist, is a litany of talismanic slogans by which friends or enemies are identified. Economic thought takes the form of the endless repetition of possible pleasures rated in terms of satisfaction. Religion is a list of commandments that no one is expected to obey and a liturgy of beliefs that no one understands. If logic is the remedy for the lack of order in these lists, it is because logic already separated "what is said" from what anyone says, has already isolated the "meanings" which the logic of classical economics, Marxist social science and Christian theology must work into a coherent body of thought. What is said has become the "proposition," detached from who says it, and the only way to avoid the chaos of an endless indiscriminate list of truths is to insist on the logical relations that separate one domain from another and rule out inconsistency. But the important step has already been taken. The Logos has been separated from the testimony of the witness, and is now only a statement or a claim that can be proven true or false regardless of its adequacy or honesty.

The atomized statements that logic reconnects in syllogisms or propositional calculi are themselves spoken, but it is by a certain kind of speaker,
a speaker who is alienated from himself, who speaks from no coherent
interpersonal experience, from no stable communal reality. It is no accident
that logic flourished when the human community had failed, when the
village had been subsumed in the city-state and the city-state dissolved in
war and economic rivalry, when the medieval consensus wracked by famine
and heresy collapsed, when international capitalism had all but destroyed
the nation-state. In each case, logic became more imperious, more desperate
to project a thought in which all can believe, a thought like a hammer to
pound into shape the common world that no longer existed, to command
the common understanding which was no longer possible, to define an evil
which no longer had any concrete shape. Logic is the thought necessary for
those who have no thought, who must, in the midst of that emptiness,
construct a substitute world of relations against disintegration, rootlessness,
homelessness, who must create a consensus without cooperative and reciprocal economic relations, familial intimacy, customs and rituals which bind
people together, art forms which express communal values in tangible form.
Given the absence of any common sense of a world durably woven out of
necessarily differing experiences, logic must seem the only alternative to
chaos and anarchy.

But the extreme conditions that make such a choice necessary are specific
historical facts: the collapse of the city-state, economic crisis, disease, hunger, and exposure to radically different cultures. They are neither necessary,
universal, nor eternal. Furthermore, men armed with the authority of logic
themselves completed the devastation, perfecting master languages insulated
from criticism, ruthlessly pursuing Sophists, heretics, witches, scarlet
women, unbelievers, Jews, extending the rule of law and truth over diversity. Wouldn't it also have been possible to repair and build, to reclear a
space for communication and discussion among the debris, to patch and
support the broken matrixes of lives? A new house, a new school, a union,
a town council, a citizens' group, a woman's center? To found institutions
that would support a coming together to an adequate understanding of what
has happened, is happening, and ought to happen? And once there and
talking, do we need logic or critical thinking to help us to reach that understanding?

In the United States Presidential campaign of 1988, a candidate won who
was not a sympathizer with women's rights, and he was supported by many
American women. There were two ideas that captured the attention of
voters more than any others and were generally credited with turning the
tide in favor of the conservative candidate. One was the fact, constantly
referred to by George Bush, the Republican candidate, that Michael Dukakis, the Democratic nominee then governor of Massachusetts, had vetoed

a Massachusetts bill that made it mandatory for teachers to lead the Pledge of Allegiance to the American flag in public schools. The other was more an image than an idea. Its source was a series of TV commercials that presented a large black man being led away by police, identified as a prisoner on furlough from a Massachusetts prison who had gone amok, raped a white woman, and murdered her husband.

The logic of these messages according to Bush was simple. Saluting the flag is the mark of loyalty to the United States, therefore if you are against it you are disloyal. Criminals are dangerous, therefore there should be no furlough program. By the necessity of this "logic," both men and women were convinced. Time and time again, with a sort of numbed persistence, prospective voters when interviewed repeated the conclusion, "Dukakis is soft on crime"; "Bush is a real American." What might have helped these voters to a better understanding of what was being said to them? Was it more sophisticated logic that would cleverly tangle the question further: the missing premise, the principle that an exception does not disprove the rule, the possible consistency of patriotism and dissent? Or were there other more important skills that were lacking, and that could be learned and taught, the skills of reading: attention, listening, understanding, responding?

These are not the same as the skills of logic; in many ways they are antithetical. If logic teaches us to ignore the circumstances in which something is said, reading asks us to consider it carefully, if logic teaches us to forget who says something and why, this is precisely what we need to know if we are to read correctly. To read Bush's attack on Dukakis's patriotism, it would have been necessary to have a grasp of the circumstances: our defeat in Vietnam, our fading economic hegemony, the global rivalry with communism in which we have cast ourselves as heroes. To read, it would have been necessary to know who Bush was, his conservative connections, his past with the CIA, his tenuous status as the anonymous Vice President of a popular President. To read what was said, it would have been necessary to know to whom Bush was speaking, to know about the electorate and their sense they were not as well off as they had been made to think they were and about their need to be told again that all was well. In the case of the black criminal who went amok on furlough from prison, another even more difficult skill was needed, the skill to reflect on ourselves as we read, and to be aware of deep-seated emotions and responses, in this case racist, that color our reading. Can logic or critical thinking based on logic teach these skills?

Logic has provided scripts for particular settings, the law court, programmed debate, theology, and science. At the same time it presents itself as universal. All men, and even women, should think logically; any communication that is not purely expressive and that aims at the truth should be logically ordered. This is the way to be critical, this is the way to guard against falsity and deception. This is the way men, and now women, should be taught to think. But retention of a list of carefully chosen facts, even when supplemented with logical rules of combination, is no guarantee of any effective response to the call to patriotism, or to the defense of the traditional family, or the policing of black criminals. The Pledge of Allegiance is the sign of loyalty to the country; if someone is against the Pledge they must be disloyal. It is such purity and simplicity at which logic aims.

A reader would have been harder to fool. She would have listened with a grasp of history that allowed her to realize that Bush and Dukakis spoke out of the failures of American foreign policy and out of the uneasy sense that the world capitalism which the United States leads is dangerously unstable. She would have heard the tone, strident, military, rigid, that demands that there can be no discussion of the rightness of anything American, no discussion of the rights of black murderers or the social reasons for crime. She would have taken account of the public to which Bush spoke, worried, shaken by the stock market crash the year before, afraid to rock the boat of an economy floundering in debt, but eager to believe in the American values that all around them had disappeared. She would have understood the reference to the color of the prisoner and his size, the black rapist who is the symbol of a sexual prowess that threatens white men in their possession of women, black like most criminals, prisoners who deserve what they get, because it must be them, these aliens, barbarians, not like us, who are causing things to go wrong. With a sense of history, she might have recognized the tone from having heard it before, in accounts of other times in which people grappled for hope and stability. She could never have read everything, no one can, but she would have read some of it. She would have read beneath the logic, she would have read the desires, the concerns, the hopes of these men, twisted as they might have become. And once having read, she might have had an answer.

If men have been the masters of logic, women may be the masters of reading. It is a skill we have perfected. We have listened and read to survive, we have read to predict the maneuvers of those in power over us, to seduce those who might help us, to pacify bullies, to care for children, to nurse the sick and wounded. We have read what men said, studied their words, heard the ambivalence and confusion in what they say no matter how univocal and logical, and having heard it we have sometimes wanted to cure it, if only by listening, and then listening more and not stopping listening until all is revealed, the final weakness, the final confession of need and weakness that is the sign of our common humanity. But there is more to speaking than listening and understanding. There is also responding, answering. And that can mortally wound. That steady subtle voice, that takes the words of another and repeats them back so we are given back to ourselves as another and we see ourselves and we have been forced to reveal ourselves in all our weaknesses. And with much pain we have given up our name, the secret name that we hoarded to ourselves, that we dreamt idolatrously would give us power over all, the name of Truth.

And only after that surrender, we might start to talk to each other. Women to women, women to men, men to women, men to men. And that talking might begin to make places in the world—homes, towns, assemblies, councils, workplaces, temples, churches—for the daughters and sons of mothers and fathers.

Index